MW00781744

Meaningful Encounters

Meaningful Encounters

Preparing Educators to Teach Holocaust Literature

Paula Ressler and Becca Chase

LIBRARY OF CONGRESS

LIBRARY OF
CONGRESS
SURPLUS
DUPLICATE

ROWMAN & LITTLEFIELD
Lanham • Boulder • New York • London

Published by Rowman & Littlefield
An imprint of The Rowman & Littlefield Publishing Group, Inc.
4501 Forbes Boulevard, Suite 200, Lanham, Maryland 20706
www.rowman.com

6 Tinworth Street, London SE11 5AL, United Kingdom

Copyright © 2019 by Paula Ressler and Rebecca Chase

All rights reserved. No part of this book may be reproduced in any form or by any electronic or mechanical means, including information storage and retrieval systems, without written permission from the publisher, except by a reviewer who may quote passages in a review.

British Library Cataloguing in Publication Information Available

Library of Congress Cataloging-in-Publication Data
Names: Ressler, Paula, author. | Chase, Rebecca, 1950- author.
Title: Meaningful encounters : preparing educators to teach Holocaust literature / Paula Ressler and Rebecca Chase.
Description: Lanham, Maryland : Rowman & Littlefield, 2019. | Includes bibliographical references and index.
Identifiers: LCCN 2018055442 (print) | LCCN 2019004003 (ebook) | ISBN 9781475822106 (electronic) | ISBN 9781475822083 (cloth : alk. paper) | ISBN 9781475822090 (pbk. : alk. paper)
Subjects: LCSH: Holocaust, Jewish (1939-1945) in literature—Study and teaching. | Holocaust, Jewish (1939-1945)—Study and teaching.
Classification: LCC PN56.H55 (ebook) | LCC PN56.H55 R48 2019 (print) | DDC 809/.93358405318—dc23
LC record available at https://lccn.loc.gov/2018055442

♾™ The paper used in this publication meets the minimum requirements of American National Standard for Information Sciences—Permanence of Paper for Printed Library Materials, ANSI/NISO Z39.48–1992.

Printed in the United States of America

In honor and loving memory of our son,
Shandi (Ressler) Hopkins, whose boundless
spirit flows through all we do.

Contents

Acknowledgments

We could not have written this book without the host of knowledgeable, supportive, patient, and loving people who shepherded us through graduate school and our teaching careers, guided us through the research and writing process, and spiritually nourished and healed us through all the vicissitudes of life that we experienced along the way.

We are deeply indebted to all the students who took the course we describe in this book. Thank you for your thoughtful and sincere work and for granting us permission to include you in our research.

Our heartfelt thanks go out to all the other people who contributed specifically to this book's research and development.

Reading Marianne Hirsch and Leo Spitzer's *Ghosts of Home* (2010), about the history and postmemory of Czernowitz, increased Paula's determination to learn more about her own extended family. Special conversations with Elizabeth (Lisa) Heineman encouraged us to let those who we have loved and tragically lost be our spiritual guides in our teaching and learning.

Katrin Paehler gave us an invaluable critique on a proposal for a summer institute on Holocaust studies teaching for secondary teachers, which Paula took the lead drafting. When we wrote Chapter 1, we incorporated her historical and bibliographic suggestions. Other members of the proposal's interdisciplinary team who conceptualized the institute include Jonathan Druker, Katherine Ellison, Elizabeth Friedman, Alvin Goldfarb, and Monica Noraian. Thanks also to the generous scholars who agreed to be part of the summer institute, had it been funded, and whose scholarship helped to shape its design: Peter Fritzsche, Elizabeth D. Heineman, Marianne Hirsch, and Sara Horowitz. We hope that a future iteration of this proposal will receive funding.

We are very grateful to our friends and colleagues who offered expertise and suggested important resources, including Shushan Avagyan, Andy Davis, Michael Dubowe, Rabbi Rebecca Dubowe, Robert Erlewine, Berenice Fisher, Sharlene Gilman, Sherry Gorelick, Sharon Leder, Gretchen Lovas, Yusuf Sarfati, Lisya Seloni, and Milton Teichman.

We also acknowledge the generous support offered by the Holocaust Educational Foundation for partially funding Paula's trip to European Holocaust sites with the 2014 Eastern Europe Cemeteries group, and the United States Holocaust Memorial Museum educators who met with us during our four-day visit to the museum.

Throughout the whole publishing process, the Rowman & Littlefield editorial staff, especially Susanne Canavan and Tom Koerner, Carlie Wall, and Brianna Westervelt, guided us patiently and respectfully. Our sincere thanks to them and the unsung heroes who saw our book through to publication.

Over the years, our colleagues in the National Council of Teachers of English (NCTE) have provided invaluable expertise and moral support in the face of professional adversity. They are too many to name. We make special mention of those NCTE colleagues with whom we have worked most closely over the years: Eileen Bularzik, Patty Dunn, Ken Lindblom, and Tom McCann.

New York University's doctoral program in English education is where we studied the pedagogical and other theories underlying our teaching and where we began our higher education teaching careers. We are forever indebted to those among our professors who also became our friends—Berenice Fisher, Irene Shigaki, and Marilyn Sobelman. Berenice has been our mentor and ethical guide since we were students in her feminist philosophy courses. Irene gave Paula the courage to make connections between her own life and her work in the classroom. Marilyn mentored us and opened her home and heart to our family during our years in New York City.

We also deeply appreciate the skillful and compassionate guidance that our other professors, Howard Coron, Margot Ely, Miriam Frank, John Mayher, Gordon Pradl, and Harold Vine, gave us. Many fellow students in our doctoral cohort we still hold dear, including Sharon Shelton Colangelo, Perry Green, Carolina Mancuso, Diana-Elena Matsoukas, Marianne Pita, David Rogers, Patricia Stephens, Dorothy Striplin, and Gail Verdi.

Berenice Fisher, Sherry Gorelick, and Linda Marks have inspired us through their commitment to actively seek peace in the Middle East, including their steadfast participation in Women in Black vigils. Our love for them is wide and deep.

There is a special place in our hearts for the mental health professionals and grief counselors who have helped us over the years cope with our son Shandi's tragic death through suicide and who guided us through our ups and downs as we wrote this book and struggled to continue our life journeys. We also are eternally grateful to the compassionate doctors and mental health professionals who treated and counseled our son when he was most in need.

We are blessed with the family members who embrace us today and encouraged us along the way. The Hopkins family—Rafi, Anne, Cecilia, Gabe, and Eli, as well as June Hopkins, David Hopkins, and David Wilson—have given us the continuity, pleasure, and future that we thought were lost after Shandi's death. The Ehrlich and Reifer cousins who came into our lives after Shandi died have happily taken up residence in our hearts: Claudy and her children, Jane, Jesse, Jimmy, Miles, Tommy, Susan, and Rachel, their partners and children, and cousin Maddie. We wish we could have known cousin Matthew, too.

We cherish Paula's sister, Joni, who we deeply miss and who was looking forward to seeing this book published. We wish her daughter Lori, son Mark, and their children and grandchildren many life blessings.

On Becca's side, the vast, far-flung Vincent clan are out there, living their incredible multigenerational saga, which she and Paula happily wander into and out of from time to time, always welcomed with open arms.

Finally, we express our unconditional love and appreciation for each other. What we each contributed to this book mirrors what we have contributed to our loving partnership over the last thirty-six years.

Preface

Paula Ressler: Teaching about the Holocaust never crossed my mind when I began my teaching career. In fact, many years passed before I decided to include even one Holocaust-related book in my syllabus. Looking back, I can pinpoint a number of experiences that led me to incorporate Holocaust studies into my teaching. Two stand out especially.

While I was still a graduate student at New York University, our professor Irene Shigaki sparked my desire to create a closer link between my life and my teaching when I attended a class in which Irene courageously shared with her students, for the first time, the story of her Japanese American family's incarceration in the Minidoka internment camp during World War II. Subsequent conversations we had about the experience and the impact of the incarceration on future generations got me thinking about my own family history.

A few years later, what finally motivated me to research that history was a conversation in which my eighty-year-old maternal cousin Herta Seiden Gutfreund asked me to investigate what happened to the family she left behind in Vienna when she was fifteen. My cousin had not heard from or learned anything about her mother, father, or sister since 1938, when my father sponsored her and her brother Artur as immigrants to the United States. Herta and Artur had Austrian passports, but the other family members had Polish passports, which meant my father was unable to sponsor them. Whether this roadblock had to do with US immigration quotas or Austrian emigration restrictions or both, I do not know.

My parents also were refugees: my mother, Hilda Seiden Planer, from Vienna, and my father, Karl Ressler (originally Rössler), from Czernowitz, then in Romania (now Chernivtsi in Ukraine). Both parents emigrated to the United States in the late 1920s before Nazism clenched in its hateful jaws so many Jews in Eastern and Central Europe. My mother's mother, Debora Planer, and my mother's brother, Arnold Planer, finally were able to leave Vienna in 1935. (I never heard the surname Planer before recently examining their passports. The surname I knew was that of my maternal grandfather, Mayer Alter, who emigrated from Vienna to the United States twenty years earlier.)

Like many other Jewish survivors and escapees from European fascism in those years, my parents did not talk with their children about what their lives had been like in Europe, how they found their way to America, or their tribulations as displaced persons. They did not discuss the families they left behind, those who did not survive—and I never thought to ask. Israeli psychologist Dan Bar-On calls this a "double wall" of silence in which "parents do not tell, and children do not ask" (1996, p. 168).

Contributing to my evident lack of curiosity about the Holocaust and my parents' lives in Europe was my own insecurity as the child of emotionally troubled parents, whose marriage was disintegrating even prior to my birth. I also shrank from seeing the nightmarish images of emaciated concentration camp survivors and mass graves on television when I was a child.

However, after Herta asked me to find out what happened to her family, I faced the fact that I knew nothing about the rest of my mother's or father's extended family members who remained in Europe, and eagerly, albeit with some trepidation, accepted the challenge. With the assistance of a paternal cousin, Jane Reifer, I contacted Gisela Wibihail, an archivist working with the Documentation Centre of Austrian Resistance in Vienna, which, as part of its mission, collects and reproduces records documenting the fate of Austria's Jews during the Holocaust. She sent me a letter and documents explaining what happened to them.

My cousin's parents and sister were among those deported from Vienna to Minsk between May and October 1942 in response to the Nazi order of April 1942 to kill the remaining Viennese Jews. Her relatives were put on a train that left Vienna on August 17, 1942, for Minsk. The order was to kill the deportees on their arrival at the Maly Trostenets estate near Minsk. Only seventeen were known to have survived these transports; Herta's family was not among them.

The news was terribly painful for Herta to receive, and it evoked profound feelings of grief. She was relieved, however, finally to know what happened. (Her Australian relatives received the same information from Wibihail at about the same time and also shared their research with her.) When Herta died a year later, I was grateful that I had been able to share with her the results of my research.

Troubled by what I was learning and recognizing that being isolated and separated from our roots had harmed our whole extended family, I was compelled to learn more. Over the next decade, I read about the Holocaust through history, trauma and psychoanalytic studies, and literary texts. I attended conferences, seminars, and workshops, including ones sponsored by the United States Holocaust Memorial Museum (USHMM); the Holocaust Educational Foundation; and the Program in Jewish Culture and Society and the Holocaust, Genocide, and Memory Studies Program at the University of Illinois Urbana-Champaign. I traveled to Europe with a group of educators to visit concentration camps, ghettos, and cemeteries.

As the years went by, and as I learned more about my extended family's troubled history—the high incidence of drug addiction, suicide, and other mental health issues, which some family members consider to be related to the Holocaust—I found it increasingly difficult and onerous to put aside my personal life in professional settings. Uncovering my family history and writing an essay that links my life with my teaching (Ressler, 2010) set me on the path I continue to follow, striving to integrate more completely all that I am into all that I do.

When I observed my students who were interning in schools as they taught Elie Wiesel's memoir *Night* and Anne Frank's *The Diary of a Young Girl*, I could see that they were unprepared to teach these texts. Their ignorance about the Holocaust as well as Jewish lives and culture sometimes even led them inadvertently to reinforce stereotypes and perpetuate antisemitism.

Realizing that my desire to better prepare my students to teach Holocaust literature dovetailed with my commitment to teach them how to develop theme-based curriculum units based on personally and socially meaningful ideas, in 2010 I made a radical decision to revamp my entire teacher education course. The literature curriculum would be comprised exclusively of Holocaust literature, while the methods curriculum would incorporate pedagogic and curriculum development strategies that education students could apply to teaching any literary texts.

Through my new curriculum, I responded to several important lacunae in my students' education. They lacked general knowledge about the Holocaust and Jewish life. They did not recognize that it is necessary to situate Holocaust literature in its historical context. They could not easily link historical to contemporary events. Pedagogically, they did not know how to develop curricula that embraces the complexity and the emotional and philosophical dimensions of any challenging subject matter. Most also were not familiar with the inquiry-based, learner-centered, social-justice-oriented pedagogies that are rooted in my teaching philosophy.

All these personal and professional reasons inspired me to deeply transform my teaching and scholarship, leading me to design, teach, and research my methods course on teaching Holocaust literature, and to write this book. Hopefully, the book will inspire educators and preservice teachers to think about, problematize, discuss, and consider whether and in what ways learning from this catastrophe might help us create a more humane and just world.

Becca Chase: The path I took to this project is quite different from Paula's. I grew up as a Christian and had only two Jewish friends until I reached college. Learning about the Holocaust, especially by viewing newsreels about the liberation of Jews in the deathcamps, profoundly unsettled me. Still, the Holocaust did not impact me directly, and I was not motivated to learn more about it.

However, from an early age I did develop a strong commitment to social justice. From the civil rights era, to the Vietnam War, the LGBTQ and feminist movements, and intersectional movements for equal rights, this commitment, and my active involvement, grew stronger. While studying English education with Paula when we were doctoral students at New York University, and teaching with her at Central State (a fictitious name), we collaborated on several research and writing projects, all of which had social justice orientations.

So, when Paula asked me to join her Holocaust education research, I agreed, but reluctantly at first. My ignorance about the subject gave me little confidence that I was qualified to act as co-investigator. As we got further into the work, however, I realized that my inexperience actually could be an asset, and I warmed to the project. I followed a path that was similar to the one Paula's students took and our potential readers might take, alternately defensive and enlightened when Paula, the data, the literature, and the resources challenged me to confront my biases and rethink my ideas. At the same time, I pushed Paula to clarify, strengthen, and, at times, revise her thinking.

To educate myself, I read the Holocaust literary texts featured in this book as well as numerous others. As our work progressed, I studied the history, culture, philosophy, literary criticism, education theory, and other texts that figure prominently in our research. When I could, I accompanied Paula to conferences and museums, including a four-day intensive visit to the USHMM, where we met with and learned from several educators who worked with students and teachers nationwide.

About our process: Paula read through the data and wrote the early drafts, chapter by chapter. Then I reviewed the data also and marked the manuscript with comments, questions, and prompts, drawing on my years of experience as an editor. After Paula revised her draft, including her early attempts to analyze the data, she sent it back to me. Then I fleshed out the theoretical perspectives. We exchanged drafts several times, working independently until satisfied that we both had developed the drafts as far as we each could. Then we worked together to create our final manuscript, arguing, researching, getting lost, and finding our way back again and again, until finally we reached consensus.

One of the biggest challenges was to sustain such deep concentration on the Holocaust over time. It was often difficult to remain both passionately connected and sufficiently distanced to withstand the subject's emotional impact. Because I have experienced personal trauma due to past abuse as well as illness and injury, the work did take a psychic toll. Yet contributing to Holocaust education, continuing in this way the exhilarating though never-ending struggle toward justice and compassionate living, also has been healing and immensely satisfying, both intellectually and spiritually.

Over the several years it took to complete this project, I became more and more committed to Holocaust studies. The strongest impact this research has had on me has been from studying ethics. How to live a moral life is a question I have pondered for many years but never conscientiously studied. In this time of great need to understand the struggle between progressive and reactionary forces in this country and the world, studying ethics and morality during the Holocaust seems particularly relevant.

I hope our readers find their work as Holocaust educators to be equally gratifying. May our efforts serve our readers well as they take on this complicated and demanding endeavor.

Authors' note: We assume full responsibility and apologize for any mistakes we might have made in interpreting or representing the scholarship we have drawn on, quoted, and paraphrased in our effort to incorporate useful and sufficient critical, theoretical, and historical background.

Introduction

While I was definitely uncomfortable talking about what happened in Germany, I was just as uncomfortable knowing that my teachers chose not to include this information in my previous experiences.

(Sandy's journal, Section 8)

This research is a case study of an English education methods course in which preservice education students prepared to teach Holocaust literature in secondary schools. The principal investigator, Paula Ressler, taught the course at a major Midwestern university with a large teacher education program. Unlike most literature methods courses, which include many genres that cover a variety of topics, this curriculum featured only one body of work: Holocaust literature.

The authors explain why the course was designed this way (see Preface), report what happened during the course, and analyze their findings. Based on this analysis and other in-depth research and experience, they discuss what teachers should consider when teaching this literature. The authors' intent is to help readers understand why teaching Holocaust literature is important today, how to teach it responsibly and ethically, and how to teach it in a way that maximizes student learning, personal development, and civic engagement.

Obviously, not all English language arts methods courses can or should focus exclusively on Holocaust literature. However, English teachers are or likely will be mandated to teach Holocaust literature during their careers. Because of this and because of its complexity and contemporary ethical implications, studying Holocaust literature and the pedagogies appropriate to teaching it should be a required component of English teachers' preparation and professional development.

However, there are no easy answers to why the Holocaust and such mass atrocities happened and continue to happen. There also are no facile solutions offered here to the obstacles inherent in teaching Holocaust studies. Taking a Freirean approach, instead we raise questions and pose problems (Freire, 1993; see Chapter 2), consider and analyze how participants responded to questions and issues that emerged, and at times make suggestions about alternative approaches.

Although they offer no formulas, still, like other Holocaust educators, the authors do specify parameters that teachers and teacher educators can follow responsibly to promote learning and teaching about this extremely demanding body of literature. While forewarning readers about potential pitfalls, the authors encourage them to embrace the ambiguities and unanswerable questions that teaching about the Holocaust inevitably arouse.

In the course studied in this research, Holocaust literature was taught interdisciplinarily, attending to historical, philosophical, psychological, and political contexts; literacy development theories and strategies; and literary criticism. The student teachers experimented with pedagogies that emphasize student engagement, critical thinking, and ethical questioning. They helped each other think critically about the texts, their contexts, and their relevance. By following along as the book recounts the path these novices took, readers hopefully will begin to conceptualize or rethink how to work together with their current or future students to explore the most meaningful ways to teach this literature today.

WHY TEACH HOLOCAUST AND GENOCIDE STUDIES?

In 1990, after a vigorous and persistent campaign by Holocaust survivors, concerned educators, and other allies, Illinois became the first state to mandate Holocaust education in all public K–12 schools in the state. In 2005, the mandate was expanded to include genocide studies. The Illinois campaign began partially in reaction to the Nazi Party of America's decision in 1977 to march in Skokie, a city of 70,000, approximately 40,500 of whom were Jewish and thousands of whom were Holocaust survivors (Oyez, n.d.).

The movement to include Holocaust studies began in the 1970s. By 1994, five states—California, Florida, Illinois, New Jersey, and New York—had passed mandates to teach about the Holocaust. It would take two decades more before several other states established commissions or passed legislation requiring that the curriculum of public schools include Holocaust and genocide curricula. Activists who support Holocaust and genocide education have been lobbying to bring such mandates to all fifty states plus the District of Columbia. Many countries around the world also require schools to teach Holocaust and genocide studies.

Regardless of whether Holocaust and genocide studies are legislatively sanctioned, scholars and educators of the Holocaust recognize that it is critically important to include such studies in school curricula. Comparative literature scholars Marianne Hirsch and Irene Kacandes (2004) provide a succinct and comprehensive rationale for teaching Holocaust studies:

> One can introduce students to philosophical debates about good and evil; to sociological theories of violence, authority, obedience, conformity, resistance, and rescue; and to psychological theories of tolerance and prejudice, of trauma, memory, and survival. The Holocaust can provide a focal point for studying the history of racism and antisemitism, of assimilation and marginality, of exclusion and genocide. [Holocaust literature] can provide . . . sophisticated interrogations of representability, of the limits of art, of speech in the face of unspeakability, and of the intersection of ethics and aesthetics. (pp. 6–7)

Because ignoring racism and ethnocentrism during the Holocaust years led to such extreme outcomes, Holocaust studies also gives students opportunities to learn more about the insidious consequences of unchecked racism and other prejudices. Also, psychologist James Waller (2002) demonstrates that when we look closely at the Holocaust's ethical dimensions, we see how power is used and abused and the roles that individuals, organizations, and nations take to perpetrate, deny, ignore, resist, or redress crimes against humanity.

Comparative literature scholar Michael Rothberg (2009) explains how this period contributed to the disintegration of civilized values. He argues that part of everyone's responsibility in a democracy is to uphold social and ethical values, learn to identify signs that suggest threats to civil rights, and know when and how to react. English educator James Farnham (1983) believes that studying Holocaust literature can assist this effort:

> Few bodies of literature are so pregnant a source of problematic issues as the literature of the Holocaust. Helping students to see these issues can stimulate them to think responsibly on ethical issues according to their own particular moral values. . . . This is one contribution Holocaust study can make to our society, for a society which does not constantly and vigorously confront ethical issues is an ethically indifferent society. It is thereby a vulnerable society. (pp. 67–68)

HOLOCAUST EDUCATION TODAY

Although most teaching about the Holocaust is done in social studies classrooms, the Holocaust learning experience that many students most remember, including the students in this study, is their reading of *The Diary of a Young Girl*. As comparative literature scholar Sara Horowitz (2012) explains, the afterlife of reading Anne Frank's diary is profound because readers respond viscerally to Frank's writing. However, English teachers generally are unprepared or underprepared to teach the book in its full historical context. Further, readers need not only to develop empathy with the victims of the Holocaust but also explore the roots of antisemitism.

This is why many Holocaust educators encourage studying Holocaust literature and history together. Unfortunately, social studies and English teachers rarely have opportunities to collaborate. Literature teachers, though charged to fulfill their schools' or states' curricula, rarely are prepared to provide historical context when they teach these and other Holocaust literary works, nor are they prepared sufficiently to unpack the texts' ethical complexities. As genocide educator Samuel Totten and Holocaust teacher educator Stephen Feinberg point out, many Holocaust teaching materials available to literature teachers are ahistorical, inaccurate, and pedagogically unsound (2009, p. 2).

In recent years, responding to the need for better teacher education and educational resources, organizations and professional development programs have contributed significantly to Holocaust education. In the United States, Echoes and Reflections, Facing History and Ourselves, Freedom Writers Foundation, the United States Holocaust Memorial Museum, the University of Southern California Shoah Foundation, and others provide educational programs, rich troves of research materials, and teaching resources.

However, professional development programs are relatively few, often restrict enrollment, and require tuition that many schools and districts cannot afford. Secondary school teachers are given little opportunity to attend such programs due to budget priorities and because little value is placed on their scholarship; so, to gain this competency, they would have to make a concerted effort to do so on their own. Most teachers, therefore, receive little or no guidance when teaching Holocaust literature, even in states where mandated to do so.

TEACHER INQUIRY

This case study is an example of teacher research, which English educator James Britton (1983) defines as "a process of discovery." In the "day to day work of teachers . . . every lesson should be for the teacher an inquiry, [and] further inquiry is also essential" (p. 90). Compositionist and teacher educator Nancy Martin (1996) analyzes the benefits of this type of research. Classroom teachers can "contribute to educational knowledge from the work they do every day. . . . Classroom enquiry carries with it the notion that teachers are learners too, and this is a big shift from the stereotype of teachers as people who know the answers to most things" (p. 49).

This book is primarily a qualitative, interpretive, naturalistic study, as defined by sociologists Liz Stanley and Sue Wise (1983) and qualitative researcher Margot Ely with Margaret Anzul, Teri Friedman, Diane Garner, and Ann McCormack Steinmetz (1991). It is naturalistic in that it attempts to present the ideas of the research population (Stanley & Wise, 1983, p. 265) and interpretive because it draws on evidence provided directly by the participants, as seen through theoretical lenses from a variety of disciplines, as well as the authors' own experiences as teacher researchers (Ely et al., 1991, p. 246).

Philosopher and organizational learning theorist Donald Schön (1984) argues that dissonant moments in teachers' practices are central to research; they are what keep teacher-researchers involved. "We are most likely to initiate reflection-in-action when we are stuck or seriously dissatisfied with our performance. Our question then is not so much *whether* to reflect as *what kind* of reflection is most likely to help us get unstuck. . . . Continuity of inquiry entails a continual interweaving of thinking and doing" (p. 280).

Reflecting on those difficult moments that were most salient to us as researchers, the authors see this study as a vehicle to improve their own teaching practices as well as to help other educators grapple especially with how difficult subjects like the Holocaust, genocide, and mass atrocities can be linked to pedagogical practices that are appropriate to the content and that can benefit all students.

The data was generated exclusively from students' written assignments, written responses to them, and field notes from the nine sections of the course taught over two and a half years. The research did not include interviews or instruments designed for research purposes. The curriculum and pedagogy were adjusted frequently as the course developed. The overall findings only became clear after the course ended, when there was time to analyze the huge amount of data collected. Often these findings cluster around a particular class section. Other times, patterns manifest across sections.

Having collaborated with each other as teachers, researchers, and writers for more than twenty-five years, the authors analyzed and wrote this book through dialogic processes, engaging in reflective dialogue until reaching consensus, as literary theorist and philosopher Mikhail Bakhtin (1986) recommends.

Specific class sections are referenced in parentheses by the numerals 1 to 9, with Section 1 referring to the first section that was taught and Section 9 to the last.

For the purposes of clarity and narrative authenticity, there are places in this book where the principal investigator/professor describes what occurred using the first-person singular and where the authors refer to themselves together in first-person plural.

PARTICIPANTS

Participants in this study, all of whom provided written consent to be included in the research and any publication resulting from the research, include students (referred to as students, student teachers, novice teachers, or teaching teams) who were enrolled in a large US public university's teacher education program, guest speakers, and the professor. To protect their identities, participants, except for the professor and one guest speaker, are identified by pseudonyms. The university is referred to as "Central State."

The university is located in a small city. Participants come from urban, suburban, and rural areas and have diverse ethnic and economic backgrounds, although a substantial majority of them are white, middle class, and suburban. Most had grown up interacting less frequently with racially, ethnically, and religiously diverse peoples than do most urban students.

A few students were either Jewish and/or had family members who personally experienced the Holocaust or World War II. Through schooling or media, most students had some, but minimal, knowledge about the Holocaust. In addition, there were a few students who came into the classes with negative views about Jews and Judaism and/or other ethnic, religious, and racial groups.

Some students were more eager to learn about and teach Holocaust literature than others. As future English teachers, the students were variously committed or not to social justice teaching. Several envisioned social justice to be at the root of their future practices; others viewed English teaching primarily as a way to teach language arts skills.

CHAPTER SEQUENCE

The chapters guide readers through the course and research. The first chapter provides historical background that enhances what students can gain from studying the literature in the syllabus. Students studied several chapters from historian Doris Bergen's *War and Genocide* (2009; 2016). (The authors draw much of their historical background information from Bergen as well as from historians Donald McKale [2002] and Saul Friedländer [1997; 2007].)

Following the history chapter is an introduction to the teaching strategies and theories framing the course, which are inquiry-based, learner-centered, and designed to maximize student learning by linking appropriate pedagogical strategies to the curriculum content.

Two chapters are devoted to examining antisemitism. The first focuses on current antisemitism, highlighted by one student's experiences. The other is about historical antisemitism as depicted by author and theologian James Carroll in the film *Constantine's Sword* (Jacoby, Carroll, Solomon, West, & Jacoby, 2008).

The three chapters following discuss the literary texts that shaped the course: *Friedrich* by Hans Peter Richter (1987); the short stories "Esther's First Born" by Sara Nomberg-Przytyk and "The Shawl" by Cynthia Ozick (both found in Teichman & Leder, 1994); and Art Spiegelman's biography/ autobiography, *Maus: A Survivor's Tale* (1986; 1992). These chapters raise some of the comprehension difficulties that arise when reading such texts, how to link what they are reading to students' lives today, and how the novice teachers in the course combined the pedagogical theories they learned with the new historical knowledge they gained as they developed and taught practice lessons about the literature.

The last chapter provides a brief look at other curriculum ideas that were not included in the research but are salient to Holocaust literature studies. It also includes recommendations for how teachers can deepen their preparation to teach the literature and how educational institutions and professional organizations can support education students and inservice teachers as they pursue that preparation. Finally, the authors encourage teachers who take up the daunting challenge to teach this complex and unsettling literature.

This book approximates a logical narrative progression from historical background to pedagogy and curriculum theory to the literature. The reader probably will want to travel back and forth among the chapters, thus replicating the recursive process of the actual curriculum. It has been challenging to achieve a workable balance, simplifying the presentation while maintaining the complexity of the learning experience.

No one book could ever suffice to prepare someone to teach Holocaust literature. This book follows one educator's experience teaching an experimental
literature methods course that focuses on Holocaust literature and the authors'
reflections on that experience. However, throughout the text, the authors cite
and quote from dozens of sources in several academic disciplines to document their background research and also to provide resource information for
readers to use as they pursue their own interests beyond this book's scope.

Sandy, in her quote at the beginning of this chapter, indicates what many
teachers and prospective teachers have expressed over the years—frustration
with the null curriculum and trepidation about bringing into the explicit curriculum what previously had been left out. While many of the students who
took this course resisted the emphasis on Holocaust texts, Sandy and others
like her were motivated to learn despite their uneasiness.

Students who willingly face the teaching problems that the Holocaust
presents inspire the authors. Meeting the needs of education students who are
committed to social justice teaching is not easy in a climate in which social
justice educators are vulnerable. Nevertheless, part of the historical struggle
of socially responsible teacher educators is to prepare preservice teachers to
practice social justice teaching. In turn, when they become teachers, these
education students will be better able to help their future students become
independent thinkers and ethical decision-makers prepared to resist injustices
and create a more equitable society.

The authors offer this book as a contribution to the efforts of the teacher
educators and their students who aspire to meet this challenge. Their intent is
to immerse readers in the complicated tangle that is Holocaust education so
that they gain awareness of how difficult this work can be. At the same time,
they hope to empower and inspire readers to responsibly introduce the next
generation to what the Holocaust Educational Foundation[1] calls the "lessons
and legacies" of the Holocaust.

NOTE

1. The Holocaust Educational Foundation of Northwestern University sponsors
biennial conferences and publishes the papers in the journal *Lessons and Legacies*.

Chapter 1

A Historical Context for Teaching Holocaust Literature

To introduce into the historical narrative not only the Jewish dimension as such but the "raw voices" of the victims. . . . These cries and whispers would puncture, so to say, the normalizing pace of the historical narrative, and jolt, albeit briefly, the distanced intellectual understanding conveyed by historical narration.

(Saul Friedländer, 2016, pp. 264–65)

The period between World War I and the Holocaust years, 1918–1933, was a time of great possibilities and ferment as the world tried to recover from what was then the most destructive war that had ever been fought. Democratic states replaced monarchies in Germany and elsewhere, women gained new civil rights and made progress toward social and sexual liberation, and the arts flourished. The League of Nations was created in the name of world peace.

Why is it that this time of promise, built out of the ashes of the devastation caused by World War I, was followed by the horrific catastrophe that was the Holocaust? How did the Holocaust happen? Why and how were the Jews, unlike other groups persecuted by the Nazis, targeted for total annihilation? Could the Holocaust have been prevented? Such questions are at the heart of Holocaust research and the teaching of Holocaust literature.

Rarely do English teachers who teach Holocaust literature have sufficient time or background to understand this literature's historical context. Because of the Holocaust's complexity and the immense amounts of documentation and scholarship associated with it, teachers who seek adequate background knowledge to make the literature about it relevant and comprehensible to their students might find this task intimidating, to say the least.

9

To introduce readers to the Holocaust and to guide readers to further study, this chapter provides a brief overview of the history of the Holocaust and the events leading up to it, along with important issues in Holocaust studies as they are relevant to the texts studied in the course. However, it includes little discussion of World War II. The focus is primarily on civilians' experiences under Nazi occupation and rule and after, paralleling the experiences of the main characters in the literary texts discussed in this book.

The goal is to introduce preservice and inservice teachers and teacher educators to the Holocaust in ways that build on what they already know, generate empathy for the victims and survivors, challenge misconceptions, and help them better understand the ethical and moral issues people faced then that relate to what people face today. It behooves all who teach Holocaust literature to learn about the context and significance of the texts they teach and how to apply what they learn to contemporary times without traumatizing students who are new to the subject matter and without trivializing or fetishizing what occurred in the past.

The Holocaust comprised one of the most violent and destructive eras of history. During this time, two-thirds of Europe's Jews were deliberately slaughtered in a state-sponsored genocide. In addition, tens of millions of others—civilians and soldiers—were persecuted, tortured, incarcerated under brutal conditions, murdered, and killed in battle. This is the period during which the National Socialist German Workers Party (NSDAP), commonly known as the Nazi Party, led the government of Germany until its defeat at the end of World War II.[1]

The Nazis called their time in power the Third Reich (Regime or Empire). The First Reich refers to the Holy Roman Empire (800–1806) and the Second Reich to the consolidation of the German nation-state under Chancellor Otto von Bismarck (1871–1918).

Historian Saul Friedländer (1997; 2007) further categorizes this period. He designates 1933–1939, the years prior to the war and before the mass annihilation of the Jews began, as the "years of persecution." During this period Adolf Hitler consolidated his power and the NSDAP became the ruling party in Germany. Germany also began to occupy and take control of other governments and passed laws and implemented policies that gradually eroded the rights and freedoms of the Jews, including citizenship.

Friedländer characterizes 1939–1945 as the "years of extermination." This is the period when World War II was fought. During this time, in Germany and countries it occupied, the NSDAP rounded up and deported Jews who could not or did not flee. Jews in Eastern Europe were first confined to ghettos and then deported to work camps and deathcamps where most died when the Nazis initiated their secretive policy to exterminate the Jews, known as "the Final Solution."

The Nazis' main target was the Jews. They also persecuted, imprisoned, tortured, and murdered countless people in other groups (as discussed in the "Years of Persecution" section in this chapter), but the Nazis slated only the Jews for total annihilation.

Social studies teacher educator David Lindquist (2012) suggests that study of the Holocaust should begin by defining it, showing how the terminology is continually scrutinized. The United States Holocaust Memorial Museum (USHMM) defines the Holocaust as "the systematic, bureaucratic, state-sponsored persecution and murder of six million Jews by the Nazi regime and its collaborators" that happened between 1933 and 1945 (USHMM, "Introduction to the Holocaust").

The appellation "Holocaust" is problematic because it is derived from a Greek term, *holokauston*, meaning "a religious burnt offering." The mass murder of Jews in the years 1939–1945 had nothing to do with religious human sacrifice. It was secular, and it was opportunistic. Despite its descriptive limitations and inaccuracy, however, "Holocaust" is the most widely recognized and most frequently used term.

The most common alternative is the Hebrew word *Shoah*, meaning "catastrophe." This term has fewer religious connotations than does Holocaust but usually refers only to Jewish victims. The Yiddish term *Khurbn*, used by many survivors to describe the Holocaust as the continuation of Jewish persecution, "refers to the destruction of the ancient temples in Jerusalem. . . . The Nazi genocide, in this context, is but the latest in a string of epic catastrophes" (Fleet, 2012, para. 9).

The very reality of the Holocaust is challenged by the Holocaust denial movement, which waxes and wanes depending on the strength of national and international far right political organizing. Historian Deborah Lipstadt discusses the persistent problem of Holocaust denial in a series of books (1994; 2006; 2016) and a film (Foster, Krasnoff, & Jackson, 2016).

Accused of libel by Holocaust denier and historian David Irving, Lipstadt and her legal team documented how he deliberately lied about the Holocaust, claiming that it did not happen. Despite Lipstadt's successful defense, Irving's attack on her fueled other such antisemitic and pseudohistorical versions of the Holocaust that continue to circulate today.

In 1944, Raphael Lemkin, a Jewish Polish lawyer, coined the term "genocide" (Greek *geno*-, meaning "race" or "tribe," plus Latin *-cide*, meaning "killing"). He created the term to describe both the Ottoman Empire's mass murders of Armenians (ca. 1915–1923) and the Holocaust. Until then, the world did not have a particular way to describe such massive events of human destruction or to speak about their common characteristics.

In 1948, the United Nations' Convention on the Prevention and Punishment of the Crime of Genocide declared genocide to be an international crime. In brief, the convention defines the term as "acts committed with intent to destroy, in whole or in part, a national, ethnic, racial or religious group" (United Nations, "Genocide").

Within the last few years, historians have identified limitations even of the term "genocide" because it does not apply to all instances of mass murder and other acts of violence against targeted groups of people. Many academic programs that originally attended only to Holocaust studies now include in their programs all mass crimes against humanity under the umbrella of genocide and mass atrocities studies.

As comparative literature scholar Michael Rothberg (2009) observes, there are aspects of genocide that are common to all specific national contexts. For example, comparative literature scholar Danielle Christmas (2015) emphasizes the parallel racial dimensions of the genocide of Africans on slave ships and plantations and the genocide of the Jews during the Holocaust. In a conference presentation (Christmas, 2014), she also pointed out how the Nazi regime modeled many of its policies against the Jews on the institution of US slavery and on Jim Crow laws, which were instituted after the Reconstruction era.

Still, genocide educator Samuel Totten and Holocaust teacher educator Stephen Feinberg (2009) argue, it is important for educators and scholars to distinguish between different occurrences of mass violence and genocides: "Rationale statements that clearly delineate the distinctions are more likely to result in a study that is both historically accurate and pedagogically sound" (p. 19). Similarly, Lipstadt (1994) cautions us against equating all instances of mass violence. While parallels do need to be drawn, when educators elide differences they overlook the significant particular lessons that each instance of mass violence can teach us (Lipstadt, 1994, p. 27).

Given the extent to which genocides and mass atrocities do share common features, and when there is limited space and time in a curriculum, it can be expedient to concentrate on the Holocaust. There are several reasons to do so.

Jewish and other victims and survivors, social scientists, and others wrote about and documented extensively what happened during and after the Holocaust years. Also, the Nazi bureaucracy emphasized careful record keeping and collecting, so massive quantities of archival materials are available for study. The legacy of over eighty years of Holocaust research, literature, and the arts provides deep insight into human behavior, particularly in relation to the perpetration of cruelty and the failures of ethical and democratic institutions. Rothberg points out that far from blocking other historical memories from view in a competitive struggle for recognition, the emergence of Holocaust memory on a global scale has contributed to the articulation of other histories—some of them predating the Nazi genocide, such as slavery, and others taking place later, such as the Algerian War of Independence (1954–62) or the genocide in Bosnia during the 1990s. (2009, p. 6)

PRECONDITIONS TO THE HOLOCAUST

Antisemitism[2]

When monotheism first appeared approximately four thousand years ago, tribes in the Middle East clashed over control of territory, scarce resources, and religious beliefs. The ancient Israelites, also known as Hebrews (they are referred to both ways in the Hebrew Bible), were one of a number of nomadic groups that settled in Canaan, an area corresponding to modern-day Israel/Palestine. (The term "Jew," which is relatively modern, first referred to the Hebrew tribe of Judah, which settled in Judea, in southern Canaan.) The Israelites established their monotheistic religion there. Due to its strategic location, the land changed hands multiple times. Eventually, most of the Hebrews were forced into exile (Seltzer, 1980, pp. 7–34).

Starting in the fourth century CE with the reign of Emperor Constantine, who converted to Christianity, anti-Jewish religious persecution increased until it reached a pinnacle during the Middle Ages with the Crusades and then the Inquisition. Crusaders slaughtered thousands of Muslims and Jews during the Crusades (eleventh to fourteenth century CE). It was during the Crusades that Christians began claiming that Jews killed Christian children and used their blood for ritual purposes, an accusation called "blood libel."

During the Spanish Inquisition, beginning in 1478, Jews variously were forced to convert to Christianity, burned at the stake, banished, or confined to ghettos. Some 150,000 first were expelled from Spain in 1492 and then again in 1496 from Portugal, where many Spanish Jews had fled, leading to a major Jewish diaspora primarily to Turkey, North Africa, and Italy.

After the fall of the Roman Empire, economic and political dimensions of antisemitism came more to the foreground. As Jews moved into Europe, they worked the land. But when agrarian and craft-based economies developed, Jews, still subjected to intense religious prejudice, were forced off the land and most were restricted from doing all but the most demeaning and dangerous crafts, such as tanning.

Some found security as merchants, developing skills suitable to a diasporic people who moved between cultures and countries and spoke a variety of languages. Rulers began relying on Jews for trade and financial services, and then, when economic conditions worsened, deflected blame for the oppressive feudal system by scapegoating Jews, characterizing them as greedy people who exploited others.

The oppression of Jews was carried out through official policies and extra-legal violence. Laws and decrees provided legal avenues to dispossess, disen-franchise, and expel Jews. Mobs that terrorized Jews by perpetrating violent pogroms,[3] particularly in Eastern Europe, did much of the other dirty work.

During the Enlightenment, sparked by the French Revolution at the end of the eighteenth century and the expansion of secularism, rulers such as Napoleon repealed some restrictions on Jewish life in a process that came to be known as the Jewish emancipation. By the late nineteenth to early twen-tieth century, many urban Jews, particularly in Western and Central Europe, had assimilated into mainstream European society.

Jews there were not segregated and confined to ghettos, although some cities continued to have Jewish quarters, a holdover from the Middle Ages when Jews were forcibly segregated from the rest of society. They engaged in many occupations and were found in every economic class (Berenbaum, 2003, pp. 4–5). Doris Bergen points out that Jewish people "often differed as much, and in many cases, more, from one another than they did from the Christians around them" (2016, p. 20).

Judaism included a broad range of religious expression, from the most insular, like the Orthodox and Hasidic branches, to the Reform movement, which emphasizes adapting rituals, practices, and lifestyles to modern times and secular culture. Many Jews, including lay leaders and liberal rabbis, "wanted to join the ranks of the German bourgeoisie. . . . [T]he collective effort of adaptation led to deep reshaping of Jewish identity in the religious domain as well as in a variety of secular pursuits and attitudes" (Friedländer, 1997, p. 80).

The Nazi Ideology of Race and Space

After World War I, antisemitism escalated again. Anti-Jewish organizations like the National Socialist German Workers' Party claimed that Jews' efforts to integrate into the mainstream constituted a Jewish conspiracy to gain con-trol over the economy as well as the cultural realm. Adopting popular social Darwinist ideas of the time, Nazis propagated a mythical stereotype of "the Jew," eliding distinctions among Jews and overemphasizing differences from the rest of the German population, including stereotypical physical characteristics.

Social Darwinism, a sociological theory that developed in the mid-nineteenth century, was a distortion of Darwin's theory of evolution and natural selection that applied the biological concept of "survival of the fittest" to a sociological context. The pseudoscience of eugenics, which promotes the idea that selective reproduction can improve human populations and societies, was developed from this theory.

To justify their racism, social Darwinists claimed that humans could be categorized into different "genetic" races. Jews, Roma and Sinti,[4] and "Aryans," for example, were considered to be separate races.[5] These theorists differentiated people by imagined and exaggerated physical and psychological characteristics.

"Aryans," Hitler claimed, were the master race. The term "originally referred to a group of people in ancient India. Hitler drew on vague theories that these people . . . were a superior group who somehow ended up in Europe" (Bergen, 2016, p. 52), thus transforming the word "Aryan" into a racist, socially constructed concept. Hitler formulated and promoted, and the Nazis adopted, his particularly virulent and obsessive strain of antisemitism, what Friedländer (1997) terms "redemptive antisemitism."

Hitler proposed that Germany, the contemporary home of the master "race," needed to acquire *Lebensraum* (living space) and resources in order for the "Aryans" to remain racially pure, thrive, and dominate. According to the Nazis, "Since each 'race' sought to expand, and since the space on the earth was finite, the struggle for survival resulted 'naturally' in violent conquest and military confrontation. Hence, war . . . was a part of nature" (USHMM, "Victims of the Nazi Era"). McKale spells out the horrifying implications of this ideology: "Opposing racial groups could never be assimilated, but only enslaved, expelled, or exterminated" (2002, p. 197).

Bergen, Friedländer, and McKale consider the Nazi focus on race and Lebensraum to be at the core of Hitler's worldview. The Nazis abandoned Enlightenment and religious concepts about goodness, liberty, equality, and fraternity and instead built their system of governance and culture on concepts such as racial purity and achieving national dominance. This system provided the framework for the moral degradation and inhumane cruelty that defined the Holocaust.

The Versailles Treaty and the Weimar Republic (1918–1933)

The German defeat in World War I humiliated Germany's military leaders. To shift the blame for military losses to explain their defeat, those who gained power after World War I and in the far right political movement scapegoated Jews, pacifists, and Communists. As the sources of the German people's postwar woes, they cited the Versailles Treaty, which set out the terms of peace at the end of World War I; the Weimar Republic, an emerging democratic state marked by social liberalization; and the Great Depression, which they saw as being precipitated by Jews.

The far right characterized the treaty as unfair because the German government did not participate in treaty negotiations and claimed that its terms led to Germany's postwar economic hardships (Bergen, 2016, pp. 41–42). Under the treaty's terms, Germany did give up about 10 percent of its territory, including some recently acquired. This included the Rhineland, the westernmost part of Germany along the Rhine River, which was designated a demilitarized zone to act as a buffer with France.

However, Germany paid little of the reparations demanded under the terms of the treaty, and the signatory nations did not enforce collection, as they were wary of provoking further conflict. The Germans did experience a year of hyperinflation, but many historians analyze that as a strategic economic move by the German government to avoid paying reparations (Bergen, 2016, p. 45).

So, while Germany's postwar economic woes were related to the war, the country actually emerged from the war as Europe's strongest country economically. This is because the war was not fought on German soil, and therefore its infrastructure and industries survived mostly intact (Weinberg, 1995, p. 51; Bergen, 2016, pp. 61–65; McKale, 2002, pp. 20–22).

The Weimar Republic (1918–1933) was established after World War I, overthrowing the monarchy and instituting Germany's first democratic constitution. The Republic also fostered social and cultural progress. For example, women benefited from significant social advances. As historian Helen Boak (2013) documents, the Weimar Constitution advocated that marriage should be based on the equality of the sexes. Women gained more reproductive rights and the right to vote. World War I also brought opportunities for women to work outside the home and be more independent, although this was less true for women in rural areas.

Historian Elizabeth D. Heineman (2002) and queer cultural theorist William Spurlin (2008) discuss the large lesbian and gay underground that thrived during this era. At the time, the imperial laws against male homosexuality remained in place but were not regularly enforced. Unlike gay men's sexual activities, lesbians' sexual activities were not criminalized. (Lesbians suffered more from the Nazi persecution of unmarried and working women [Heineman, 2002, pp. 34–35].)

Conservative and nationalist Germans hated the republic. McKale writes, "Hitler denounced the Weimar regime as foreign and alien to Germany, born of revolution and forced upon its people, and the product of a Jewish-Marxist plot against the nation" (2002, p. 20). Historian Dagmar Herzog (2005) adds, "All the complexities and contrary political and social impulses of German life between 1919 and 1933 were obscured and displaced by an image of Weimar as a hothouse of decadence and promiscuity" (pp. 20–21).

Hitler and his allies longed for the return of what they considered to be proud German values, including authoritarianism. The Nazis instituted a propaganda campaign, ran for offices, and established the *Sturmabteilung* (Stormtroopers, or SA), a paramilitary police force that used violent tactics to help destabilize the Weimar Republic. The SA continued to operate for the first years after Hitler came to power.

Contrary to common belief, Hitler did not attain his position at the head of the German government primarily on the strength of his charisma. Bergen points out that "Hitler was not swept into power by a stampede of German voters hypnotized by his oratorical skills, nor did he seize power by an illegal coup d'état" (2016, p. 61). Nor was the NSDAP's ascendancy a natural outcome of Germany's defeat or the Great Depression. The Great Depression, precipitated by the US stock market crash of 1929, affected Germany as it did the rest of the world.

Rather, in the end, political maneuvering on the part of the German political, military, and corporate establishments backfired, leading to Hitler's succession to power. In 1930, facing a major economic and political crisis, the German president, Paul von Hindenburg, under pressure from the right, invoked an article of the constitution that allowed Hitler to govern by decree.

Following this, the Nazis gained seats in the Reichstag (Parliament), as did the Communists. Hitler, meanwhile, lost his bid for the presidency, with only 37 percent of those who voted casting their ballots for him. Conservative industrialists and nationalists, however, argued that appointing Hitler as chancellor, which Hindenburg did in 1933, was the best way both to control the far right and to "defuse discontent among workers and prevent any increase of Communist strength" (Bergen, 2016, p. 67). But once Hitler was at the helm, the Nazi Party took complete control of the government.

THE HOLOCAUST YEARS

Years of Persecution (1933–1939): The Nazi Party in Control

This is the period coinciding with the first Holocaust text the students read in the course, Hans Peter Richter's *Friedrich*. In his novel, based on the author's boyhood experiences, Richter investigates the relationship between a Jewish and non-Jewish family who live in the same building. He narrates, from a youth's perspective, many aspects of the years of persecution, showing how this period in German history affected individuals, families, and a community.

Like other urban Jews in Germany and elsewhere, the Schneider family lived an assimilated life in a German city. All this changed in 1933, when Hitler became chancellor and took over legislative and executive powers through the Enabling Act, which disempowered the Reichstag and gave him dictatorial powers. Hitler no longer had to seek the Reichstag's approval to implement directives. His first move was to outlaw all political parties but the Nazi Party.

Hitler was now positioned to move ahead with his efforts to rid society of any people who presented obstacles to the Nazi campaign to achieve "Aryan" domination and imperial conquest. The NSDAP's first victims were Communists, other leftists, and trade unionists, who the Nazis either murdered or imprisoned in the first concentration camp, Dachau. Following this initial purge of their political enemies, the Nazis turned to other marginal groups previously discriminated against in society: people with disabilities, Jews, gay men and gender-nonconforming women and men, Sinti and Roma people, African Germans, Jehovah's Witnesses, antifascist clergy, and other political resisters.

This campaign was carried out predominantly by the SA, headed by Ernst Röhm; the *Gestapo*, the secret state police force comprised of members of the Nazi Party and headed by Hermann Göring; and the *Schutzstaffel* (SS), headed by Heinrich Himmler, which was an elite guard formed to provide security for the Nazi leadership. (SS members later were placed in charge of the concentration and deathcamps.)

"In all its major decisions the regime depended on Hitler," writes Friedländer (1997), but he cautions not to accept the common and reductive viewpoint that Hitler was solely responsible for determining the trajectory of the Third Reich. Hitler did not make decisions without consulting his inner circle. His initiatives "were molded not only by his worldview but also by the impact of internal pressures, the weight of bureaucratic constraints, at times the influence of German opinion at large and even the reactions of foreign governments and foreign opinion" (p. 3).

Hitler tested the waters of public opinion especially in this first year but also throughout the era of the Third Reich. For instance, people put up little resistance when his social restructuring agenda included attacking homosexuals. There already was precedent in Paragraph 175 of the criminal code, that made sexual relations between men illegal, and many Germans considered homosexuality to be deviant and immoral. The persecution of homosexuals provided an emotional social outlet for people who were against the liberalization of social mores that happened during Weimar.

On the other hand, a boycott of Jewish businesses in 1933 met with public disapproval and was discontinued. The SA aggressively enforced the boycott, but many Germans, motivated by self-interest and uncomfortable with the SA's violent tactics, defied it. They continued to patronize Jewish shops, and, internationally, human rights activists and Jews threatened a counterboycott of German goods.

Catholic and Protestant Church leaders and victims' relatives strenuously protested the systematic killing of children and adults with mental and physical disabilities that began in 1939 and which the Nazis speciously characterized as euthanasia, implying that killing people with disabilities was a humane way to end their suffering. Responding to the resistance, the Nazis continued the killing, but in secret. (This is also discussed in Chapter 4 under the heading "Class Discussion.")

Beginning in 1933, the Nazis sterilized about four hundred thousand people with disabilities, alcoholics, Roma and Sinti, and people of mixed African and German heritage. Some Catholic clergymen and victims' relatives also protested the "eugenic" sterilization program, but ineffectively.

The Nazis were able to attract public support for the fascist government from many non-Jewish Germans by taking over youth groups and doling out favors and rewards to adults who joined the Nazi Party, including access to good housing and high-paying jobs. The government also created jobs through public works programs and rearmament and sponsored mass production of low-cost consumer items such as radios and Volkswagens. The Nazis even set up a travel and leisure activity agency to persuade Germans to associate fascism with pleasure.

Heineman and Herzog emphasize how the Nazi regime garnered support by providing opportunities for heterosexual and gender-normative pleasure while simultaneously dismantling women's rights and the greater sexual freedom attained during the Weimar era. Bergen adds, "Members of the general public were more likely to participate in or at least tolerate attacks on minorities if they stood to gain . . . from such initiatives" (2016, p. 78).

From 1934 to 1937, the Nazis consolidated their power. After withdrawing from the League of Nations, in July 1933 Hitler signed a concordat with the Vatican. In it, Pope Pius XI pledged to support the Nazi government in exchange for the government's protection of church organizations, such as Catholic schools, and Jews who had converted. The Nazis normalized violence and coercion as ways to gain control over civilian enemies and to secure citizens' compliance.

In 1936, Hitler tested Europe's willingness to fight back when his troops invaded the Rhineland, the zone between France and Germany that had been demilitarized under the terms of the Versailles Treaty. Meeting with no resistance from France, Hitler proclaimed the government to have "restored the full and unrestricted sovereignty of the Reich" (quoted in Bergen, 2016, p. 98).

The government began to institute anti-Jewish policies when Hitler came to power and continued to do so throughout the years of the Third Reich. The German Parliament passed the anti-Jewish Nuremberg Race Laws in 1935. These laws forbade sexual relationships between Jews and "Aryan" Germans and defined Jews genealogically rather than according to religious practice. The laws were expanded in a flurry of further legal prohibitions that affected every aspect of life. Jews were fired from professional jobs, expelled from public schools, and evicted from their homes. They were stripped of citizenship.

These laws and practices effectively isolated Jews from Gentile mainstream society, making it easier for non-Jewish Germans to turn their backs on their former neighbors and associates.[6] *Friedrich* illustrates this process, showing what happened to Jews and how most ordinary non-Jewish Germans, aside from a minority of rescuers and resisters, went along with Nazi policies. The laws eventually expanded to countries invaded by Germany and its allies, paving the way for the concentration camps and genocide. "Once Jews were defined, it would be much easier to isolate, rob, deport, and eventually kill them" (Bergen, 2016, p. 94).

Besides instituting and enforcing laws restricting Jews, the new regime stepped up discriminatory practices against other minorities. For instance, the Nazi government revised Paragraph 175. Paragraph 175a provided more explicit and more inclusive descriptions of punishable sex acts and increased penalties, including concentration camp imprisonment and castration. Even suggestive glances and affectionate words directed to someone of the same sex were considered criminal behavior. To enforce the law, police often raided gay clubs and bars and needed only denunciations or tip-offs to make arrests (Herzog, 2005, p. 89; McKale, 2002, p. 357).

Once the majority of non-Jewish Germans accepted the initial wave of violence and legislation that brought Hitler to power, they became increasingly compliant. Millions of ordinary people endorsed and overtly or covertly supported the regime. After the Malicious Practices Act (1933) was instituted, which banned remarks that offended or subverted Nazi authority, people reported on suspected resisters to demonstrate loyalty, secure promotions, attack outsiders, or as retribution for past disagreements.

On a day-to-day basis, even those who did not support the NSDAP or benefit from Nazi patronage were complacent. "The Nazi regime only needed most people to obey the law, try to stay out of trouble, and promote their own interests as best they could under the current circumstances" (Bergen, 2016, p. 97).

Many non-Jewish professionals—teachers, journalists, doctors, lawyers, and judges—found it advantageous to serve the Nazi cause. These citizens, especially those in the legal professions, legitimized the Reich in the eyes of many international observers and ordinary Germans. For professionals who continued to associate with Jews, however, charges of *Rassenschande* (racial shame) led to the destruction of their relationships and careers. (In the United States, this also happened to whites who allied themselves with blacks during slavery and afterward.)

Shortly before Germany invaded Poland, the Nazi Party orchestrated a pogrom, known as *Kristallnacht* ("The Night of Broken Glass"), to increase pressure on the Jews. On November 9, 1938, the Nazi Party ordered or encouraged the SA, members of Hitler Youth, and fascist partisans to attack Jewish communities across Germany, including in the Sudetenland (the northwest region of what was then Czechoslovakia) and Austria. Many ordinary non-Jewish people got caught up in the mobs and joined the destruction.

The attackers torched synagogues and destroyed ritual objects such as Torah scrolls. They smashed windows of Jewish businesses, trashed Jewish homes, beat and raped their occupants, and stole and vandalized Jewish personal belongings. During the pogrom about one hundred Jews died and some thirty thousand Jewish men were arrested and deported to concentration camps.

Many Gentiles, horrified by what they were witnessing, rushed to the aid of those under attack and even rescued precious artifacts from synagogues. The Nazis got the message that a significant portion of the public disapproved of the chaotic and disturbing nature of the events; this pogrom was the last time non-Jewish Germans witnessed widespread public displays of antisemitic violence.

During the prewar years, about half of Germany's Jews emigrated, the majority leaving after Kristallnacht, because they worried that current conditions made it too dangerous to stay. However, some saw it as a pogrom that eventually would die down as others had in the past. Many assimilated German Jews who identified as German citizens first refused to leave their own country. Others would not leave elders behind who were too frail to travel. Many more had no resources and were unable to escape in time.

It also became increasingly difficult to find a place that would accept them as immigrants. By 1939, many doors were closed, and last-ditch efforts, like that of the *St. Louis* ocean liner that was refused entry first to Cuba and then the United States, often were thwarted. One of the few successful collective efforts was the *Kindertransport*, organized by the British government in response to Kristallnacht, which succeeded in saving ten thousand Jewish children whom the parents sent away so those children could survive. Most of the children never saw their parents again.

Years of Extermination (1939–1945): War and Genocide

As early as 1933, the regime began to rearm, secretly at first, but by 1935 openly, and through conscription and manufacturing built up the armed forces. After retaking the Rhineland in 1936, Hitler appointed Hermann Göring to oversee a four-year plan to prepare Germany economically and militarily for war. He purged the old military elite and consolidated his hold on the armed forces, installing his own officers and assuming the position of minister of war.

In 1938, Germany annexed Austria unopposed in the operation known as the *Anschluss*. The regime succeeded in conquering Czechoslovakia the following year with no military opposition. Now, with the German war machine fully prepared, the Third Reich was ready for full-scale military invasion of Poland.

The "Final Solution": The Functionalist/Intentionalist Debate

Before 1941, forced emigration and resettlement were the main tactics used by the Nazis to rid Germany and the lands it conquered of Jews. The mass killing began in the 1930s, but it was not until 1942 that the Nazis perfected and implemented mass murder on a vast scale and embarked on what they called the "Final Solution," with its goal being the total annihilation of Jews. Approximately 75 percent of the Jews who were murdered during the Holocaust died between 1942 and 1945 in a many-pronged campaign throughout Nazi-occupied territories. Historian Gerhard Weinberg (1998) emphasizes the connection between World War II and the annihilation of the Jews. He claims that the genocide could not have been carried out without the camouflage of war. McKale agrees: "This was a 'shadow war' in which they would eliminate millions of Jews—a people whom the Nazis hated more than anything or anyone else" (2002, p. 2).

Who instigated this policy of mass murder, and what was the process by which the Nazis implemented it? This is a matter of considerable debate among Holocaust historians.

In *Mein Kampf,* published in 1923, Hitler blamed twelve thousand or so "Hebrew corrupters of the people" for Germany's defeat in World War I and proposed that if this group had been gassed, millions of other Germans would not have died (quoted in McKale, 2002, p. 23). After he came to power, however, Hitler never did sign any document specifically ordering the extermination of Jews through mass murder.

Intentionalists, among them historian Lucy Dawidowicz (1986), present evidence that Nazi leaders circulated ideas about exterminating the Jews even before Hitler came to power.

Functionalist historians, including Raul Hilberg (1961/1985) and Hans Mommsen (1991), assert that once it became evident to Nazi planners that the complicated strategy of evacuating and resettling Jews was impeding their goal of Lebensraum, they saw genocide as their best practical option.

Other scholars, such as historian Christopher Browning (1992), see merit in both explanations. They recognize that Hitler and his inner circle were virulently antisemitic and supported murdering Jews even early on but that approval for the genocide grew out of their frustration that previous solutions for ridding Europe of the Jews had failed.

Ghettoization enabled mass murder by physically weakening potential resisters and gathering the Jewish population for easy deportation to killing sites. Historians also point to the mass killings of Jews that spiked in 1941–1942, coinciding with the invasion of the Soviet Union. Rooted in anti-semitism, these massacres were perpetrated by local officials, trained Nazis, and ordinary Germans who organized into paramilitary units that had considerable autonomy to make their own decisions. Once the genocide became an overt goal of the Third Reich, German bureaucratic and industrial efficiency enabled the genocide to occur on a massive scale.

The Concentrationary Universe

After reading *Friedrich*, students turned to the experiences of Jewish women and children in the deathcamps, represented in two short stories: "Esther's First Born" by Sara Nomberg-Przytyk and "The Shawl" by Cynthia Ozick (both in Teichman & Leder, 1994), discussed in Chapter 6. They also read about Auschwitz in Art Spiegelman's *Maus* (1986), discussed in Chapter 7.

David Rousset, a Buchenwald political prisoner from France, coined the term "concentrationary universe" to describe the brutal totalitarian environment of the concentration and extermination camps, called *Lagers* (the German word for "camp"). Holocaust scholars also have come to include in this "universe" the ghettos where Jews were relocated and the transport centers where Jews were forcibly gathered to await deportation.

The Nazis opened Dachau in 1933, and other Lagers opened during subsequent years. The camps first were designated for Germans and were located in Germany, but after the war began, the Nazis established hundreds of ghettos, concentration camps, transit centers, and eventually, killing sites scattered across all occupied territories.[7] These places could be anything from a forest clearing where people of a village were rounded up, shot, and buried in open pits, to huge facilities like Auschwitz-Birkenau, where thousands of people were gassed and cremated daily.

They were sites of torture, extreme degradation, disease, and murder, where victims were killed one by one or in large groups. In concentration camps the prisoners were forced into slave labor while simultaneously being tortured and starved to death. People were warehoused in transit centers before being transported on cattle cars or trucks to extermination camps. Many people never made it to the extermination centers. They were marched off of trains and trucks and gunned down on the side of the road and tracks or gassed in vans.

As noted above, when the Nazis invaded the Soviet Union in 1941, murder squads called *Einsatzgruppen* (special action groups), paramilitary police, and civilian collaborators killed as many as two million people. These special forces were tasked to move across the countryside, stirring up pogroms and systematically killing as many Jews, Communists, Roma and Sinti, and other targeted people as possible. People they captured were transported to extermination centers, where they were unloaded and marched to their immediate deaths (Browning, 1992).

The top officers and officials in the camps were recruited from Nazi police units like the SS and Gestapo. Guards and others in functionary positions, both men and women, were recruited from the non-Jewish population through advertisements that promised job security and high wages. Doctors who examined prisoners to determine whether they were fit to work or should be selected for extermination, and medical researchers who performed grisly experiments on prisoners, were persuaded that they were doing their patriotic duty.

The Nazis recruited or conscripted many other functionary workers from within the prison populations. The *kapos* were guards who enforced the rules; many committed brutal atrocities. Other prisoners also occupied low-level positions and in exchange received favors. Professionals, such as doctors and accountants, often were forced to serve the Nazis. Jewish women also were conscripted as sex slaves, despite the laws against "Aryans" having sexual relations with Jews. Then there were the *Sonderkommandos*, who manned the gas chambers and crematoria.

Many prisoners resisted, revolted, and tried to escape. Most of these were murdered. Others surreptitiously documented the horrors of the camps in photographs and diaries that survived the war and provided valuable evidence for war crimes trials and historical research. About 450 participated in the largest insurrection at Auschwitz-Birkenau. There, Sonderkommandos blew up part of a crematorium, but in the fighting that followed, the SS killed all who participated in the rebellion (McKale, 2002, pp. 376–78).

Jewish Passivity and Resistance

Holocaust literature scholar Lawrence L. Langer describes how his students raised the same questions semester after semester over the years: "How could the victims have been so passive? How could they let them do that without fighting back?" These questions are echoed time and again among the general population, despite the evidence of widespread resistance. My students also posed similar questions. Langer concludes that many of their questions indicate "a naïveté about individual behavior and forces of history" (2000, p. 196).

Antisemitic Germans "wanted to show Jews as weak, to highlight their own strength and portray Jewish death as almost inevitable" (Bergen, 2016, p. 265). The judgment that people make even today—that Jews were passive, even fatalistic—also is grounded in antisemitism (albeit, for some people, probably unconscious) and shifts the blame from perpetrator to victim.

There were good reasons why many Jews could not or did not resist individually or militarily. Elders and children, especially, could not defend themselves. The vast majority did not have the skills or resources to engage in combat. Many of those who did, leftists and social reformers, were arrested early on. What some describe as Jewish passivity is related also to the different ways people understood and coped with their oppression.

Even when Jews did not stand up to the Nazis, they did not succumb "like sheep to slaughter," to use a scornful expression often used to describe Jewish behavior when they were thrown out of their homes, forced into ghettos, loaded onto freight cars, and led into the gas chambers.[8] Many understood the inevitability of their doom but also that if they resisted they likely would be tortured and shot on the spot and also would put their families and neighbors in mortal danger.

Some Jews believed that rumors of extreme and inhumane cruelty could not be true and held on to their faith in humanity to the bitter end. Many of them maintained a strong sense of their dignity, self-worth, and Jewish identity. In *An Iron Wind: Europe under Hitler* (2016), historian Peter Fritzsche writes that these Jews refused "to be defined by their enemy" and go to their deaths "degraded and dejected" (p. 209).

Art Spiegelman's father, Vladek, who is the main protagonist in *Maus*, vividly describes this problem. After Vladek tells Art about the gruesome slaughter of Hungarian Jews at Auschwitz, Art asks why the Jews did not resist. Vladek replies, "In some spots people did fight . . . but you can kill maybe one German before they kill fast a hundred from you. Then it's everyone dead" (Spiegelman, 1992, p. 73). He confirms the extreme forms of retaliation the Nazis employed to suppress the populations they subjugated.

Despite the risks, Jews and non-Jews did resist, individually and collectively. For family or personal reasons, religious and moral principles, or political beliefs, people privately or openly criticized or actively countered the Nazis. Individuals and subversive networks hid Jews and facilitated their escapes. Partisan underground actions included sabotage and anti-Nazi intelligence gathering, ghetto uprisings, and various forms of resistance in the concentration camps. Antifascists and Jews enlisted in the armies of countries fighting the Nazis. In all, many thousands of Jewish and non-Jewish resisters defied Hitler's regime.

However, all these acts of resistance together were unable to stop the organized and relentless drive of Hitler and the fully militarized Third

Reich to achieve their goals of completely racializing society and attaining Lebensraum through colonial occupation and imperialist conquest, massively enriching those in power.

STUDENTS RESPOND TO *WAR AND GENOCIDE*

After completing the unit on antisemitism that began the course, and to prepare to study and teach *Friedrich*, students read the first three chapters of *War and Genocide*.[9] In those chapters, Bergen discusses the preconditions to the Holocaust, Hitler and his inner circle, the Nazification of German society, and the drive toward war. Students then wrote journal entries about what surprised them, what questions they still had after reading the chapters, and, after reading *Friedrich*, how reading Bergen affected their understanding of the novel.

Many students who had studied World War II had never questioned the popular theory that the Versailles Treaty caused egregious harm to the German people, the Weimar Republic destroyed the economy and undermined German moral and cultural values, and that these were the primary reasons for Hitler's rise to power. They noted Bergen's explanation that these reasons were used as a false pretext for Nazism and that a fascist reaction to Weimar and Versailles was not inevitable (Bergen, 2016, pp. 61–64).

Actually, Nazis and right-wing nationalists disseminated propaganda and took paramilitary actions to foment popular resentment about the Versailles Treaty, thus deflecting blame from the military for Germany's defeat. To undermine the Weimar Republic, destroy the reforms that led to more social equality, and pave the way for fascism, the Nazis played on people's fears of communism and socialism. As stated earlier, Germany's economic woes had to do more with the Great Depression than with reparations and the progressive moves toward social and economic equality under Weimar.

The idea of the inevitability of fascism in Germany, successfully transmitted even to our students today, does not hold up when we compare how progressive policies instituted after the Russian Revolution, many of which were similar to those of Weimar Germany, did not lead to fascism there. Nor did the Great Depression, coupled with liberal social and economic reforms, lead to fascism in England and the United States. Despite this argument, however, some students were not convinced and continued to assign blame to the treaty and Weimar rather than to Nazi propaganda about the Versailles Treaty, Weimar, and political and paramilitary maneuvers.

Not many of these English preservice teachers showed strong interest in the political background of the Holocaust, though, except as it pertained to Hitler. In their journals, more students commented on Hitler than on other historical or political aspects of the Holocaust. They mentioned his problematic psychological profile: his self-aggrandizement, insistence on eliminating or unseating anyone who disagreed with him, antisemitic rage, and virulent racism.

However, reading Bergen caused them to question the myth that Hitler was popularly elected and was just a madman who brainwashed everyone into playing along with his scapegoating of the Jews. It helped them understand the importance of the functionalist-intentionalist debate and how it both explains and tempers the importance of Hitler's influence. The Holocaust, they saw, was not the responsibility of one man, a unique historical aberration that could never happen again. Knowing that Hitler did not act alone but rather was part of a group of like-minded fascist co-conspirators was important new information for many.

Further, the students better understood that the Holocaust was not a catastrophe that happened only during the war but gradually evolved over the course of the years between the wars. The changes instituted by the Nazis incrementally ate away at the rights and dignity of Jews and degraded the morality of many Gentile citizens over several years before the years of extermination began.

How fascism correlates with racism was another topic students discussed. Historians have an overall concern about "the role of racial and political ideology as a motivator for German atrocities and behavior on 'ordinary' Germans" (McKale, 2002, p. 10). To what extent were perpetrators acting out of ideological belief in fascism, and to what extent were they manifesting fanatical antisemitism and racism?

Racism can and does exist separately from fascism. However, given its assaults on democratic values and institutions, its national chauvinism, and its imperialist aims, fascism does tend to have a strong racist component. Such considerations are key to unraveling the complexity of the Holocaust and the literature that emerged from it.

Questions and Answers

How to compare fascism to racism and other questions students raised when discussing Bergen and the literature's historical contexts throughout the semester, along with what their questions implied, revealed what they most needed to learn but also that the students did not easily retain and apply what they studied from one session and one text to another. However, by articulating and posing their own questions, students indicated that they were aware of many issues, were thinking critically about them, and were situated to pursue future research.

Q: "Since the Jews were so few in number, why was getting rid of Jews
   part of the Nazis' race and space ideology?" Bergen discusses this in
   her section on Hitler's worldview (2016, pp. 52–53) and elsewhere.
   The answer, discussed below, also lies in the history of antisemitism,
   which we studied before reading *War and Genocide*.

A: Jews had been scapegoated, discriminated against, and slaughtered
   for centuries, so there was precedence. Orthodox Jews who had not
   assimilated were easily targeted because many lived in isolated rural
   areas or urban enclaves and ghettos. Even those Jews who were highly
   assimilated still were singled out as different because of their cultural
   and religious differences from the majority populations in Europe.
   Hitler and his propaganda specialists racialized these differences by
   setting up false comparisons between what they claimed to be Jewish
   and "Aryan" physical features.

Also, the Nazis exaggerated Jewish influence on society. They
overemphasized and criticized the noticeable Jewish presence in certain
professions, such as finance and business, the arts, the academy, and the
industrial labor movement. They claimed that these Jews were trying to take
over society. Such conspiracy theories, fueled by intense state-supported
propaganda and linked to the *Protocols of the Elders of Zion* (originated
in 1903; USHMM, "Protocols of the Elders of Zion"), a fraudulent Czarist
document that describes an alleged international Jewish conspiracy for world
domination, quickly gained traction among non-Jews.[10]
It is true that the percentages of Jews working in these occupations, rela-
tive to the size of the Jewish population as a whole, was greater than the
percentages of the general population similarly employed. However, this was
because Jews were banned from many other jobs and professions due to the
history of European antisemitism, not because of any conspiracy. They had
always been shut out of high-ranking government and military positions.

Q: "How was homophobia related to Nazism?"

A: This question is related to the widespread myth that Hitler was
   gay and acted out his internalized homophobia violently. The
   myth provides a way for people to blame Nazi brutality on another
   persecuted minority, a point that Bergen raises in her book. There
   is no credible evidence that Hitler was anything but heterosexual
   (2016, p. 48). Nevertheless, unlike Himmler, who was intolerant of
   and hypersensitive to the homoeroticism inherent in the masculinist
   ideology that encouraged male bonding among the military and police
   forces (Boden, 2011), Hitler tolerated homosexuals in the upper
   echelons of his elite.

In 1934, however, Hitler ordered the SS to assassinate openly gay Ernst Röhm, head of the SA, and Röhm's closest allies. Now that the Nazis could legally persecute liberal and leftist individuals and organizations, they no longer needed the extralegal Stormtroopers, who had become a liability because of the violent tactics they used to suppress the opposition. The Nazi leadership, playing to its base, used the charge of homosexuality as a cover for the killings, calling it "a necessary measure against decadence and perversion" (Bergen, 2016, p. 89).

Bergen raises similar concerns about the myth, for which there is no credible evidence, that Hitler had a Jewish grandparent and thus could be considered Jewish. She explains that through these rumors, some of Hitler's critics cast aspersions on Hitler, playing both on homophobia and antisemitism. Both rumors aim to discredit Hitler, because each group was considered to be inferior and evil (Bergen 2016, p. 18).

Strengths and Limitations

Even after reading the chapters in *War and Genocide*, some students still held on to inaccurate or biased antisemitic or pro-Nazi viewpoints about the history of the Holocaust. This became evident in some of the journals they wrote and lesson plans they created and taught. They often found corroboration for these perspectives in deceptive online sources they used to help them prepare their own practice lessons.

When some students learned for the first time that the Nazis also persecuted other groups besides Jews, they suspected that people who taught them about the Holocaust must have been biased against others who were persecuted. There may be some truth to this claim. Teaching about homosexuality is still taboo in many high schools; so is discussion about communism and socialism. Despite the gains of the disability rights movement, this topic rarely makes it into the curriculum. Other minorities who were persecuted, such as Roma and Sinti, are also hardly on the radar in the United States.

Within the constraints of curricula, the tendency to concentrate on Jews, who were the only group targeted for total extermination, is understandable. Paying no attention to these other victims and survivors, on the other hand, is not acceptable. Students grappled with the problem of how, in their curricula, teachers could balance the important fact that persecution of the Jews was at the center of Nazi ideology and that the Jews were the only group marked for total extinction with the fact that Nazi persecution also devastated many other stigmatized minorities.

Their reading and discussion of the three chapters in Bergen's book did seem to make a difference to most students. While they could not assimilate immediately all the new information they were learning, they did realize that there are no simple explanations for the Holocaust. In particular, they learned how ordinary people became perpetrators. They realized that citizens' resistance was limited. Acquiescence became routine. Non-Jewish Germans often willingly participated in or were complicit in antisemitic attacks, if not for ideological reasons then for financial gain or social benefits.

Still, reading three chapters in an historical overview, though instructive, was insufficient. For more historical information and teaching resources, students were directed to the rest of Bergen's book and websites such as the USHMM's "Resources for Educators" and "Topics to Teach," Echoes and Reflections, the University of Southern California Shoah Foundation, and Facing History and Ourselves.

LEARNING THE HISTORY UNDERLYING
THE LITERATURE

There is no easy fix to the problem of how best to prepare English teachers to understand the historical context of Holocaust literature. To enhance their preparation, inservice teachers could take advantage of workshops and professional development opportunities offered by museums and other organizations (see Chapter 8). They also could read other detailed histories. We primarily consulted Bergen's *War and Genocide* (2016), McKale's *Hitler's Shadow War* (2002), and Friedländer's 1997 and 2007 texts on the years of persecution and extermination.

Teachers also can supplement their study by reading or viewing testimonies. Several websites offer access to films and videos of survivors' testimonies, including the Fortunoff Video Archive for Holocaust Testimonies at Yale University, the Steven Spielberg Film and Video Archive at the USHMM, and the Visual History Archive at the University of Southern California Shoah Foundation.

Carefully vetted supplemental reading and research should accompany any curriculum that incorporates Holocaust literature. However, it is not easy to choose the best texts and other resources. There are many sources, particularly on the internet, that contain Holocaust-denial or ultra-right-wing propaganda, which students may not recognize if they discover those sites on their own. Providing students with easy access to resources teachers have vetted by consulting reliable websites or the works of recognized scholars, many of whom we mention in this book, will reduce the risk of students going to inaccurate websites on their own.

No one could expect high school English teachers to read all the texts recommended herein, view even a small percentage of the testimonies available, attend workshops far from home, and also prepare themselves culturally to teach a Holocaust literature unit. At best, a highly committed teacher might accomplish much of this preparation over several years. At least, teachers should study the main historical trajectory of the Holocaust and the salient issues and questions in Holocaust studies before teaching any Holocaust literature—an effort this book is intended to assist. This chapter focuses on historical context. Chapters 3 through 7 provide cultural context specific to the literature discussed in each chapter.

NOTES

1. The National Socialist German Workers' Party formed in the early 1920s. The word "Socialist" in its name was used to deceive workers, many of whom were socialists and communists.

2. We prefer "antisemitism" to "anti-Semitism." The term "Semitic" refers to a group of related languages, including Hebrew, and the people who speak them. There is no such concept as "Semitism." "Antisemitism" refers specifically to animosity toward Jews.

3. Pogroms originally were described as organized mob violence, including massacres, against Jewish communities in Russia in the late nineteenth and early twentieth centuries. The definition has since been extended to include other such anti-Jewish attacks throughout history and occasionally to similar attacks against other ethnic minorities.

4. Two branches of an ethnic minority believed to have originated in India and often referred to collectively as "Gypsies," which is a misnomer associated with prejudice. The Roma generally resided in Austria, the Balkans, and Eastern Europe, and the Sinti in Germany and Western Europe (USHMM, "Who Were the Gypsies?").

5. In the United States, where eugenics originated, social Darwinists applied this theory to justify subjugating African Americans.

6. In this book, the descriptors "Gentile" and "non-Jew" are used interchangeably to connote anyone who is not Jewish. The term "gentile" does not have to be capitalized but we do so because we are discussing Gentiles in relation to Jews and do not want to privilege either one over the other.

7. The Florida Center for Instructional Technology's online "A Teacher's Guide to the Holocaust" provides maps that pinpoint these sites, as well as other teaching resources.

8. Resistance recruiter Abba Kovner used the phrase "sheep to slaughter" to shame young Jews in the Vilna ghetto to "die fighting" (Bergen, 2016, p. 265).

9. Students read the 2009 edition of *War and Genocide*. All passages quoted in this book are from the 2016 edition.

10. The *Protocols* originated in Russia and was first translated into German around 1920. Exposed as a fraud in the 1920s, and periodically denounced even by governments, for more than 120 years antisemitic conspiracy theorists have continued to employ the document as propaganda.

Chapter 2

A Pedagogical Framework for Teaching Holocaust Literature

The reader, the student, the literary work . . . these terms are somewhat misleading, though convenient, fictions. Actually, there is no such thing as a generic reader . . . or . . . literary work. . . . [E]ach reader is unique, bringing to the transaction an individual ethnic, social, and psychological history.

(Rosenblatt, 1995, pp. 24, xix)

Philosopher and educational reformer John Dewey (2004/1916) posits that the type of schooling we develop in society is linked to the type of society we value. At its best, democratic schooling can prepare young people to be engaged, creative, independent thinkers who want to create a more just world; but those in power can also manipulate schooling to serve their interests. For example, as curriculum theorists Daniel and Laurel Tanner (1995, p. 302) explain, in the 1950s and 1960s the US government subverted the comprehensive mission of public education by elevating science and math curricula in a bid to attain supremacy in the Cold War and the space race.

A much more extreme example of government control occurred in Germany during the Third Reich, when education, organized to reinforce the Nazi worldview, shaped all aspects of social and academic life to serve the racist, sexist, nationalist, imperialist, and militarist goals of the NSDAP. Party officials shaped public education to win over and indoctrinate the youth.

Historian Lisa Pine (2011) explains that the curriculum was tightly controlled and was reinforced with pedagogical strategies designed to prevent students from thinking for themselves or questioning the authority and ideology of those in power. The Nazis infused the curriculum with the pseudo-science of eugenics, claiming "Aryan" racial superiority. Textbooks reflected

Nazi ideology. "While censors removed some books from the classroom, old books were revised to meet Nazi party standards, and new textbooks . . . promoted love for Hitler, obedience to state authority, militarism, racism, and antisemitism" (USHMM, "Indoctrinating Youth").

By 1936, almost all teachers had joined the Nazi Party. Teachers were expected to be authoritarian and to emphasize nationalism and total allegiance to Hitler. "The teacher would enter the classroom and welcome the group with a 'Hitler salute', shouting 'Heil Hitler!' Students would have to respond in the same manner, often eight times each day—at the start and end of the day, as well as the beginning and end of each lesson" (London Jewish Cultural Center, "The Holocaust Explained").

Historian Michelle Mouton (2007) explains that fascist ideas also were promulgated through family policies in which Nazi leaders revived traditional gender roles, some of which had been challenged during the Weimar Republic. These ideas also were reinforced through Nazi youth organizations. "Aryan" girls were to concentrate on motherhood and the domestic sphere. "Aryan" boys were to prepare for military service and fathering "Aryan" children. By 1939, all "Aryan" youth were required to join Hitler youth groups.

In contrast to the ways in which the Third Reich used education, this book creates strong links between content, pedagogy, and educating for democracy and social justice. The reasons for doing this are to better prepare educators to teach about the emotionally disturbing and historically demanding worldview that pervaded Nazi-controlled societies, juxtapose Nazi education to education in democratic societies where people can more easily resist irrational or militaristic solutions to problems and injustices, and challenge rigid thinking and racist social structures and ideologies when they arise.

To teach and interpret Holocaust and other similarly complex literature requires interdisciplinary analysis, cultural sensitivity, and finding a balance between empathic and cognitive engagement. This chapter focuses on pedagogical theories that help teachers meet and address these requirements and integrate content and meaning-making with literacy skill building. In it, the authors feature a number of theorists who take constructivist approaches to teaching and learning.

English teacher educator John Mayher (1990) characterizes pervasive skill-based pedagogies "that break down complex processes like reading into a set of behaviors that must be mastered" as "commonsense." These pedagogies primarily emphasize literacy skills acquisition instead of "meaningfulness or the reader's interest in the texts" (p. 55). The methods we follow and teach are strongly influenced by what Mayher calls "uncommonsense" educational philosophy, which underlies constructivist teaching.

Teacher educators Jacqueline Grennon Brooks and Martin G. Brooks (1993) explain that in constructivist classrooms, teachers create environments to encourage student inquiry and dialogue. "Problems constructed around 'big ideas' provide a context in which students learn component skills, gather information, and build knowledge. Attempts to linearize concept formation quickly stifle the learning process" (pp. 48–49).

Constructivist educators value intrinsic learning and authentic assessment practices that de-emphasize grading and fragmentation. Students thrive in classrooms in which constructivist teachers are well prepared and supported and communicate regularly with each other, administrators, parents, and community partners about meaningful teaching and learning (Brooks & Brooks, 1993, pp. 120–26).

PEDAGOGICAL CONTENT KNOWLEDGE

Teacher educator Lee Shulman explains in a 1986 article that "pedagogical content knowledge represents the blending of content and pedagogy into an understanding of how particular topics, problems, or issues are organized, represented, and adapted to the diverse interests and abilities of learners, and presented for instruction" (p. 8). To help students in the course learn how to synthesize content knowledge and pedagogy, the course's curriculum moved along parallel tracks, linking one Holocaust text to another, one pedagogical strategy to another, and simultaneously linking content to pedagogy and to students' lives and interests.

For a historical perspective on pedagogy, students read and discussed teacher educators Margaret J. Finders and Susan Hynds's (2006) analysis of the major literacy paradigms that English teachers practiced from the 1950s through the late 1990s (pp. 54–78).

Finders and Hynds explain that student-centered methods that are constructivist, process-oriented, inquiry-based, and culturally responsive— methods that attend to cognitive development as well as personal growth, which began developing in the 1960s, and which progressive educators still use today—are akin to Paolo Freire's (1993) and Dewey's (2004) educational philosophies. These methods coexist uneasily with teacher-centered text-based approaches that used to dominate education in the United States and still are widely practiced today.

This course emphasized such constructivist and social-justice-oriented pedagogies. In the practice lessons they developed, students were directed to apply student-centered methods and craft inquiry-based lessons designed to engage students in "reading the word and the world" (Freire & Macedo, 1987) and to meet the needs of all learners. The course introduced participants to these methods, applying them to the teaching of Holocaust literature.

The goal was for these preservice teachers to achieve pedagogical content knowledge, have confidence that they could become competent teachers of Holocaust and other literature, and have the courage to teach Holocaust literature while still being novices, with the understanding that teachers are always learners. The course also emphasized that it is important for teachers to discern and emphasize how Holocaust literature is significant today without trivializing or distorting meaning.

CHALLENGES FACING TEACHER EDUCATORS AND EDUCATION STUDENTS

To gain the competence necessary to teach Holocaust texts, educators need pedagogical content knowledge, cultural competence, and strong comprehension skills. They also need to acquire the ethical fortitude to navigate potential hazards such as Holocaust denial, trauma, trivialization, and reproducing antisemitism. The process to gain this competence, challenging in itself, was further complicated by several factors related to problems in teacher education.

Each student brought a wide range of educational experiences to the course. Therefore, what each one already knew and believed about teaching and learning was unpredictable. Complicating the situation was the school's imperative to incorporate new standards and to clear licensing and accreditation hurdles like edTPA (a nationally based teacher performance assessment that education students are required to pass). Further, the students' other teachers had ideological differences concerning the place of social justice education in a system that tends to reproduce socioeconomic, cultural, and political norms (Bourdieu & Passeron, 1990).

The social justice aspects of the course are addressed in the following chapters. In this section of Chapter 2, we discuss two factors that complicated the course: student-teacher anxiety and standards.

Teacher as Learner

Knowing that they lack experience, content knowledge, and pedagogical skills, and fearing that they will not become competent classroom teachers, many education students understandably fall back on formulaic ideas about teaching that they assimilated through their own schooling. As English teacher educator Sheridan Blau points out, education students often think that "if they haven't been taught a literary work, they won't know how to teach it" (2003, p. 26).

Especially if they subscribe to a teacher-as-expert model, these students become anxious when they feel incompetent. They sometimes resist the curriculum, get angry, or disengage if it does not include specific directives on how to teach particular texts. Their anxiety is understandable, as compositionist Ellen C. Carillo (2006) explains, because "texts [are] situated as stable repositories of meaning and, by extension, teachers [are] cast as the masters and safeguards of these meanings" (p. 31).

Therefore, teaching unfamiliar literature heightens new teachers' perceptions that they are inadequate and unprepared. To maintain their teacher-as-expert personae, some stay safely within the bounds of their limited understanding. They shy away from or circumscribe responses to literature that are intensely emotional, require attention to social justice, and/or raise complex questions that lead to multiple, ambiguous, often incomplete, and unsettling answers.

Blau (2003) and English teacher educator Pamela Grossman (2001) both reject the teacher-as-expert model with which most students are familiar. It is characterized by teacher-led recitations and the teacher's questions, followed by students' short responses, followed by teacher evaluations and elaborations. Grossman instead recommends decentering teacher knowledge and holding discussions in which the teacher is a coexplorer instead of examiner (pp. 421–24).

In such classrooms, the teacher does not rely on lecturing to provide background knowledge but gives everyone a chance to study background information, write about what they find, and discuss what they have learned with their peers. Following this process, everyone works together to build a classroom culture characterized by literary reading and critical thinking (Blau, 2003, p. 55). In this course, students experienced what learning through these processes is like and observed how their professor created a student-centered literature classroom.

To encourage education students to experiment with these methods, and to help them build self-confidence, English teacher educators Thomas M. McCann, Paula Ressler, Diane Chambers, and Judy Minor (2010) recommend that teacher educators use a collaborative model to prepare student teachers. Compared to models that isolate preservice teachers, their approach helps beginning English teachers form "more reflective and nuanced public selves, and come to understand that teacher identity is an ongoing process of development and refinement" (p. 11).

Their model relies on student-teaching partnerships between schools and colleges of education and puts preservice teachers in classrooms together, teaching and observing each other teaching. Teams composed of student teachers, cooperating teachers, and university mentors review what worked and what did not, according to agreed-on criteria. They then prepare the next day's lesson together based on what they learned from their collaborative analysis.

Although the course studied in this research lacked the field component, students collaborated when they developed and taught their practice lessons. They worked in pairs and triads and then received feedback from the class as a whole.

To model the teacher-as-learner paradigm, I explained how I prepared to teach the literature in this course, which still was somewhat unfamiliar to me. I was transparent about my learning process during the semester and collaborated with students to research answers to our questions. However, many of the big questions about the Holocaust have no definitive answers, so teachers and learners alike are faced with the need to accept the uneasiness that ambiguity engenders. Seeing their teacher also learning gave many students confidence to do the same.

What's the Use of Standards?

The demand to factor standards into pedagogy is almost ubiquitous in teacher education programs throughout the country. When this Holocaust methods course was first offered, the university's English teacher education program required instruction for using the NCTE/IRA Standards for English Language Arts (National Council of Teachers of English, 2009), along with the state's literacy standards. During the time of this research, Central State's teacher education programs adopted the Common Core State Standards (CCSS). Therefore, the Holocaust methods curriculum also incorporated standards.

The developers of what language arts educators Stergio Botzakis, David L. Burns, and Leigh A. Hall (2014) and literacy teacher educator Brian V. Street (1995) call "autonomous" standards (those like CCSS that are developed by outside agencies and imposed on educators) disingenuously attempt to sever literacy from ideology. Street argues that reading and writing within social institutions are "embedded in an ideology and cannot be . . . treated as 'neutral' or merely 'technical'" (p. 1).

Botzakis, Burns, and Hall also explain why relying on standards can impede literacy development. Literacy is more than a "one-size-fits-all, hierarchical skill set in the same way every time regardless of context or purpose" (2014, p. 224). Taken at face value, standards offer no insight into *why* a particular skill might help students develop their literacy; nor do they indicate *how* to use the standards to get to meaningful literary experiences.

When standards are applied as a generic checklist to cover isolated skills, teachers forget that for all students to reach their highest potential, teachers must attend to diversity. They "must teach contemporary children in ways that are relevant to *their* needs and the world *they* will live in" (Botzakis,

Burns, & Hall, 2014, p. 224). The Common Core and similar standards represent only a small fraction of what students are able to learn in English language arts classrooms. They leave out some of the most valuable reasons to develop language arts skills, such as:

> self-expression; releasing the imagination; creating works of art; developing social networks; engaging in civic discourse; supporting personal and spiritual growth; reflecting on experience; communicating professionally and academically; building relationships with others, including with friends, family, and other like-minded individuals; and engaging in aesthetic experiences. Most important perhaps is education for social and civic participation. (NCTE, 2009)[1]

Standards also have a great deal in common with New Criticism, developed in the 1930s, in which literacy instruction is focused on the text only. Referring to New Criticism and CCSS, Carillo (2006) writes, "Both pedagogies insist on the existence of objectivity and, by extension, objective readings. . . . [B]oth eschew the role of feeling when reading and interpreting" (p. 29). Therefore, "Common Core misses opportunities to help students connect, understand, and empathize with others. . . . In the end, students are robbed of their voices, agency, and any sort of dialogue about meaning that should characterize classroom discussions" (p. 34).

Keeping these caveats in mind, teachers still can use standards as springboards to think about linking curriculum and pedagogy with literature, emphasizing the whole-to-parts approach that constructivist educators recommend. Standards *can* challenge teachers to reflect on why they choose particular texts and which elements of a text might help students get to the literal and implied meanings of that text. However, standards *do not and cannot* specify the appropriate pedagogy to attain education goals, nor do they help students find the social and personal significance a text might have for them.

National and state standards will never provide all the criteria teachers need to consider while planning and assessing learning for all their students. Standards ignore the needs of students with learning disabilities, those whose home language is not English, and native speakers for whom standardized English is not their primary discourse. They impede teachers' efforts to use universal design, which includes qualitative, creative, and holistic assessments such as portfolios and project-based learning. Such practices are beneficial for all and critically important for many students with disabilities.

When students in the course designed lessons that were driven by standards, they tended to ignore their original objectives and the meaning and significance of the texts and had more difficulty planning student-centered lessons. When students assigned standards that were appropriate to the lesson *after* they developed their plans, attending to standards often did help them fine-tune those plans. For many, referencing autonomous standards was immaterial to their lessons' viability and success.

To meet the education school's and the students' future administrators' requirements, it was important for these education students to practice applying standards. However, when teaching the course, I always emphasized that achieving and demonstrating pedagogical content knowledge was the priority. Most often, the students found that having to deal with the standards impeded that effort.

MAJOR EDUCATIONAL CONCEPTS AND STRATEGIES

In addition to emphasizing the importance of integrating content with pedagogy, this chapter introduces the course's other major pedagogical concepts. During the course, the students studied these concepts prior to and alongside reading and working with Holocaust literature in its historical context.

Cambourne's Conditions for Literacy Learning

The first concept the students considered is literacy educator Brian Cambourne's conditions for literacy learning, as presented in English teacher educators Lynn Meeks and Carol Austin's *Literacy in the Secondary English Classroom* (2003, pp. 3–7), which was this course's principal language arts theory and pedagogy textbook.[2]

Cambourne (1988) delineates eight phases of learning that promote children's oral and written language abilities and that lead to what Meeks and Austin call "barrier-free" learning. While Cambourne developed these conditions for young children based on what he saw as the processes of natural language acquisition, Meeks and Austin claim they can and should be adapted for secondary classrooms. The authors of this study agree that Cambourne's taxonomy for literacy is applicable to other types of learning and all age levels.

The eight conditions, adapted for all learning levels and summarized, are:

1. Immersion—Immerse students fully in the subject matter, presenting it several times in different ways.
2. Demonstration—Teachers demonstrate to students and then students demonstrate to each other the concepts they are learning.
3. Expectations—Establish clear and realistic expectations and requirements for students' work.
4. Responsibility—Students take responsibility for their own learning and for teaching their peers.

5. Practice or Approximation—Students practice what they learn in a risk-free environment, approximating expertise to the extent they can.
6. Response—Students receive timely feedback from teacher and peers, using agreed-on criteria for assessments while learning self-assessment skills.
7. Application—Students apply new knowledge with opportunities to think metacognitively about their work.
8. Engagement—Engagement occurs when all the other conditions for learning are in place, because the learner has invested time and energy and is interested in the subject and intrinsically wants to acquire more knowledge.

The course curriculum, as a whole, models and incorporates Cambourne's conditions for literacy learning. Students immersed themselves in the study of literature and pedagogy, valuing and assessing their initial transactions with new literature and what they learned by discussing texts with their peers. Rather than following strict guidelines for their assignments, students had room for their own interpretations and experimentation, allowing them to approximate how to develop and teach lessons.

Integrated Language Arts Pedagogy

To meet these conditions for literacy learning, English language arts teachers need to employ a variety of language modes (writing, reading, talking, listening, viewing), media, and academic disciplines. This integrated language arts pedagogy originates from the 1966 Anglo-American Conference at Dartmouth College, where prominent English educators and scholars met to define the field of English and the best ways to teach it (Dixon, 1975; Loban, 1976). Since then, English language arts teachers, scholars, and professional organizations such as NCTE have emphasized that effective language arts instruction requires using multiple language modes and theoretical lenses.

Inquiry-Based Learning

For the first couple of weeks, we studied and practiced a number of effective inquiry-based guided reading activities. These included predicting and questioning techniques (Meeks & Austin, 2003, pp. 79–103) and collaborative pretelling and retelling to stimulate students' imaginations, to foster learning communities, and as another way to pay close attention to texts (pp. 155–78). Students explored these prior to reading the Holocaust texts and were encouraged to incorporate them into their own lessons.

In both their learning and teaching, students in the course used writing-to-learn strategies, as described by English teacher educators John Mayher, Nancy Lester, and Gordon Pradl (1983). Among these were learning journals and exercises using wall texts and text tours (Meeks & Austin, 2003, pp. 63–78) in which groups of students recorded their ideas on newsprint sheets that they then posted around the classroom and shared with their classmates.

Literary Theory

Reader response theory is the most flexible and inclusive literary theory to employ when taking an integrated language arts approach to literature. By guiding students through the reader response process, as promulgated by English teacher educator and literary theorist Louise Rosenblatt, teachers can create beneficial learning conditions. This is the key literary theory the students studied.

According to Rosenblatt (1969, pp. 43–45), literature becomes meaningful through a transaction between the author, the text, and the reader. The reader is not merely a passive recipient of an author's ideas that are implanted in the text. The teacher encourages learners to begin with their own unmediated responses to a text before delving into literary structures, multiple layers of meaning, or background information.

Reader response analysis nurtures a love for reading and develops the skills and motivation needed for people to become lifelong readers. They also become more savvy readers. Research shows that "students who begin with personally inflected reading responses can be prompted—often more successfully than students who don't—to fuse what they always already bring with them to ultimately move their thinking to a more critical place" (Carillo, 2006, p. 32).

Rosenblatt (1993) distinguishes between efferent and aesthetic reading experiences. Efferent reading happens when "the reader's attention is primarily focused on the information to be acquired, the logical solution to a problem, the actions to be carried out." In aesthetic reading experiences, "the reader's attention is centered directly on what he is living through during his relationship with that particular text" (p. 380). But she also warns against dualistic interpretations that separate efferent and aesthetic readings.

One of the major problems with Common Core State Standards is its emphasis on efferent reading. Such an emphasis distorts efforts to engage students in reading for personal, emotional, and intellectual growth and for pleasure.

Rosenblatt breaks down the process of reading and interpreting literature in education settings into three components: spontaneous response and reflections on the initial reading, shared response, and rereading to form a discriminating response. These responses ideally lead readers to a fourth component, which is tied to the third—pursuing background research and applying other critical literary strategies.

To have a genuine aesthetic experience with literature, readers first need opportunities to respond to a text spontaneously and without mediation. Often, teachers direct students to write journal entries as a way to articulate these responses. As individuals read a text through the lenses of their life experiences, their spontaneous interpretations inevitably will be different from others'. These differences are unearthed when students share with others their disparate responses.

After comparing responses, all study the text carefully together and discuss where their responses reveal and enhance the text's meaning and when they are reading into the text something that is not there or misunderstanding what is there. Through these processes they will realize that there are multiple interpretations but also see that not all interpretations hold up when they check evidence from the text.

When the reading community has reached its limit of understanding, the readers do background research and also subject the text to further literary analysis, drawing on other literary theories as appropriate. The teacher guides readers as they explore literary devices, sociohistorical and biographical contexts, gender issues, and the like. Other literary theories that factored into the study of Holocaust literature conducted in this course were New Criticism, New Historicism, critical literacy theories, and feminist and queer theories.

Practitioners of New Criticism believe that the primary way to understand a text is through closely reading the text and studying its structure. The author and reader are peripheral to the text's meaning. Rosenblatt stresses that author, reader, and text should be considered together when practicing reader response but that a discriminating response requires some close reading. Students were most comfortable with close reading, so they often incorporated this strategy into their lessons.

New Historicism entails understanding literature in its historical contexts and understanding history through literary study. It not only emphasizes the historical and social contexts of the literary work but also helps us see cultural nuances that cannot be addressed merely through historical information. In the course, students read history, studied historical documents and images, and read essays to help them situate the literature. They compared Holocaust-related texts and considered how the times and places described in the texts they studied and in which the authors wrote influenced the texts.

Critical theory, which examines cultural, historical, and institutional perspectives and power inequities, came into play when students investigated the texts' social and political contexts. The course emphasized how reading through this lens could influence students' abilities to engage with civil society, meet challenges to democracy, and uphold universal values.

Chapter 6 introduces feminist and queer theories. Through these lenses students examined how characters in literature are affected by gender and sexuality. They also studied how the treatment of women, girls, boys, and men during the Third Reich was steeped in misogyny, homophobia, and masculinist ideologies. A few students designed lessons that employed gendered perspectives for both the short stories and *Maus*.

Applying Reader Response Theory

As a way to articulate their initial responses, course participants wrote one journal response for each text they read. Questions they addressed include: What is your first reaction or response to the text? In what ways does the text connect or not to your own life experience? What else did the text remind you of? What do you think is the most important chapter, excerpt, scene, line, or word, and why? What do you think the author was trying to accomplish with this text, and what evidence in the text supports this?

These parallel the basic line of questioning set up by English teacher educator Robert Probst. In his book *Response & Analysis* (2004, pp. 81–100), Probst provides an engaging, thoughtful, and accessible framework for applying Rosenblatt's theories to the classroom.

After writing their initial responses, students met in small groups to discuss the text and their journals. Then they wrote addenda to the journals, answering additional questions: How was your response similar to or different from that of other group members? Did your own response change as a result of your interactions with your group members? Why or why not? What would you need to research further to better understand the text? If you were asked to write about something in this text or related to this text in some depth, what would you choose?

With this reader response process as a base, students built a foundation on which to construct their practice lessons. They and I did, however, face problems inherent when applying reader response theory too rigidly.

Having the locus of control as much as possible with the readers empowers them and stimulates them to read more and read attentively, as long as the text is not so unfamiliar as to be inaccessible. For this reason, reader response theorists caution against frontloading the study of literature with a lot of introductory material, such as historical, sociological, or cultural contexts, or author biography. However, not supplying any introductory information carries the significant risk that students might seriously misinterpret the literature.

This risk is quite high when teaching Holocaust literature. Because most students in the course were ignorant about the Holocaust and/or had absorbed inaccuracies and distortions from mainstream culture and society, it seemed necessary to provide some initial context. This is why the curriculum begins with an introduction to the history of antisemitism and Jewish culture. Students studied the history of the Holocaust along with the literature.

The preparatory study helped most students better understand the literature. Unfortunately, this did not prevent some students from reinforcing pervasive stereotypes about Jews or reiterating reactionary interpretations of history. This happened most frequently when reading and teaching the first book in the course, *Friedrich*.

No teacher can foresee every problem, nor can students integrate new background knowledge readily. Teachers must continually ask: What do readers need to discover for themselves in order to have authentic literary experiences? Do readers need to know anything about a work of literature before reading it? How does what they learn affect their understanding of the text, their lives, and the world?

Specific to Holocaust literature, which terminology, historical information, and theoretical concepts should teachers introduce to students through lecture, film, and primary and secondary texts, and when? When students write about and discuss texts and expose their ignorance and prejudices, what should their teachers do? When students repeat antisemitic ideas, or give credence to Nazi ideology, for example, how should teachers respond? How do the ethical issues students encounter make a difference to them and to their understanding of the world today?

How can teachers ready themselves for the curveballs that inevitably come their way, knowing that they can never anticipate them all? There are no definitive answers to any of these questions, but the following chapters demonstrate how the students and professor wrestled with them throughout the course.

Authentic Discussions

Reader response as an educational strategy relies heavily on dialogue. In many middle and secondary schools, little time is spent engaging students in discussion, even though research tells us that such practices are critically important components in building literacy skills. Authentic discussions, writes compositionist and rhetorician Martin Nystrand, feature dialogic instruction, when "teachers and students alike contribute their ideas to a discussion in which their understandings evolve during classroom interactions" (2006, pp. 399–400).

I invited my colleague Tom McCann, an expert in dialogic instruction, to conduct a workshop in my class. McCann helped the class understand how to conduct, observe, and evaluate discussions that are inquiry-driven, that limit teacher talk, and in which a majority of students participate. The students practiced asking questions that have no single answer, not accepting "I don't know" for an answer, rephrasing questions and offering choices to encourage more students to respond, paraphrasing responses, calling on other students to answer questions, and asking follow-up questions (McCann, Johannessen, Kahn, & Flanagan, 2006).

During the next session, students learned about and practiced other questioning techniques that avoid leading questions, closed questions requiring yes-or-no answers, and questions imbued with value judgments, all of which stifle discussion. They also read about related questioning techniques developed by other English education theorists.

Leila Christenbury and Pat Kelly's schema of intersecting critical questioning circles, which they illustrate as a Venn diagram, helps teachers generate complex questions about a text (Christenbury & Lindblom, 2016, pp. 342–43). The teacher asks questions about the content, the reader's personal reality and external reality, and about intersections of these circles of inquiry, not necessarily in any particular order. Where all three areas intersect is where dense questions arise, linking all areas of inquiry and varieties of perspectives.

A dense question could follow from earlier questions about the text, how this idea relates to the reader's life, and how it relates to the world. Or it could come early, "circumvent[ing] the usual . . . movement of a hierarchical questioning schema" (Christenbury & Lindblom, 2016, p. 343). A dense question about *The Diary of a Young Girl* might focus on what the memoir can tell us about a young Jewish girl and her family forced into hiding: "What damage can unchecked discrimination and persecution do to individuals, families, communities, and the world?" This type of questioning complements a reader-response approach that highlights transactions between the reader and the text.

Curriculum theorists Grant Wiggins and Jay McTigue (2005) and English teacher educator Jim Burke (2010) also recommend asking nonhierarchical essential questions to stimulate critical thinking and discussion about literature. They eschew lower- to higher-order questioning taxonomies. They recommend that teachers focus on questions about meaning rather than on behavioral objectives and teach literacy skills by engaging students in meaningful discussions.

To foster successful classroom discourse, the teacher also needs to build a safe and respectful social environment for people from different social, ethnic, economic, and educational backgrounds. Over the years, we have, along with our students, developed discussion guidelines based on feminist discourse that enable everyone to respect each other's unique and important perspectives. This becomes particularly important when disagreements arise and biases surface due to a curriculum's social justice content. The following are some of the guidelines for feminist discussion the course participants made an effort to follow:

- Contribute to the conversation by adding new information and ideas to topics others raise, or take the conversation in a new direction. Refrain from speaking again until all others who want to speak have taken their turn.
- Pay close attention, showing you have listened by validating speakers to whom you respond. Summarize what they said as accurately as you can, and ask for clarification if necessary.
- When responding to a point of view with which you disagree, critique the idea, not the person expressing that idea. Ask a question, counter with other evidence, or add to the evidence already given.
- If a speaker hurts or offends you, use an "I" statement, for example, "When you say _____, I feel _____ because _____."

English teacher educator Douglas Barnes (1992) further explains how, through small-group exploratory talk, learners "make connections, re-arrange, re-conceptualize, and internalize the new experiences" (p. 6). A discussant may have a vague idea but cannot articulate it. Yet when faced with the necessity to do so in the group, suddenly the idea comes into focus and the discussant can verbalize it.

English teacher educator James Britton calls this "shaping at the point of utterance." A speaker involved in exploratory talk makes a claim, "and perhaps it is the social pressure on the speaker to justify his claim that gives talk an edge over silent brooding as a problem-solving procedure" (1982, p. 139).

Cultural Competence and Cultural Relevance

One of the biggest obstacles Holocaust literature teachers and students face, and that often is revealed in classroom discussions, is that they often know little about the people involved in the Holocaust and carry many misconceptions and biases regarding them. Meeks and Austin (2003), and multicultural educators such as Gloria Ladson-Billings (1992; 1995) and Carol Lee (2007), stress that teachers need to understand their own culturally based perspectives and biases and how these may come into play in their teaching. Developing such self-awareness was a major endeavor for everyone involved in the course.

Students created their own "cultural eyes"—diagrams, based on a Meeks and Austin activity (2003, pp. 28–30), that identified their spiritual beliefs, education, race, age, gender, social class, political beliefs, marital status, and sexual experience, and shared them in small groups. The Meeks and Austin template left out some stigmatized or sexuality identity categories such as sexual orientation and gender identity and expression. The students included these categories and discussed problems that might arise if they did so in high school classes.

The cultural eye activity helped them make important distinctions between their life experiences and those of the characters they would be encountering in Holocaust literature. They saw how the various components of their identities defined who they were. This better situated them to relate what they were learning to their own lives without either overly identifying or overly distancing themselves from the people characterized in the literature they were studying.

The activity informed the lesson plans they created and helped them critique their peers' lessons when stereotypes and biases appeared. Seeing how Debby (Chapter 3) and Arlo (Chapter 4) related their own identities (Debby identified as Jewish and Arlo as Christian) to the subjects of current anti-semitism and the history of antisemitism demonstrated how understanding one's own cultural perspectives can contribute to understanding other people.

An important sociolinguistic and literacy viewpoint that Meeks and Austin introduced, critical to developing cultural competence, is linguist James Paul Gee's explanation of primary and secondary discourses. Gee defines "discourses" as "ways of being in the world; they are forms of life which integrate words, acts, values, beliefs, and attitudes, and social identities as well as gestures, glances, body positions, and clothes" (1989, p. 6).

Primary discourse is our first social identity, our initial understanding "of *who* we are and *who* 'people like us' are, as well as what sort of things we . . . do, value, and believe in when we are not 'in public'" (Gee, 1996, p. 143). Secondary discourse originates in "local, state, and national groups and institutions outside early home and peer-group socialization" (p. 137). How close a person's primary discourse is to a secondary discourse can help determine how successful the person is within that secondary-discourse community.

This theory helps explain why, for working-class and minority students, academic success sometimes is difficult to attain. (See also, Heath, 1990; Delpit, 1998; and Gilyard, 1991.) Meeks and Austin (2003) recommend that teachers integrate activities comparing primary and secondary discourses into their own curricula to bridge the gaps between discourses.

To better understand this idea and why it is important to help students connect home and school, students did a workshop in which they had to identify and analyze their own primary discourse and a secondary discourse and then teach someone a skill based on a discourse with which the other person was unfamiliar. Several students tried to apply Gee's concept to lessons they created. Students experimented with an unconventional application when teaching *Friedrich*, described in Chapter 5.

When constructing their own lessons about the Holocaust, students were faced with whether and how their cultural and linguistic identities intersected and differed from characters in the literature they studied and what intersections and differences their future students might have. Examining these differences was relevant to their own development as readers and teachers of Holocaust literature and would be to their future students.

Integrating Cognitive and Affective Learning

Traversing the often-brutal psychological terrain of Holocaust literature tends to evoke deep emotional responses. When trying to understand what happened in the Holocaust, students may make inappropriate comparisons between themselves and Holocaust victims and survivors, thus distorting and trivializing what occurred. English teacher educator Mary M. Juzwik (2013) warns that this may happen when teaching texts with deeply disturbing historical themes.

To address such concerns, Juzwik recommends contextualizing Holocaust literature socially and historically rather than adhering exclusively to the confines of the text. Perhaps because they had gained a little historical background before delving into the literature, students in the course rarely made inappropriate comparisons. When they did, the students and I critically analyzed the qualitative differences between, say, a teenager choosing whether to keep a curfew or violate it and a mother in a deathcamp choosing whether to save her child or herself.

Juzwik favors taking a rhetorical approach through which students engage in studying how texts "work persuasively to take ethical stances on persons and events of the Holocaust years." She suggests we ask students, "How do texts represent a difficult-to-represent past? What are the (ethical) consequences (intended and unintended) of those representations?" This helps students "engage with the moral complexities of the Holocaust . . . as a set of historical events being represented to various audiences in writing and other artistic forms" (2013, pp. 296–97).

Acknowledging the dangers of inappropriate comparisons, Totten advocates against role-playing activities related to the Holocaust (2001, pp. 243–52). The Anti-Defamation League ("Holocaust Education") and USHMM ("Guidelines for Teaching about the Holocaust") alert educators to the potential hazards that employing such pedagogies present. The USHMM warns that Holocaust experience can be trivialized and victims and survivors disrespected when teachers employ "gimmicky exercises" such as games and simulations that try to approximate actual events for the purpose of eliciting and exploiting students' emotions.

Comparative literature scholar Shoshana Felman (1992), however, cautions that whether or not a teacher takes a purely cognitive approach to teaching Holocaust literature, studying these texts can cause students psychic distress. She still encourages teaching, reading, and viewing Holocaust literature and testimonies but recommends that teachers warn students in advance that doing this work can be disturbing and that they be ready to intervene if students get upset.

We agree that attention-getting and affective approaches that gratuitously evoke primarily emotional responses, thus encouraging uncritical personal identification with victims and survivors, can distort reality and oversimplify current and historical occurrences of mass violence. Nevertheless, strictly rational approaches do not engender empathy, which is critically important to Holocaust studies.

It takes empathy even to raise the universally asked question about genocide, "How can people treat other people so cruelly?" Part of the answer lies in the decision to deny the humanity of people who are very different from ourselves, claiming that those "others" do not warrant dignity and respect, especially if doing so appears on the surface to be in our self-interest. When we do not connect meaningfully to strangers, we tend to overlook injustices perpetrated against those who are not like us. Without empathy, people are vulnerable to the arguments of Holocaust deniers and nationalists who scapegoat "outsiders."

Feminist educational philosopher Berenice Fisher argues that emotions are important to cognitive learning. The consciousness-raising movement showed how "emotions have a decidedly rational content—a cognitive or evaluative aspect that is part of the way we understand and respond to the world." As Fisher advises:

> We should not romanticize or separate emotions from reason: Sometimes we express anger to keep from addressing the underlying issues that make us angry. Sometimes we feel pity in order to distance ourselves from people whose problems feel too much like our own. When we assume that given emotions have a self-evident meaning we encourage the cathartic and sentimental use of the emotions. (1987, p. 76)

The solution she offers is to balance and integrate the cognitive and affective in educational inquiry, always analyzing how they are intertwined.

Educational Drama

Educational drama provides a powerful way to link cognitive and affective learning that involves the student intellectually, emotionally, and physically. Experienced drama teachers avoid exploiting emotions and trivializing and oversimplifying human experiences. They include metacognitive activities to help students process what occurs during the dramas and deal with any distress that arises. Besides leading to deeper understanding of the issues involved, drama can help students build empathy and foster a deeper connection to humanity.

Process drama, also called drama across the curriculum, was developed and popularized in educational settings outside the United States, primarily by drama theorists and practitioners Dorothy Heathcote and Gavin Bolton (1995), Cecily O'Neill (1995), and Jonothan Neelands (1990). In this style of educational drama, students work toward resolving a conflict or problem while in role, usually directed by teachers who are also in role. By stepping into roles, students explore viewpoints of people unlike themselves.

In a process drama developed and conducted by English teacher educator Esther Cappon Gray and high school drama teacher Susan A. Thetard (2010), students stepped into roles as people who worked in a bakery in Munich during the Holocaust. In the process, students tackled big questions that arise in Holocaust literature, such as what it is like to hide one's racially marginalized identity in a racist society, whether to endanger oneself and one's family to help others, and what makes people comply with perpetrators or go along with the crowd despite misgivings.

This role-play demonstrates how teachers can contextualize history and literature, drawing students into an experience that successfully integrates affective and cognitive learning. However, when teachers who are unfamiliar with drama pedagogies and have limited understanding of the Holocaust engage in activities that simulate atrocities or set up parallel scenarios, difficulties arise. Role-plays that reproduce authoritarian behaviors, for example, or simulate what it was like to be packed into railway cars bound for deathcamps, can be emotionally dangerous and trivializing.

Even experienced teachers can misstep. Teacher educator Simone Schweber (2004) relates how a teacher tried to enliven a history lesson through a dramatic role-play that simulated what victims of the concentration camps experienced. The teacher stepped into the role of an authoritarian, bullying disciplinarian. Emotions eventually overshadowed informational learning, replicating oppression (p. 99).

This drama activity was not about coming to realizations together; rather, the teacher focused only on her objective that students feel what people in concentration camps experienced. As theater educators Jan Cohen-Cruz and

Mady Schutzman (1994) point out, such activities do not really help students see multiple viewpoints, nor do they allow for reflection during the process of the role-play. A similar role-play is described in Chapter 5.

Other drama educators have developed socially critical drama strategies in which the teacher plays a less directive role. Drama theorist and political activist Augusto Boal (1985/1974) developed Forum Theatre, a form of Theatre of the Oppressed (based on Freire's *Pedagogy of the Oppressed* [1993/1979]) in which a group of actors play out an oppressive situation to a point of crisis and then invite audience members (whom Boal calls "spectactors") to step into roles, trying out different tactics to empower people as they struggle against oppression.

Educational drama educators Brian Edmiston (2013) and Jeff Wilhelm (2002) apply theater techniques such as role-playing and improvisation to explore a subject or a text from different angles. They ask students to adopt roles as researchers and as people from conflicting points of view or experiences. These techniques also highly motivate students to develop integrated literacy skills (see also, Edmiston & Wilhelm, 1998; Schneider, Crumpler, & Rogers, 2006; and Wagner, 1998).

Over the years I have often incorporated process drama and critical role-playing into my curricula (Ressler, 2002). For this course, concerned that there was insufficient time in which to help my students develop the many complex skills this course already required that they learn, and because of Holocaust educators' warnings about role-plays, I made the choice not to teach drama pedagogy or to encourage drama activities.

Yet quite a few students incorporated role-plays and simulations into their lessons. Novice teachers want to try games, simulations, and role-plays, having learned about them elsewhere or, as students themselves, having found them entertaining. While I did not recommend these approaches, neither did I prevent their use. Better that they experiment in the education classroom/laboratory, where they can reflect on what works and does not work and discuss alternatives with peers and professors, than in secondary classrooms where they might be on their own and with little time to reflect on their practices.

All education students would benefit from a course in educational drama. It would help teachers discern the difference between drama strategies that probe deep levels of meaning and those that are superficial and potentially harmful. Such distinctions are particularly important when working with emotionally intense subject matter like the Holocaust.

Such courses, when available, usually are taught only at the graduate level. However, national organizations, particularly the NCTE and American Alliance for Theater in Education, frequently offer educational drama workshops during conferences. Through these organizations, teachers also can find information about special workshops and courses available elsewhere.

INTEGRATING THEORY AND PRACTICE

Each student in the course planned and taught one lesson related to each literary text they studied. For each lesson, the classes divided into pairs and triads. The teaching groups agreed on themes and learning goals based on their journal discussions. From there they planned fifty- to seventy-five-minute lessons, wrote formal lesson plans, and taught their lessons.

Guidelines were designed to help them progress toward pedagogical content knowledge by synthesizing literary, literacy, and cultural and historical content goals with pedagogical theories and their applications. In addition to the subject matter and themes they would emphasize from the texts, the teams were tasked to employ whichever teaching methods they deemed appropriate to the content and teaching context. They were to explain how the lesson would help their students develop literacy skills, build their learning community, and qualitatively assess student learning.

They scaffolded their work on a basic lesson plan template along with directives to feature specific language arts concepts based on the learning theories studied to date. The plans had to include two lesson goals, one related to the themes of the book and the other to a language arts skill. They also included brief rationales justifying their thematic and pedagogical choices in terms of learning theory and literary content.

Furthermore, they were to address how the lesson might take into consideration one or more different needs of students based on their racial, ethnic, language, economic backgrounds, and sexual and gender identities. Each had to incorporate principles of universal design, and they had to identify at least two standards, choosing from CCSS, NCTE/IRA, and state language arts standards.

Each group sketched out the sequence of their lesson and situated the lesson within a larger curriculum unit. The lesson included a qualitative means to assess the lesson's effectiveness and the students' learning, and a hypothetical homework assignment that could reinforce, enhance, and/or synthesize the major learning objectives. Finally, they cited any outside sources or resources they used or adapted.

At the end of each session, everyone wrote for a few minutes to give the teaching team feedback related to the theme, how the lesson integrated history and literature, the language arts skills it addressed, what further research might be beneficial, and how the groups might improve their lessons. The post-lesson discussion began with the presenters talking about the challenges they faced in planning and teaching the lesson. After that, their peers and instructor gave the teachers oral feedback.

CONCLUSION

The conceptual trajectory of the course was for both the class and professor to work toward pedagogical content knowledge by studying and practicing a major pedagogical concept for every curriculum unit while building on those introduced in previous units. In actuality, the process was quite a bit messier than that. Often the curriculum needed to be adjusted based on what transpired as the semester progressed, moving back and forth between the literature, the pedagogy, and background research.

Students sometimes embraced methods of studying and teaching literature with which they were unfamiliar and other times reverted to formulaic, teacher-centered techniques. Some made the effort to develop their competence in regard to Jewish culture, Holocaust history, and related issues. Others crafted lessons to build literacy skills that had no meaningful content, thereby avoiding opportunities to stretch themselves intellectually and emotionally. All the students developed their teaching skills as well as their understanding of Holocaust literature, and a few moved progressively closer to developing substantial pedagogical content knowledge.

In Chapters 5 through 8, we investigate in detail how participants studied and put into practice the pedagogical theories and processes introduced in this chapter. Prior to applying these ideas and methods, however, participants first looked into the history of antisemitism and into contemporary antisemitism, and so we report on those experiences in the following two chapters.

NOTES

1. Retrieved from an NCTE web page that is now defunct but is cited in the reference list.

2. Several other English education textbooks also were used in the course and/or are referenced in this book, by Blau (2003); Christenbury (2000); Christenbury and Lindblom (2016); Finders & Hynds (2006); Meeks & Austin (2003); Milner, Milner, & Mitchell (2012); and Smagorinsky (2002; 2007).

Chapter 3

Jewish Culture and Contemporary Antisemitism

That's what happened to the majority of my family. And I'll be totally honest, I wish with every part of my being that I did not have to know that. . . . It's why when John drew that swastika on the board, I was just like, oh my God.

(Debby's talk, Section 2)

The defeat of the Third Reich did not eliminate fascism, Nazism, and anti-Jewish prejudice. As this text is being written, neo-Nazis and white supremacists in the United States and Europe, who believe that minority rights movements and the influx of migrants threaten their race and socioeconomic status, are reenergized. Their actions, and slogans such as "Jews will not replace us" and "Blood and Soil," chanted in Charlottesville, Virginia,[1] and elsewhere, harken back to the years of persecution and genocide of the Third Reich.[2]

This course was offered prior to the escalating anti-immigration sentiment that fueled the Trump campaign and presidency and the ascendancy and renewal of right-wing extremism in Western democracies. However, the need to raise students' awareness about historical and contemporary antisemitism was no less urgent then. Therefore, the course began with a workshop about Jewish stereotypes adapted from one designed by economist Gerald Weinstein and organizational consultant Donna Mellen (1997, pp. 175–77). This exercise was conducted to establish not only a cultural and historical context for the course but also a classroom environment in which all could safely and productively dialogue cross-culturally.

Weinstein and Mellen's goals are to understand "the historical development and dynamics of antisemitism . . . how antisemitism is manifested in our personal lives as well as in our society," and to "identify and discuss actions we can take to interrupt antisemitism" (1997, p. 175). Students brainstormed anything they had ever heard about Jews. Then, in groups, the students listed the results of their collective work on large newsprint sheets and posted them where everyone could see. The class participants then reflected on the group processes and what everyone learned.

While creating their wall texts, students were told not to censor themselves but to be aware of hurt feelings that might arise. The purpose was to learn about the origins of antisemitism and its prevalence today, not to perpetuate bias or to judge one another based on the stereotypes that are still pervasive in the world and seep into so many people's conscious or unconscious minds.

Most groups began their lists with stereotypes about money and physical characteristics, such as "greedy" and "stingy" with "big noses" and "Jew-fro" hair. They listed ways in which Jews are blamed for the world's problems: Jews "caused economic unrest in Germany before World War II," "faked the Holocaust," are "responsible for ALL wars," "killed Jesus," and "would do it again (given the opportunity)."

They are all "communists," "Arab killers," "sneaky and controlling," and "complainers" who "see themselves as victims" and have "domineering mothers." While the students seemed aware that Jewish stereotypes are pervasive, they did not realize how deeply embedded these were until they saw that each group listed similar stereotypes.

They also noticed how contradictory they were, such as accusing Jews of being weak and cowardly at the same time that they are accused of being murderers, or labeling Jews as communists at one moment and greedy capitalists at another. They also were surprised to notice that attributes can be considered positive for one group but negative for another. For example, being thrifty is considered a virtue for some groups and individuals, but when applied to Jews, the same behavior may be defined as being cheap.

Some students were familiar with a number of Jewish religious and cultural practices, artifacts, and holidays, such as Passover and Chanukah, Torah, menorahs, yarmulkes, and "breaking a glass at weddings." They mostly listed these nonjudgmentally, with some notable exceptions, such as "they wear funny yamacas [sic]." (The adjective "funny" belittles the *yarmulke* or *kippah*, a skullcap worn traditionally by Jewish men as a sign of religious observance.) One group recorded that Jewish men are "good husbands (treat wives well)," a simplistic stereotype, albeit a positive one. One student also mentioned the importance of "jewish [sic] community."

In class, students then read Weinstein and Mellen's antisemitism timeline (1997, pp. 177–91), which helped them place into historical context the Jewish stereotypes they had articulated. Following the exercises, the students discussed what they learned and asked questions, commenting on how shocking it was to see the continuing prevalence of these stereotypes. I elaborated on some of the points they needed clarified, and students who had relevant personal or academic knowledge contributed their thoughts.

As the antisemitism workshop demonstrated, most students had little previous knowledge about Jewish culture and history, nor were they aware of antisemitism's historical roots. Most students had little or no experience interacting with Jewish people. Thinking about Jews and antisemitism had been of little or no concern to them before. To prepare to teach their students about the Holocaust, these students would not only need to learn more about the historical context of the 1930s and 1940s; they also would need to develop their own cultural awareness and literacy (see Chapter 2, "Cultural Competence and Cultural Relevance").

A JEWISH STUDENT INFORMANT
SPEAKS TO THE CLASS

Jews comprise a tiny minority at Central State and in the local community. Only a few students openly identified as Jewish during the five semesters in which I taught the course, one of whom was in the process of converting from Judaism to Christianity. A few students had familial connections to the Holocaust: one student's grandmother-in-law was a non-Jewish survivor of Nazi slave labor camps, another had a non-Jewish German grandfather who remembers being so hungry he ate plaster from the walls during World War II, and another student's Polish grandmother was a member of a Nazi youth group.

While antisemitism can be confronted and reduced through textual study, interpersonal interaction has a great impact, so having an informant is beneficial. I was usually the primary informant in the course, which was both advantageous and disadvantageous, as discussed in the reflections at the end of this chapter. During the first year the course was offered, a Jewish student in the class also acted as a valuable informant.

On day one, after I introduced the syllabus and explained that we primarily would be studying Holocaust literature and ways to teach it, Debby came to my office to speak with me. "I'm Jewish," she told me, "and I'm not sure I want to be in a class where there would be so much discussion about Judaism." She had experienced too much antisemitism in her life, Debby explained, and was afraid that she would be subjected to it again because of the course content. I suggested that she wait a bit before deciding to switch sections but assured her that I would support whatever decision she made and invited her to check in with me anytime.

After the session on Jewish stereotypes and the history of antisemitism, Debby told me she was now very glad to be taking the course. However, around midterm she told me that after she came out as Jewish during class, one of her peers commented that he was surprised to learn that she was Jewish because all the Jewish girls he knew in high school had been "stuck up." Debby was disturbed that her peers believed that antisemitism was just a thing of the past, that this student still harbored stereotypes, and that he and others were insensitive to her feelings.

Anxious about the Passover holiday that was approaching, which her peers knew little about, Debby asked if I would talk to the class about it. I agreed to do so and asked if she would also speak to the class then about her own experiences with antisemitism. She enthusiastically accepted the invitation.

Explaining Passover

Passover for me had been a yearly ritual in which I participated but only superficially understood. Therefore, before the next class session, I discussed Passover (in Hebrew, *Pesach*) with a more religiously observant Jewish friend who practices Reconstructionist Judaism and then shared what I learned with the students. What follows summarizes the lecture I presented to the class.

The eight-day holiday carries spiritual, sociocultural, and sociopolitical significance. It is the Jewish celebration of spring and renewal, but it also is linked to the history of the Israelites'[3] enslavement in and liberation from Mitzrayim,[4] as narrated in the Book of Exodus in the Hebrew Bible. On the first two nights, families usually gather together to share a ritual meal called a Seder. Jewish tradition encourages families to reach out to and welcome strangers to the Seder, a reminder that Jews also once were strangers in the land of Egypt.

During the Seder, families read from a Haggadah, which tells the three-thousand-year-old Passover story of when the Israelites escaped slavery as if it were happening now to the people around the table and to other people around the world. "Pesach is not simply a commemoration of an important event in our past but an event in which *we* participated and in which we *continue* to participate" (Levitt & Strassfeld, 1999, p. 5). The Haggadah also includes prayers, songs, and commentary about slavery and freedom.[5]

Participating in the Passover Seder is one way that Jews today connect with their ancestors and oppressed people around the world. As Rabbi Alfred Kolatch writes in his *Concise Family Seder* (1987): "May the problem of all who are downtrodden be our problem; may the concern of all who are afflicted be our concern; may the struggle of all who strive for liberty and equality be our struggle" (p. 7).

This story about oppression and liberation has sustained many victims of antisemitism and racism, who use it as a metaphorical tale. One of the songs many American Jews include in the ritual Seder is the antislavery spiritual "Go Down Moses," with Pharaoh symbolizing slave owners and Moses referring to liberators such as the conductors of the Underground Railroad, particularly Harriet Tubman, who is known as the Moses of her people for leading so many people of African descent out of slavery. Identifying with the biblical story of the Exodus is an important commonality between African Americans and Jewish Americans today.

The Passover Seder represents paradoxes inherent in any struggle for liberation. It is a time to reflect on freedom and redemption and also to remind us that we are neither free nor redeemed and cannot be until everyone is. Yet we also feast together in community to celebrate the continuing joys of life.

Symbolic foods are part of the meal. During Pesach, religiously observant Jews follow strict dietary laws, eating only foods that are deemed kosher for that holiday. Many less observant Jews avoid foods made with yeast or leavening, symbolizing the escape through the desert when there was no time to let bread rise. At the Seder, we eat and drink the symbolic wine of freedom and share the symbolic matzoh (unleavened "bread of affliction"). We also share other ritual foods, which are displayed on a special plate: parsley, hard-boiled or roasted egg, horseradish, and lamb shank bone.

Parsley sprigs symbolize spring and renewal, but at the Seder they are dipped in salt water, representing the tears of the oppressed. The egg reminds us of new life and also is dipped in salt water, to remind us of life's pains. Horseradish is the bitter herb symbolizing slavery's harshness, but often the horseradish is eaten with charoset, made of chopped fruit, nuts, wine, and spices. While it tastes sweet, charoset also embodies a paradox because it symbolizes the mortar the ancient Israelites used to build their enslavers' monuments. The shank bone represents sacrifice, a visual reminder of the days of animal sacrifice. Vegetarians today substitute a beet.

Some people include recent additions to the plate, such as an orange, representing the particular struggles of women and LGBTQ people who have been marginalized in the most traditional branches of Judaism; and an olive, representing the Palestinians' olive trees that have been uprooted over decades during the Israel/Palestine conflict.

Questioning and discussion are integral components of Seders. Questioning provides children and adults a way to maintain the Passover story's relevance today. I invited the students to save their questions about Passover until after Debby spoke about her personal experiences with antisemitism.

Debby's story is an example of how, for Jewish people, past and present struggles for freedom and against oppression are interconnected. Her personal experiences with and awareness of antisemitism were more extensive and intense than most American Jews in her generation before Charlottesville and the murders of Jewish congregants at the Tree of Life Synagogue in Pittsburgh on October 27, 2018.

Debby's Story[6]

I do not live in an Orthodox home, a super religious home; we don't keep kosher in my family. I grew up in a town in which there was a church on every corner and the closest temple was about four towns away. One of the things that I had in my life was a family member, my grandmother, who was actually in the concentration camps. From a very young age I knew about the atrocities that had gone on there and basically the ins and outs of the most terrible things that you can imagine happening.

I know about her siblings who couldn't be with us today because of the experiments the Nazis did [referring to the sadistic medical experiments Nazis inflicted on many concentration camp prisoners]. That's what happened to the majority of my family. And I'll be totally honest, I wish with every part of my being that I did not have to know that.

So, at a very young age I knew that being Jewish was not the easiest thing in the world, but I was also told that it was a very special thing. In the neighborhood we lived in we were the only Jewish family. My parents would fight because my dad wanted to move but my mom was on this crusade to stay there. "You know I'm Jewish, I'm proud."

You remember being friends in kindergarten: "Hey, you want to be my friend? Let's go." Sometimes I wasn't allowed to go to friends' houses because I was Jewish. Sometimes when I would get to friends' houses, the mom would introduce me to the dad as "This is Debby, she's the Jewish one." Even as a little kid, you know that that's not right. I mean, whenever I brought friends home I wouldn't say, "This is Kimberly, the Christian one."

A couple of years later, I was probably eight or nine years old, there were a few Jewish families living in our neighborhood. There was one that we called the poster family for Judaism. They were outspoken about being Jewish, which was fine. We did not deny the fact that we were Jewish at all, we just didn't go around like, "Yay Jews."

This family had a menorah on their lawn during the holidays, because when you go to the store you don't see Chanukah lights. You don't see dreidels[7] that can be strung up and down the house. You see Christmas lights or snowmen. They had made this menorah out of piping and all kinds of lights that they lit up on the correct days. Honest to God, it was the coolest thing I had ever seen, about two people high and two people long.

One night someone stole the menorah and lit it on fire in a field across from their house. I remember my parents sitting me down and talking to me about what had happened. "There are a lot of people who aren't okay with who you are, but never be ashamed of who you are," and all that stuff. But what really was surprising is, the people this happened to, the very next day they went out and made another one. And luckily it never happened again, but the police that were there never put it in the paper. It wasn't on the news. It was kept very hush-hush.

Then I went to Outer State University [a fictitious name] for two years and you think how your freshman year in college was, how great that is. You have all this freedom and your parents aren't around, and everyone's going to love you. My first year at Outer State was the most perfect experience I ever had in my life [*said sardonically*]. First of all, I was the first Jew that anyone had ever met. A new friend of mine said, "Oh my god, you're Jewish, what do you eat? How do you sleep? Do you sleep standing up?" You can't believe some of the ignorant comments that are made.

I will admit it became tedious, but it was really funny. I thought, boy, you guys are really dumb. I gave them slack and everything, but, you know, there were a lot of other things that happened that weren't as laughable. Early on, I was on a bus to go to the other side of campus, and this guy was staring at me. I thought, "He's into me, this is great." All of a sudden he just makes this face like he's about to vomit. He comes up to me and he started sniffing me. Literally, sniffing me, and I was just like, "What the hell are you doing?" He looks at me, pulls the string to get off the bus, calls me a "dirty kike," and leaves the bus.

I don't know if you guys have ever heard the term "kike." It's the most derogatory term you could ever call a Jew. It's like calling a black person the n-word. I don't know how to this day he knew I was Jewish. I wasn't wearing a shirt that says, like, "Jews do it for eight nights."

[Her joke is a reference to Chanukah, which memorializes the time when the Jews reclaimed the temple of Jerusalem from conquerors who had suppressed their religion. The story goes that there was only enough oil to light the eternal flame (a ritual light in front of the ark that contained the Torah) for one night, yet it remained lit for eight nights. Later, Debby said that probably the man had seen the *Magen David* ("shield of David," the six-pointed Jewish star) she had drawn on the cover of a notebook she was carrying.]

A little while after that, I was seeing somebody who was my first serious relationship and I went to meet his parents. Before I could say, "Hi, my name is Debby, I love your son and blah blah blah," he says, "This is Debby, she's not Jewish. Don't worry. She might look Jewish but she's not Jewish, she's Italian."

At that point I had no idea that he had this huge problem with me [being] Jewish; but I was so in love with this guy that I stayed with him for a lot longer. Everything we ever fought about turned into a fight because I was Jewish. I lent him some money because he didn't have enough for textbooks. And about two months later I said, "Are you ever going to get that money back to me?"

"You only want it because you're a greedy Jew."

It turned into this huge fiasco. I was in such a state of mind that I was almost ashamed that I was cursed with this religion and that I could be hated for something that I can't control.

My second year of college, it was Chanukah and unlike the majority of the people in this room [who spend Christian holidays with their families], I don't get to spend the Jewish holidays with my family. Like today [the first night of Passover] is a high holiday and I'm leaving after class to drive almost three hours home, so I can be with my family for dessert.

I wasn't at home with my family, so I was really, really upset. My friends brought me Chinese food because a lot of people think that Chinese food is national Jewish food since all the Jews go to Chinese restaurants on Christmas Day. So, they brought me Chinese food and I had this great night with these great friends who were ignorant enough to bring me Chinese food.

[Her friends were acting on a common stereotype based on the actual relationship between Jewish and Chinese immigrants in the late nineteenth and early twentieth century in New York City's Lower East Side neighborhood. Jewish and some Chinese immigrants were among the few non-Christians in New York, so Chinese restaurants usually were open on Christmas Day. Because Chinese cuisine did not mix meat and milk, which is forbidden in Jewish dietary law (*kashrut*), Jews were able to appear to be more cosmopolitan and assimilated while still obeying kashrut (Plaut, 2012, pp. 65–86).]

The next morning I open my door and from top to bottom it was covered, and I mean *covered*, with swastikas: swastikas with polka dots, swastikas with curlicues, swastikas that were italicized, everything in permanent marker.

I called the police. I called the head of the residence hall. [They told me] I couldn't get another door for two months. I put white contact paper over the door but you could still see the black swastikas come through. The police didn't do anything about it. They didn't put it in the papers. They didn't make an announcement to anyone in the dorms, which also aggravated me. But, that's a hate crime. A lot of people have tried to argue with me that it wasn't a hate crime, that it was artistic expression. It's a hate crime! And the fact that the police didn't do anything about it only makes it that much worse.

When I tried to learn how they knew I was Jewish, I found out that somebody had hacked into the files of the residence halls. Your religion and ethnicity are posted on that file. The only reason I found this out was because during Black History Month, every black student woke up to find a noose on their door handle. That's how they concluded that this happened to my door.

I never heard of any other Jews that this had happened to, but there were maybe three Jewish students at Outer State at that time. Finding a Jew there was like finding a needle in a haystack, and luckily they found me every time!

My mom wanted me to leave Outer State immediately because of what happened to me and because of previous antisemitic incidents my family experienced. So that's when I came to Central State.

That's my experience—that antisemitism is real and it's at large. It's why when John drew that swastika on the board, I was just like, oh my God. [John had drawn the swastika as part of a lesson plan his group created.] And I totally got why you did it, so I'm not saying that I thought [*pause*], but the swastika does not sit well with me. So, that's what I wanted to talk to you guys about today.

Questions and Answers

After the presentation, Debby invited the students to share their questions. In response to queries about her outlook on life, Debby said everyone is affected by their own life experiences and that her outlook definitely is rooted in Judaism. When asked if her experiences with antisemitism affect her ability to be open about being a Jew, Debby replied that she reveals her identity if asked.

"There are a lot of times I keep my mouth shut about it, because you never know whom you're telling and you never know what could happen from it. Coming into this class was really, really hard. The first couple of days I said to myself, 'I'm not saying a word. I don't know how this is going to go.' And then, after a while, it was like, 'I'm Jewish, I have an opinion about something, hold on.'"

When faced with antisemitism now, Debby explained, "A lot of the times I get so heated I can't help myself and I pretty much lose control and start, 'Are you kidding, what's wrong with you?' But there have been some times that I've really tried to hold my tongue. That it's so upsetting that I'm not going to get involved in getting into it."

Debby explained that she doesn't want to blame people who are anti-semitic. "I blame where they came from. I really try my hardest not to hate a person because of how they feel about it, because they have to get it from somewhere. There are definitely people who make it very difficult to do that. Like, for example, Mel Gibson. He is out against the Jews.[8] I don't know why. It started with his father and his father's family. I don't hate Mel Gibson. It all started somewhere and it could lead all the way to Hitler."

On the other hand, Debby felt that her exposure to antisemitism has made her more tolerant of differences. "It has definitely had an impact on how

I look at pretty much everyone else. I really don't like to judge people. That's not how I was raised."

The discussion provided a great opportunity for students to ask questions about Jewish culture too. "I've always wondered about the word 'Jew' versus 'Hebrew,'" a student said, "and what is correct or preferred." I explained that "Hebrew" refers to a language and an ancient people. It is not used to identify Jews today.

The term "Jew" is not inherently derogatory, as is "kike," which definitely is an ethnic slur. However, "Jew" historically has been used pejoratively, so that even Jews tend to be uncomfortable using the term. To avoid this problem, often people use only the adjective "Jewish," as in "Jewish people," instead of the noun "Jew." Journalist Mark Oppenheimer, in a *New York Times* op-ed article "Reclaiming 'Jew'" (2017, April 22), argues that Jews should reclaim the noun as a positive identifier (which we have done in this book).

Students asked Debby whether she considered attending a school that had more Jewish students. She had checked out a predominantly Jewish school, but the tuition was prohibitive, and because of how vulnerable she was feeling, she wanted to be within driving distance of her home. Still, she was shocked because "some people I met at Outer State literally had never seen someone who was black. And some friends told me they had never met a Jewish person."

The conversation then returned to holidays. "Do you get offended when people say "Merry Christmas?" Debby retorted sarcastically, "Oh, I don't get offended. . . . It just annoys the crap out of me. It drives me nuts. At Macy's last year a clerk said to me, 'Merry Christmas.' And I said, 'No, Happy Holidays.' And I was in a bitter mood. Oh no, we don't say 'Happy Holidays' here, we have to say 'Merry Christmas.' And that offended me.

"We never get holidays off. In elementary school, they didn't put the Jewish holidays on the assignment notebook. They are required to put in all holidays. It was a whole big thing that ended up going to trial and somebody sued the school, because how could they not do that?"

Debby interjected, "I have a cousin, a second cousin. We aren't super religious, clearly. My second cousin decided out of nowhere that he wanted to be a Hasidic rabbi. Hasidic men are the guys all in black with curlicue sideburns [*payot*].[9] I don't know where [my cousin's decision] came from. I don't know why."

I took this opportunity to explain that there are many different ways to be Jewish. Orthodox and Conservative Jews are the most theologically traditional and incorporate a number of rituals into daily life. The Reform and Reconstructionist movements generally are more open to adapting traditional norms and rituals as a way to blend in with modern society. A substantial percentage of US Jews define themselves as Humanist or secular, and observe few religious traditions and rituals.

In general, religiously observant Jews, no matter what branch of Judaism they follow, study the Hebrew Bible, otherwise known as the Tanakh. This consists of the Torah, or the five books of Moses; the Nevi'im (Prophets); and the Ketuvim (Writings)—corresponding to what Christians call the Old Testament. Religiously observant Jews also study the Talmud, an ancient collection of rabbinic writing that contains interpretations of the Tanakh.

After a little more discussion, Debby excused herself, saying she had to leave for the long drive home to her family's Seder. As she left, the class thanked her and burst out in applause and cheers. With some time left in the session, the class peppered me with more questions about cultural and religious topics.

"Who is defined as being Jewish?" Even though Judaism is traditionally patriarchal, heritage is passed through the mother; that is, if your mother is Jewish you are considered to be a Jew. This understanding comes from Judaic law (*halakhah*), which is derived from the Torah. Halakhah laws are most strictly observed in the Orthodox and Conservative traditions. Reform, Reconstructionist, and Humanist Jews tend to interpret halakhah more liberally, for example, identifying children of Jewish fathers as Jews, also.

"My friends, who were Christian and Jewish, couldn't find a rabbi to marry them," one of the students commented. I explained that interfaith marriage is a point of much contention in many congregations, and while many rabbis will perform interfaith marriages and many congregations welcome interfaith families, others do not. Acceptance of LGBTQ couples in many Jewish religious communities is less prevalent, although these days more rabbis are performing same-sex marriages and more congregations are welcoming to LGBTQ people. The problems facing interfaith and queer couples in Judaism are similar for interfaith and queer couples in many Christian denominations.

Finally, with the time left for the session dwindling, I returned to the theme of antisemitism by reciting "Growing Up Haunted," a poem from Marge Piercy's *The Art of Blessing the Day* (1999, pp. 108–9). The poem mirrors the distress Debby felt when she found out about the horrors her grandmother and grandmother's siblings experienced during the Holocaust. Piercy also cautions the reader not to think naïvely that the threat of antisemitic violence is past. She implies that only through our words can we partially represent the Holocaust and the unrealized potential of the ancestors we lost then.

REFLECTIONS

Being an Insider/Outsider

Debby, as a Jewish outsider within the dominant Gentile world and insider as her fellow students' peer, was well positioned to help the students understand how antisemitism did not die with the Nazi defeat. As a result of her intervention, the students became much more sensitive to the ways in which the literature they were reading is still relevant today.

Working with Debby as an informant and, in other semesters, working with a Gentile guest speaker (see Chapter 4), I better understood how my own vantage points as outsider in relation to my students (as a Jew and teacher) and insider (as a Jewish woman within Holocaust studies and as a teacher researcher in my own classrooms) were sometimes advantageous and sometimes not.

As a passionately engaged teacher who is related to Holocaust victims, survivors, and escapees, and has personally experienced antisemitism, I am deeply connected to the subjects of antisemitism and the Holocaust. This *insider* position gave me the ability to respond spontaneously to many of my students' questions. And, because of our shared identity as Jews, I could support and encourage Debby in particular ways.

However, being an *outsider within*, a Jewish woman in a predominantly Gentile university, in some ways interfered with my ability to teach freely and most effectively. To teach responsibly, I had to expose my students to unsettling ideas, but doing so sometimes alienated or intimidated them, putting them on the defensive and offensive. Consciously or unconsciously fearing antisemitic backlash, at times I withheld helpful experience and knowledge.

There was a history to my fears, not only from my family background and life prior to Central State but also at Central State. Three examples come to mind immediately, although there were others.

Prior to developing the Holocaust studies methods course, I had incorporated one Holocaust text into my methods curriculum, Holocaust survivor and Nobel laureate Elie Wiesel's memoir *Night* (2006/1960). A student in that class blamed the Jews for what happened to them because they did not leave before they were killed. He called them "stupid." The other students and I tried to explain to him why many Jews stayed in the face of danger and that his language was derogatory, but nothing that his peers or I said seemed to sway him.

Whether or not the problem lay in this student's disposition for teaching, his ignorance of history, and/or antisemitic beliefs he held consciously or unconsciously, this experience only strengthened my conviction that bringing Holocaust literature into the methods course was the right thing to do. Seeing that studying and teaching *Night* as an isolated text insufficiently prepared education students to teach Holocaust literature was one factor contributing to my decision to teach multiple Holocaust texts.

Once I made that decision, a department administrator tried to stop me, even though there was no precedent for such curriculum control in our English Education program. This administrator claimed that even my college students—let alone their future students—were not mature enough to handle the subject matter I wanted to teach. Only after I informed this person that the state mandated teaching Holocaust and genocide studies in public schools, and laid out some of the rationale given in this book's introduction, did the administrator relent.

In the final semester I taught the course, Deena (Section 5) protested that she had never before been told that her lessons had to engage students with topics that were significant to the students while they developed their language skills. Previous education teachers, she claimed, said focusing exclusively on building literacy skills is fine, and the only reason I was teaching the course with a focus on Holocaust literature was that I am Jewish.

Deena seemed to imply that if I were not Jewish, I would not have focused on Holocaust literature and therefore would not have required students to create meaningful lessons! Taken aback, I did not even try to address her resistance to linking skill-building lessons with meaningful ideas. I just apprised her of the fact that most people who teach about the Holocaust are not Jewish.

Such encounters as these might be understood as microaggressions, a term defined by psychologist Derald Wing Sue and his co-researchers as "brief, commonplace, and daily verbal, behavioral, and environmental slights and indignities," often automatic and unintentional, which are marked by "a dynamic interplay between perpetrator and recipient" (Sue, Capodilupo, & Holder, 2008, p. 329). The term, originally coined by Chester M. Pierce to describe instances of racism against African Americans, has since been extended to include similar behavior on the part of members of the dominant culture against other minorities as well.

Taken individually, a microaggression would seem to be harmless. However, the cumulative impact of many such aggressions "is traumatic and detrimental to the mental and physical well-being of the recipient" (Sue, Capodilupo, & Holder, 2008, pp. 329–30). Further, they are insidious exactly because they are covert or unconscious, go unrecognized and unacknow-ledged by many perpetrators and witnesses, and so cannot be linked directly to institutionalized and systemic discrimination.

The aggregate effect of the microaggressions I experienced over the years undermined my abilities as a knowledgeable informant. Fortunately, I did have a good support network, a group of minority women faculty and staff members who met regularly. One book that we read together, *Presumed Incompetent: The Intersections of Race and Class for Women in Academia* (Gutierrez y Muhs et al., 2012), validated our daily wrangles with discrimination and helped us all stay on track. This support, and my conviction that integrating Holocaust literature into teacher preparation courses is crucial, gave me the courage to press on.

Being an Ally

It is important to acknowledge and honor the many non-Jewish educators who teach Holocaust studies. Anyone who teaches Holocaust literature has a great deal to learn about the historical context as well as the continuing manifestations of antisemitism today. While Jewish Holocaust studies teachers may be subjected to antisemitic backlash, non-Jewish teachers who lack substantial background knowledge about Jewish culture and religion face other challenges.

To gain the knowledge and experience necessary to do this work might seem like an overwhelmingly daunting task, but this is no reason to be discouraged. As is the case with acquiring any difficult skill or new knowledge base, overcoming and addressing biases like racism, sexism, homophobia, antisemitism, and ableism entails the willingness to make mistakes and to fail. Many non-Jews become successful Holocaust studies teachers, filling knowledge gaps through study, overcoming internalized antisemitism through intercultural exchanges, and reflecting on their practices.

Feminist activist Gloria Yamato (2004) provides a helpful taxonomy of racism and encourages those who are not subjected to racism and are moved to take on the responsibility to recognize and confront it in all its forms. "Assume that you are needed and capable of being a good ally. Know that you'll make mistakes and commit yourself to correcting them and continuing on as an ally, no matter what. Don't give up" (p. 103). *Teaching What You're Not: Identity Politics in Higher Education* (Mayberry, 1996) also contains inspirational essays about teachers being allies and becoming scholars in fields that embrace identities different from their own.

CONCLUSION

As Debby's experience made clear, the antisemitism workshop at the beginning of the semester was helpful but insufficient. In subsequent semesters, and as a result of her suggestions and presentation, I became more attentive to students' lack of basic knowledge about Judaism and Jewish life throughout the course. I saw the value of using knowledgeable informants as resources and tried to overcome my fears so as to become a better informant myself.

Studying historical antisemitism and relating it to today's world is crucial to reading and interpreting Holocaust literature and understanding its relevance. The antisemitism workshop and Debby's presentation addressed the first two concerns of Weinstein and Mellen's antisemitism unit: learning the history of antisemitism and seeing how it is manifested today. As for Weinstein and Mellen's third goal—discussing how to "interrupt" antisemitism—that would have to wait until we viewed *Constantine's Sword* (Chapter 4) and read *Friedrich* (Chapter 5).

NOTES

1. On August 11–13, 2017, white supremacists rallied in Charlottesville, Virginia. Clashes between them and counterprotesters ensued. On August 13, one of the white nationalists drove his car into a group of counterprotesters, killing one and wounding nineteen others.

2. "Jews will not replace us" refers to the social Darwinist argument that races are at war with each other for finite land and resources, and the strongest one must win in order to survive. "Blood and Soil" refers to Nazi claims that the strongest races have agricultural roots, necessarily excluding Jews because they historically had been excluded from owning land. This echoes the Third Reich's fixation on racial and territorial domination (USHMM, "Origins of Neo-Nazi and White Supremacist Terms").

3. An ancient people, not citizens of the modern state of Israel. Citizens of Israel are called "Israelis."

4. Strictly translated from the Hebrew as "narrow place," usually translated as Egypt but not synonymous with today's Egypt.

5. There are many variations of the Haggadah, but all share these elements.

6. This is an abridged version of the transcription of Debby's talk.

7. A four-sided spin top with symbolic Hebrew letters that is used in a game played at Chanukah.

8. Referring to the actor's reputed history of antisemitic remarks and his involvement with the controversial film *The Passion of the Christ* (Davey, Gibson, McEveety, & Gibson, 2004) as producer and director.

9. Hasidism is a branch of Orthodox Judaism. Other Orthodox men also may dress in black clothes and have payot.

Chapter 4

Constantine's Sword
Inviting Passionate Dissonance

I went to a christian [*sic*] school for ten years, and in the ten years I was
there I never learned any information that was presented to us in the film. . . .
Constantine's Sword is a good example of a film that tells people things they
may not want to hear, and I found it to be important and interesting.

(Flora's journal, Section 8)

I am too distracted by the openly anti-evangelical tone of the film to
respect it. . . . Rather than feeling more educated about Crusades and the
history of antisemitism, I felt blamed and guilty for something that is
associated with me only because I call myself a Christian.

(Alicia's journal, Section 8)

The Nazi genocidal campaign against the Jews was not based on religion,
but the Nazis exploited preexisting and continuing religious antisemitism
while also promoting extremist racialized anti-Jewish prejudice. Therefore, it
is necessary to address both the religious and racialized dimensions of antisemitism when teaching Holocaust literature.

As Flora and Alicia indicate in their journals quoted above, however,
Christian students are particularly sensitive when it comes to discussing
religious antisemitism. These novice teachers, most expecting to teach in
public schools, were hesitant to teach about this, fearing that they would be
subject to repercussions and violate the separation of church and state. To
address both the historical background and the pedagogical issues associated
with teaching about antisemitism, I chose to show the film *Constantine's
Sword* (Jacoby, Carroll, Solomon, West, & Jacoby, 2008) and enlisted a

self-identified Christian high school teacher who taught the film to lead a discussion following the viewing.

James Carroll's book *Constantine's Sword: The Church and the Jews, a History* (2002) explains what he has learned about the Christian roots of antisemitism. Carroll, a practicing Catholic and ex-priest, explores why the Jews, and not the Romans, were and still often are blamed for killing Jesus, who appears to have been a devout Jewish teacher. He shows how Christians justified discrimination and violence against non-Christians beginning in the fourth century CE. Carroll also illustrates how antisemitism still exists today and, like racism, often goes unrecognized or is denied by people who are not subjected to that particular form of discrimination.

While the course could not accommodate such a lengthy book, the film based on the book seemed like a manageable follow-up to the lesson on antisemitism that is discussed in the previous chapter.

THE FILM

The documentary opens and closes with scenes from the United States Air Force Academy in Colorado Springs, where, in 2005, members of Rev. Ted Haggard's evangelical New Life Church, with the cooperation of the academy's administration, openly proselytized to cadets, especially targeting Jews. One Jewish cadet's father filed a lawsuit, leading to a ban on religious proselytizing at the academy. Carroll interviews several of the key people involved and characterizes Haggard's activities at the academy as contemporary state-sponsored antisemitism.

Moving from the present to the distant past, Carroll traces the evolution of the cross as Christianity's major religious symbol. A painting of Constantine I, when he was a Roman general in 310 CE and Rome was still polytheistic, shows him having a divine vision of the cross as a sword. This vision was worked into a design to adorn his troops' shields. Constantine consolidated the Roman Empire, defeating all his foes, converted to Christianity, and ruled as emperor from 306 to 336.

Carroll challenges the idea that the cross has intrinsic religious meaning because of its secular origins and Constantine's use of the symbol to consolidate his own power. The cross, Carroll claims, did not become a significant Christian symbol until 326, the fish being adopted earlier.

The film and book present incident after incident when the Catholic Church and various states with the church's blessing, or at least compliance, targeted Jews for persecution, but also times when the church saved them. Jews who lived in Rome when popes held secular power were alternately protected or persecuted, depending on the pontiff.

Pope Paul IV (1476–1559) established one of the earliest Jewish ghettos in 1555. (Venice's ruling council established the first Jewish ghetto in 1516.) This Roman ghetto was a tiny walled-in district in very poor condition. In 1882, after the Papal States were incorporated into Italy, the Roman ghetto was almost completely demolished. Later, the Nazis replicated, in the Eastern European countries they invaded, many of the conditions of the Italian Jewish ghettos.

The Vatican was the first foreign power to sign a treaty with Hitler, in 1933. Pope Pius XI demanded, in return, that Hitler protect Jews, but only those who had converted to Christianity. The Nazis did not honor even that agreement. The film highlights the case of the nun Edith Stein, who had converted from Judaism but was nevertheless sent to Auschwitz and murdered there.

In 1965, the Second Vatican Council, initiated by Pope John Paul XXIII, directed the church to stop promulgating the idea that the Jews killed Christ. In the *Nostra Aetate* (*In Our Time*), the pope states, "Jews should not be presented as rejected or accursed by God." It also renounced its centuries-old policy that it was a duty of Catholics to convert Jews. The film tracks the church's response to its antisemitic history until the term of Pope Benedict XVI (2005–2013), whose relationship with Jews was again very troubled.

VIEWER RESPONSE JOURNALS

After viewing the film, students posted their online responses to a writing prompt: "What in *Constantine's Sword* made you uncomfortable from a religious or nonreligious perspective and/or from the perspective of your own religious identity? What previous exposure to the issues the film raised have you had? How does your response address what we have discussed from the perspective of cultural awareness and reader response theory?"

Knowing that many students were practicing Christians, including Evangelicals and Roman Catholics, and that the film would likely affect them personally, I emphasized that this assignment would not be graded. My purpose was to give students a chance to express their reactions in a way that did not entail too much personal risk. To receive credit, they only had to write and post a response to the questions.

A majority of students commented that the film promoted critical thinking and successfully linked thought and feeling and therefore might be a good film to show in their future classes, although even they expressed trepidation about showing the film because of its religious themes. Others pushed back intensely, harshly criticizing the film and Carroll and questioning his scholarship. They found the film inappropriate even for a college-level course.

Sonia and Mindy praise Carroll's film for its empathy toward Jews. By bringing in various viewpoints, they write, the film recognizes people's feelings and opinions as well as facts, and emotional responses as well as critical analysis. They and Cynthia, Kendall, and Barry also point out that the film showed how Christians still hold animosity toward Jews. All five were disturbed at the way the church's evangelical members tried to convert the cadets, and they expressed shock that Jews are still being blamed for Jesus's death. (All the students quoted and paraphrased in this chapter, other than Flora and Alicia, were enrolled in Section 9.)

On the other hand, Dennis, Charles, and Barry claim that the film ignores "the great things Christianity offers" and "how Christians were persecuted"; "humanizes Jews more than Christians"; "portrays Christianity as a tool of hate"; and "fails to recognize that men are responsible for waging war, not Christian doctrine."

Charles further claims that "the church should not be held responsible for what happened and should neither be villainized nor idolized for its role during the Holocaust." He argues that because the Germans kept evil hidden from the world, it was hard to speak up when there was so much danger, and the pope did not have much power. This group of students also questioned whether Carroll's scholarship was legitimate. Others merely dismissed the film, saying that the film is "about the past," and denied that antisemitism is still a problem despite the film's evidence to the contrary.

Rather than respond individually to each student's critique, I wrote one response to all the journals. I did this to decenter my teacher authority, stimulate further discussion and inquiry, bring students into dialogue with each other and with me, and ensure that any conflict that arose during the discussion would not be personal but rather about ideas. In my response, I pose a few questions that synthesize what seemed to reflect their overall major concerns:

- What does it mean to criticize your own religion while still embracing it?
- How do we find scholarly sources of history and evaluate critiques of Carroll's viewpoints?
- How do learning experiences in which teachers allow or even encourage controversy, creating discomfort and cognitive dissonance, compare to those in which teachers suppress or avoid conflict?
- How might teachers use questions such as these to guide students to the critical analysis phase of reader response?

This strategy effectively postponed further discussion until a social studies teacher at a local high school could join us. I had contacted the teacher, Arlo, after someone defaced a poster in the hallway of my classroom building. The poster announced that a speaker would be giving a presentation about his mother, who had survived Nazi slave labor camps. Someone had written on the flyer that the Holocaust was a lie. Arlo, responding to a message about the graffiti that circulated on the English department's listserv, mentioned that he shows *Constantine's Sword* in his classes. How fortuitous! I invited him to visit the class, and he accepted immediately.

CLASS DISCUSSION

To provide background, and with my students' permission, I gave Arlo copies of their written responses as well as my response letter. My hope was that the students would be more open to Arlo's perspective on Carroll, as a self-identified Christian, than to mine, as a self-identified Jew.

Reviewing several points made in the film and in earlier discussions about the roots of antisemitism, Arlo emphasized that stereotypes about Jews still abound, many having their origin in the religious persecution they faced during the Middle Ages. He reviewed the origin of Jewish stereotypes about money, explaining that Jews were the only people allowed to engage in the financial industry, which was critical for industrialization, but which most Christians considered a "detestable occupation." Jews were forbidden to pursue most other professions and could not own land.

Arlo mentioned examples of current antisemitism, including the Mel Gibson film *The Passion of the Christ* (Davey, Gibson, McEveety, & Gibson, 2004), which blames the Jews for Jesus's crucifixion, for which there is no historical evidence. Another example: Sarah Palin characterized as "blood libel" the accusations that her rhetoric incited Jared Loughner to shoot Rep. Gabrielle Giffords in Tucson in 2011 (Whitesides, 2011). After the Affordable Health Care Act bill passed in 2010, she had urged her followers to "reload." Palin posted on a website an electoral map with crosshairs on key Democratic congressional districts, including Giffords's.

During Easter services in many churches, Arlo noted, priests still reference the Jews as Christ killers, despite evidence to the contrary. Several students in the class confirmed that this still occurs in their churches. He also mentioned Pope Benedict XVI's efforts to reinstate four conservative bishops who had been excommunicated. One, Richard Williamson, denied that millions of Jews were gassed to death (Donadio, 2009).

The ensuing debate about the film was quite spirited, but students worried that the explicitly religious orientation of the film "would offend people." Most students, even those who thought that it was important to teach about how antisemitism is still practiced today, voiced general concerns about whether the topic of religion should be broached at all in public schools, given the separation of church and state.

To clarify the law, Arlo explained that *Constantine's Sword* does not promote religion and that it is legal to talk *about* religion in public schools. The PEW Forum on Religion and Public Life (2007) clarifies that teaching about religion in schools is "constitutionally permissible and educationally appropriate," while inculcating religious beliefs in public schools is illegal. Teacher educator Robert Kunzman (2012) adds: "Teachers need to be intentional and persistent in . . . encouraging civic multilingualism in their students, creating a classroom culture in which conversations about religion and other deeply held beliefs are seen as integral to the education mission" (p. 48).

Complicating his argument, Arlo told an anecdote about a time earlier in his career when, in frustration, he gave an evangelical student who persistently interrupted the class and vehemently objected to the film permission to preach against the film using biblical evidence to refute Carroll's argument. Arlo framed his decision as a way to contain the disruptions and protect the other students, explicitly giving the boy only ten minutes to speak.

According to Arlo, this assuaged the disruptive student while also reducing the influence he had on others. Technically, this strategy to let his evangelical student preach might be considered in violation of the separation of church and state. However, the tactic served to limit the damage caused by the student's previously continuous disruptive behavior.

Such incidents highlight the potential pitfalls inherent in teaching controversial texts such as Carroll's. As much as teachers and administrators would like to eliminate controversy, no amount of teacher-proofing the curriculum can succeed. Teachers will have to analyze difficult learning situations in the moment and make decisions on the spot that might or might not be the most appropriate or effective. These incidents exemplify James Britton's "process of discovery" (mentioned also in the introduction, "Teacher Inquiry"), in which teachers are researchers who "must make a hundred and one decisions in every session" (1983, p. 90).

Today, Arlo might not solve the problem he had with his evangelical student the same way. However, his spontaneous decision illustrates one way this teacher might respond to a very human teaching dilemma: in this case, how to protect other students from having their own religious beliefs imposed on by the hostile religiosity of one of their peers. His response exemplifies how teachers sometimes experiment, diverging from usual classroom routines, even employing ethically or pedagogically questionable strategies as a way to move difficult situations forward.

Teachers often can avert such difficulties by fostering civil classroom discourse. When classroom talk does go awry, teachers can dialogue and work with their students through writing and other active learning strategies to mitigate any negative aftereffects. Sometimes what seems like a crisis can lead to important learning opportunities that would not otherwise occur.

Arlo then went on to describe how his high school students individually responded differently to the film based on their own social contexts and identities. This discussion fit in well with the work the English education students had been doing exploring and reflecting more on their own cultural contexts, including their "cultural eye" activity.

In general, Arlo reported that the film upset his very religious students, while secular students found it informative. The Catholics in his classes were troubled by the anger of Christians toward Jews as well as the Catholic Church's collusion with the Nazis. Evangelicals were shocked to hear that the Catholic Church sometimes fought antisemitism and promoted it at other times. They also were troubled by accusations that Rev. Haggard's church was illegally proselytizing. The Jewish students in his classes previously had no idea that some of their Christian friends viewed Jews so negatively.

Regardless of their religious beliefs, however, those who were not usually engaged in school and did not seem to care about other topics found the film and the ensuing classroom discussion fascinating and intellectually stimulating. Discussions of such controversial topics are a good way to engage otherwise reluctant learners, Arlo observed.

He also pointed out that the Holocaust was not about religion, something that confuses most students. Similarly, when he teaches about the Armenian genocide, he says that he thinks about ways to broaden it beyond it being an example of a religious conflict.

Arlo reported how the religious press responded to *Constantine's Sword*. For instance, Harry Forbes and John Mulderig, in a 2008 Catholic News Service online review, characterized the film as the vehicle of an ex-priest with an ax to grind. Eugene L. Pogany, a Jewish correspondent writing for *Interfaith Family*, recognizes critiques of the book's scholarship but nevertheless sees it as an important appeal to the Catholic Church's hierarchy to "find its conscience and capacity for self-reflection" (2012).

Evangelicals "get hammered pretty hard" in the film too, Arlo acknowledged, noting that some of his Protestant students feel insulted at the end. Even though the film is controversial among students and critics, and even though he does not agree with everything Carroll says, Arlo still thinks that showing the film is worthwhile. He emphasized that teachers should not avoid controversy if it can stimulate inquiry and analysis.

Barry and Tammy objected that teachers should maintain neutrality and not share their own moral beliefs with their students. They were concerned that dealing with controversial issues in the classroom would require criticizing what students think. Arlo countered that teachers cannot ignore the ethical issues raised in the Holocaust. If we do not express our outrage at certain acts of violence and disregard of moral values, he said, we would lose our credibility and students' trust.

In response, Tammy reasserted that teachers should not express their own opinions or criticize students' ideas. "The Nazis didn't think they were evil, but that what they thought was right and true." During the Holocaust, Arlo rebutted, the Nazis' decisions and actions were not based on notions of good and evil, right or wrong, but on what the Nazis considered to be expedient.

He compared the difference in social responses to the Nazis' T-4 "euthanasia" program to kill people institutionalized with mental disorders and disabilities with responses to the mass murder of Jews, which began at around the same time. Arlo pointed out that Pope Pius XII, made pontiff in 1939, along with some other Catholic and Protestant clergy, objected strenuously to the T-4 program but less so to the persecution and mass killing of Jews. As a result, Arlo said, the Nazis stopped the program. (Bergen clarifies that the T-4 program never really stopped; it was just hushed because of Catholic and Protestant leaders' negative responses [2016, pp. 163–65].)

As a teacher, Arlo lives for the debates that are generated by texts such as *Constantine's Sword*, he told my students, but he acknowledged that they would have to find their own comfort zones as professional educators. He also understood why they would be hesitant, because it is hard to analyze antisemitism and racism, and people who do not experience these forms of discrimination do not always recognize their manifestations.

Concluding his presentation, Arlo addressed the students' skepticism about Carroll's claim to be a Christian. He compared Carroll's perspectives on Christianity with Dr. Martin Luther King Jr.'s and Frederick Douglass's views about the wrongs committed by the US government.

For example, in his 1967 "Beyond Vietnam" speech, Dr. King, risking ridicule and hatred and putting his own life at risk, charged that the greatest purveyor of violence was his country's government. Similarly, Frederick Douglass, in an 1847 speech, defined a true patriot as "a lover of his country who rebukes and does not excuse its sins." In these ways, Arlo linked James Carroll to other thinkers and activists who dedicated their lives to demonstrating the harm that can come from blindly following a religion or supporting a government, even their own.

UNIVERSAL VALUES OR MORAL RELATIVISM

The discussion about whether and how to teach about religion and antisemitism was characteristic of many conversations education students have about teaching any literature that broaches social justice themes. Many do not know what to say, do not understand the issues, and have no experience discussing them from multiple perspectives. They feel vulnerable, worrying that raising such issues would offend people and get teachers in trouble with parents and administrators.

Rather than taking up the challenge and meeting their responsibility as teachers in democratic classrooms to learn about these subjects alongside their students, these prospective teachers retreat. When it becomes impossible to avoid controversy, as when Holocaust studies are mandated, they use moral relativism as a shield.

Taking a moral relativist position—simply put, that everyone's perspective has merit and so none should be challenged—shuts down any possibility of dialogue in which people can learn from one another and come to appreciate their differences. "Relativism of that sort isn't a way to encourage conversation; it's just a reason to fall silent," argues philosopher Kwame Anthony Appiah in *Cosmopolitanism* (2006, p. 31). He claims that all cultures share universal values and that we should rely on these to help us manage conflict. (We come back to Appiah's ideas in Chapter 5.)

History teacher Jonathan Gold (2016, pp. 24–25) applies to pedagogy a philosophical stance similar to Appiah's. He writes that attempting to be a neutral teacher puts him in an ethical and philosophical quandary as he tries to situate himself between the extremes of moral relativism and absolutism. He suggests that we need to be aware of our own subjectivity, acknowledge it to our students, and avoid preaching.

However, Gold continues, we also need to challenge views that are based on faulty reasoning or false information or are morally repugnant. Not all ideas are equally valid. "By owning our morality and demanding rigor in our classrooms, we can knowingly, mindfully, and progressively develop students' abilities to articulate and assess the human experience" (p. 25).

Historian and social justice activist Howard Zinn extends this line of reasoning in his memoir (2002), explaining why it is important for teachers to inform their students about their own life experiences, beliefs, and ethics to the extent that these are relevant to the curriculum.

> I have often wondered how so many teachers manage to . . . never reveal who they are, what kind of lives they have led, where their ideas come from, what they believe in, or what they want for themselves, and for the world. Does not the very fact of that concealment teach something terrible—that you can separate the study of literature, history, philosophy, politics, the arts, from your own life, your deepest convictions of right and wrong?
>
> I would always begin a course by making it clear to my students that they would be getting *my* point of view, but that I would try to be fair to other points of view. I encouraged my students to disagree with me. I didn't pretend to an objectivity that was neither possible nor desirable. "You can't be neutral on a

moving train," I would tell them. [I meant] that events are already moving in certain deadly directions, and to be neutral means to accept that. (pp. 7–8)

These are words to remember when comparing how neighbors and coworkers complied when the Nazis persecuted the Jews and others during the Holocaust years to how people today support or ignore policies that promote prejudice and discrimination.

Gold's sweet spot between pedagogical moral relativism (the student is always right) and absolutism (the teacher is always right) only can be found through reflective practice. Similarly, Zinn's confidence that he could be open about his lifetime of social activism and his radical beliefs without intimidating his students was developed through years of teaching experience.

It is never easy for teachers to challenge resistant students' ideas without losing their trust or turning them against their instructors. As social justice teacher educators, we encourage teachers to welcome difficult dialogue in their classes. However, even we sometimes avoid challenging our own students, fearing a backlash (as discussed in Chapter 3). But when students express opinions and ideas that contradict universal moral values, we challenge ourselves, as we do our education students, to push through the fears and maintain our moral compasses.

Philosopher John K. Roth, in his 2008 lecture "The Failure(s) of Ethics," explains why it is so important that Holocaust educators do so:

The Holocaust did not have to happen. It emerged from human choices and decisions. Those facts mean that nothing human, natural, or divine guarantees respect for the ethical values and commitments that are most needed in contemporary human existence, but nothing is more important than our commitment to defend them, for they remain as fundamental as they are fragile, as precious as they are endangered. (p. 31)

TEACHING ABOUT CHRISTIAN ANTISEMITISM

Christian students' resistance interfered with their critical abilities to analyze the film and to focus on how the history of religious antisemitism is relevant today. I did not anticipate all their objections, and I did not want to argue with individual students about Carroll's scholarship and his Christianity, fearing that this would create a rift between us. I hoped that writing one response to the whole class rather than individual responses to their journals and having a Christian guest speaker would enhance their learning rather than heighten their resistance.

I see now that there are other ways I could have mitigated the friction that occurred. Had students read reviews of the book and film, they would have realized that Carroll has both detractors and supporters. For example, theologian Charles R. Morris's review of Carroll's work in *The Atlantic* (2001), and Andrew Sullivan's in the *New York Times* (2001), would provide the students with more background through which to examine Carroll's scholarship. Texts by theologian Franklin Littell (1975) and Harry James Cargas (1991), a literature scholar and theologian, are less accessible to high school students but useful for teachers, who could summarize Littell's and Cargas's arguments for their students.

Cargas spells out how he thinks the church should take responsibility for its actions during the Holocaust. He points out that Nazi leaders were not condemned or excommunicated by the Roman Catholic Church, and he believes that the Holocaust was, in large part, the result of misinterpreted and erroneous Christian theological teachings about the Jews (1991, pp. 109–20). Littell asks how Christianity can survive the terrible truth that Christians carried out mass murder and torture during the Holocaust (1975, p. 2).

Both Cargas and Littell expose historically inaccurate and antisemitic sections of the Gospels and rebut supersessionists. Littell writes: "The cornerstone of Christian Antisemitism is the superseding or displacement myth, which already rings with the genocidal note. . . . To teach that a people's mission in God's providence is finished, that they have been relegated to the limbo of history, has murderous implications" (1975, p. 2).

Other educators also have experienced their students' resistance based on religious beliefs. Theologians Mary Todd, a Christian, and Rochelle L. Millen, a Jew, cowrote about their experiences teaching Holocaust studies in different settings (2014). Todd mentions how little her students knew about the backgrounds of their own faiths in relation to antisemitism and discusses the challenge to expose them to this knowledge. She ends with a quote from a student who says that she is "left with more questions than answers . . . questions that I previously wouldn't have asked" (p. 114).

Millen stresses how her students came to more nuanced understandings of concepts such as sin, forgiveness, redemption, and salvation by studying Holocaust survivor Simon Wiesenthal's anthology *The Sunflower* (1998/1976), which juxtaposes Christian and Jewish approaches to these concepts. This being their first exposure to the Christian roots of antisemitism, the students in my course also lacked perspective about the prevalence and importance of this dialogue within Christianity and between Christians and Jews. They, too, would have benefited from studying *The Sunflower*.

Todd's and Millen's ethical approaches emphasize how important it is for students not just to gain a critical understanding of what occurred but also to develop empathy and realize that the choices people make are important.

CONCLUSION

From the data gathered in this research, the film's long-term impact on the students cannot be determined. When students' basic values and beliefs are questioned, they often need a maturation period to assimilate what they have learned, during which time their life experiences interact with text-based learning. Certainly, there are other good films the students could have viewed that would give them information about antisemitism and the Holocaust. Part I of *The Longest Hatred* (Wistrich, 1992), for instance, deals with some of the same history of antisemitism as does *Constantine's Sword*.

Despite its flaws, *Constantine's Sword* provides a visually stimulating and memorable introduction to the history of antisemitism and its manifestations today. Studying it brought a number of important ideas into play: the distinction between teaching about religion and proselytizing, the recognition of how little the students knew about the history of antisemitism and how that still influences their views about Jews and Christians today, and the value of and difficulties inherent in teaching controversial texts.

Watching and discussing the film gave even the students who most resisted Carroll's ideas opportunities to consider other perspectives. When reading, responding to, and teaching the literature they read during the rest of the semester, students who thought the film too contentious nevertheless did not avoid controversy and became more open to critique. Still unable to recognize subtle antisemitism, some students might have benefitted from more study in this area. Regardless, for most students, what they learned from the film and the antisemitism unit laid a solid ground for their study of *Friedrich*, which came next, and for the texts that followed.

Chapter 5

Friedrich

The Erosion of Jewish Rights and Gentile Ethics

> When we forget that all groups have differences, and emphasize the differences of a specific group above all others . . . it creates a social climate that allows for events such as the Holocaust to occur.
>
> (Cora and Jesse's lesson plan, Section 5)

The students now were oriented both historically and pedagogically. They had explored their cultural background knowledge, or lack thereof, regarding Jewish stereotypes and Jewish culture. They had discussed historical and present-day, and religion-based, economic, and racialized antisemitism.

They had studied reader response theory and other applicable literary theories, culturally responsive teaching, and Cambourne's conditions for literacy learning. In addition, they had been introduced to a number of other significant pedagogical methods designed to develop students' literacy while engaging them in active and relevant meaning-making.

Making sense of the literature about the experiences of Jewish and non-Jewish Germans during the years of persecution (1933–1939) still remained a challenge. Even those students who had studied the Holocaust in history or social studies classes or had read literature about the Holocaust in college, high school, or middle school had not been exposed to what life was like for Jews in Germany prior to the Nazi takeover and after, as Jews lost their civil rights and their quality of life deteriorated.

The Holocaust texts taught most frequently in middle and high schools are various versions of Anne Frank's *The Diary of a Young Girl* (we use the "Definitive Edition," 1995), about a young Jewish teen in hiding with her family in the Netherlands from 1942 to 1944; and *Night*, by Elie Wiesel (2006/1960), about the deportation of the Hungarian Jews to Auschwitz in

1944. Neither book provides much historical background or gives students a sense of the specific ways in which European Jews were persecuted in different countries and different times under Nazi rule.

Most recently, some middle school teachers have adopted into their curricula *The Book Thief*, by Markus Zusak (2007), about a non-Jewish German girl who befriends a Jewish man her foster parents are hiding; and John Boyne's *The Boy in the Striped Pajamas* (2007), about the son of a concentration camp commander who develops a friendship with a Jewish child in the camp. Neither of these books offers insights about the rise of fascism in Europe or the gradual subjugation and persecution of the Jews during the Third Reich.

In Samuel Totten's anthology *Teaching Holocaust Literature* (2001), I found the text I was looking for: *Friedrich*, by Hans Peter Richter (1987), discussed in middle school teacher and Holocaust educator Rebecca Aupperle's article (2001, pp. 73–102). The novel meets the requirements that none of the books mentioned above do. I also was looking for a literary text with which both my students and I would be unfamiliar, allowing me to be a learner alongside my students as a way to challenge the teacher-as-expert paradigm (see Chapter 2).

For those who want an example of what an in-depth unit on the Holocaust might look like in middle or secondary schools, Aupperle's article, based on her long-term experience teaching Holocaust literature, provides a useful model. It is important to note that her *Friedrich* unit included multiple sessions to build background knowledge and link Nazi racism to racism in the United States.

ABOUT *FRIEDRICH*

Friedrich begins in 1925, in an unnamed German city. At this time, prior to Hitler's appointment as chancellor, antisemitism exists, but most Jewish people are assimilated and integrated into German society. They live and work in the same neighborhoods and workplaces as do Gentiles. The narrator, who is unnamed, is the non-Jewish German neighbor of a German Jewish family, the Schneiders, whose son, Friedrich, is the narrator's best friend.

The book follows the trajectory of German history between the wars. The Nazi government institutes racial laws, depriving Jewish people of all citizenship rights, public education, and employment. The reader watches a community drastically transform from one in which Jews are integrated into one that is openly hostile. The book ends in an ironic tragedy when the Allied forces bomb the city, killing the eponymous Jewish protagonist.

Based on Richter's own childhood experiences, *Friedrich* is written from the perspective of a non-Jewish German boy. The book reveals how ordinary Gentile Germans—neighbors, friends, and civic leaders—become, in some cases, resisters of antisemitic persecution but, more often, are swayed by Nazi propaganda, peer pressure, and economic advantages to become bystanders, collaborators, and perpetrators.

The book also contains short chapters on a number of important topics. (We refer to the chapters by their titles in the discussion below.) Richter describes how Jewish adults lost jobs and Jewish children the right to public education and how Jews were scapegoated for the economic crisis in Germany. He narrates the development of Hitler youth groups and the segregation of public facilities and spaces. And he vividly describes a pogrom representing Kristallnacht.

In her chapter on Richter's trilogy of autobiographic novels, of which *Friedrich* is the first, literary scholar Hamida Bosmajian (2002) investigates Richter's motives for writing the book. Due to the age of the protagonists, and because it is linguistically accessible to young adult readers, it would seem plausible that Richter was writing for young adults, but Richter denies this. "I do not write for children or for teenagers or for grown-ups—I simply write" (p. 50).

Whether or not Richter's intent was to write for young adults, Bosmajian and others point to evidence that reading *Friedrich* is complicated for any audience. Throughout, he is ambivalent about the extent of his narrator's culpability for his antisemitic behavior. Therefore, reading and teaching the book are challenging. Young readers could miss the book's irony and subtlety. Adult readers could misinterpret the text and overlook places where Richter reinscribes and rationalizes antisemitism.

Yet the book provides a powerful depiction of Jewish persecution and suffering due to the policies of the Third Reich and at the hands of ordinary non-Jewish Germans during the years of persecution and leading into the years of extermination. The ambiguity reflects real and persistent challenges to universal moral values and opens up space for meaningful dialogue.

JOURNALS, DISCUSSIONS, AND LESSONS

The students began working with *Friedrich* by reading the book and writing journal entries based on Probst's dialogue-with-a-text reader response exercise (described in Chapter 2). In their journals, students asked questions about ethics and morality while linking the book to today's world and their own lives and hypothesizing what children at different ages can and should learn about the Holocaust.

They wondered about cultural and historical background, noticed literary features, and reported new information they were learning. Richter's mixed messages and the text's ambiguities confused them. The students wondered why so many non-Jews accepted the Nazis' persecution of their Jewish neighbors and tried to justify the non-Jews' behaviors. In my written and oral responses, I engaged them in dialogue, answered some of their questions, raised other questions, and encouraged them to inquire further.

Teaching *Friedrich* requires educators to have substantial cultural awareness and historical background knowledge in order to teach it accurately and without reproducing and reinforcing the Jewish stereotypes prevalent in the text. The students' journals reflected their lack of cultural and historical understanding. So, after the students had their first unmediated encounter with the text, they then read and responded to the first three chapters of Bergen's *War and Genocide* (discussed in Chapter 1). They also reviewed the timeline in *Friedrich* (pp. 139–49), which highlights some of the major anti-Jewish laws and decrees that the Nazis instituted.

After a short exercise in which they applied Cambourne's schema for developing literacy learning environments (see Chapter 2) to teaching *Friedrich*, each class divided into pairs and triads to plan and teach lessons. The students and I divided the book into three sections of sequential chapters, and each group chose one of these. In addition to the lesson criteria (also found in Chapter 2), they were to incorporate something they learned from Bergen's history and Richter's chronology.

Ethics and Morality

In their journals, most students address topics related to ethics. (In this book the terms "ethics" and "morality" are used interchangeably, except when a speaker, writer, or character specifies one or the other.) Many focus on whether ordinary non-Jewish Germans shared culpability for the persecution of the Jews in Nazi Germany.

The narrator's non-Jewish perspective was helpful because the students saw how ordinary Gentile Germans responded to the growing influence of Nazism. This perspective also was problematic because Richter was ambivalent about the extent to which non-Jewish Germans were culpable. Most students did not recognize the complexity of Richter's positionality.

Some students stated or implied that the non-Jewish population was helpless to counteract Nazi aggression. Barbara (Section 5) reports on the conversation in her group in which the students defended the narrator and other non-Jewish characters: "Above all, my group believed that the author was ultimately trying to show that despite Hitler, some Germans did sympathize with Jews. This can be seen through the teacher's actions and the narrator's father telling Herr Schneider that they should leave the country." (This scene is described later in this chapter. That Barbara does not identify the Jews as also Germans is discussed later too.)

Ann, who was also in that group, writes, "We see how emotional the narrator's family gets when Friedrich is in trouble and how much they care about him." At times, the narrator and his family show sympathy and provide minimal covert support for the Schneiders. For example, in "Vultures" (pp. 126–28), after the Nazis have arrested Friedrich's father, the narrator writes that he and his father and mother could not sleep, Mother cried, and both parents agreed that they had to prepare Friedrich before he came home to find his father missing.

However, this group overlooked the fact that the family only goes so far to resist the Nazis. Social expedience trumps moral principles. The son betrays his best friend by joining the *Jungvolk* (the Hitler youth group for boys) three years before all "Aryan" boys were required to join. Father joins the Nazi Party to gain material advantages. The son joins a mob that ransacks a Jewish home. The family does not harbor Friedrich after his mother dies and his father is arrested. Along with the other Gentiles in the air raid shelter, the family eventually capitulates to their Nazi landlord's authority when Friedrich's life is at stake.

Cora (Section 5) writes, "The narrator experienced and witnessed the poor treatment and gradual degradation of Friedrich's family, yet he was unable to do anything to stop it. He was virtually silent, and completely powerless against the system that was victimizing his friend." Cora does not consider that the narrator's silence might represent a choice and that his behavior might not be inevitable, although the narrator's age is a mitigating factor.

The narrator responds differently as the book progresses and the boys get older. As an eight-year-old, the narrator says nothing when the Jungvolk leader shames Friedrich in front of his peers, and Friedrich leaves the meeting alone (pp. 32–38). At age thirteen he does not intervene when Friedrich is taunted at a public swimming pool, but he does leave with him (pp. 74–77). Later that year, he turns from passive bystander to perpetrator when he participates in a pogrom (pp. 88–95).

At age sixteen he has to choose whether or not to tell authorities about the rabbi whom the Schneiders are hiding. He fears that his family could be punished if the authorities find out he knows about the rabbi (pp. 114–17 and pp. 123–25). One year later, he does not stand up for Friedrich when his friend is denied entrance to the air raid shelter, and subsequently Friedrich dies in the Allied bombing (pp. 133–38).

Cora, Barbara, and Ann seem to read *Friedrich* as Richter's apologia, defending what the narrator and his family—and by extension many non-Jewish German citizens—did or neglected to do during the Holocaust in reaction to the persecution of Jews. Ann writes that Richter's goal was "to show that the Holocaust and WW I made victims out of German Gentiles too, and not just Jewish people."

They did not understand that, while World War I and the economic depression leading up to Hitler's takeover did indeed bring great suffering to everyone, Gentiles were not persecuted as were Jews. Many gained advantages by going along with the Nazi agenda, among them the narrator's family. Richter's distancing stance, reporting without analyzing, makes it difficult for readers to understand this. *Friedrich* illustrates the distinctions between Jewish and non-Jewish experiences, but with sufficient ambiguity that many students could not recognize or would not acknowledge these distinctions.

The students had difficulty recognizing the bitter truth that ordinary people not so different from themselves complied with the Nazis. As social psychologist Rona Novick (2010) explains, powerful social forces influenced what people thought and did, even those who would have refrained from such inhumane behaviors in another era. "Each dehumanizing act made further acts of violence and degradation that much more acceptable, until Jewish victims were seen not only as responsible but also deserving of their disastrous fate" (p. 85).

Perhaps the students who had difficulty accepting ordinary Germans' culpability also were influenced by the Christian redemption narrative, which ascribes redemptive qualities to tragic stories. Those who write Holocaust literature for children and want to shield their readers from the full brunt of atrocities often use this trope, as do Zusak in *The Book Thief* and Boyne in *The Boy in the Striped Pajamas*.

Similarly, teachers often present Anne Frank's diary simplistically, whichever version the students read, view, or perform. The stage version of *The Diary of Anne Frank* (Goodrich & Hackett, 1986/1955) decontextualizes some of Anne's last thoughts before she is arrested. The play ends with Anne's father, Otto Frank, reading a fragment from her diary—"In spite of everything I still believe that people are really good at heart"—which downplays the tragedy. In the actual diary entry, Anne seems aware of her family's terrible circumstances but does not want to lose hope that things might improve.

Wendy Kesselman's (2000) adaptation of the original play mitigates Goodrich and Hackett's false positive by adding Anne's fate in the Bergen-Belsen deathcamp. As the play concludes, Mr. Frank says that when last seen, Anne is "naked, her head shaved, covered with lice. . . . A few days later, Anne dies. My daughters' bodies are dumped into mass graves. . . . All that remains. (*Slowly he opens the diary. . . .*)"

In *Friedrich*, a redemptive narrative is just not there. Jesse (Section 5) recognized the problem with redemptive themes in Holocaust literature. In his journal, he writes that he identifies strongly with both Friedrich and his friend and cannot understand why Gentile Germans treated their Jewish neighbors so badly. As he grew up, Jesse, who describes his childhood as "wonderful" and "innocent," also struggled to accept a world in which "war, corruption, and . . . hatred seem to be everywhere."

He explores this theme intertextually, contrasting the stark reality of *Friedrich* to redemptive fantasies like *The Chronicles of Narnia* (Lewis, 2001), wherein the villain is completely evil and "the children . . . rally together in order to destroy the evil force and return balance to the world" (Jesse's journal). Jesse points out that in *Friedrich* there are no precise boundaries between good and evil, there is no balance, and no one is saved.

After reading Bergen, Cora moved beyond her initially simplistic interpretation. In a lesson she and Jesse taught, they explained how the Nazis exaggerated and falsified distinctions between Jewish and non-Jewish Germans. They designed an activity to help students understand that the Nazis promoted the belief that "Jews were completely different than Germans, using Jews as Scapegoats based on socially constructed stereotypes, when in reality the two groups held more similarities than differences" (Cora and Jesse's lesson plan, referring to Bergen's discussion about this [2016, pp. 18–20]).

First, they showed antisemitic Nazi political cartoons found in Bachrach and Luckert's *State of Deception* (2009) and discussed with their students "how this Propaganda perpetuates the Jewish stereotypes learned about in the previous class during the Bergen discussion."[1] Then they worked with the class to create three Venn diagrams, representing where Jewish and Gentile Germans' lives intersected and differed in relation to economics, social relations, and religion. With this more systemic analysis, they and their peers could better understand the characters' complex values and behaviors.

Moral Relativism

Denying the Gentile characters' culpability reflected some students' inclinations toward moral relativism (see the discussion of universal values and moral relativism in Chapter 4). Flora and Annette (Section 8), in their lesson plan for "Reasons" (Richter, 1987, pp. 68–73), write that they want the students to see that "not everyone always has a choice, and that sometimes the lines between right and wrong can become very blurry." They chose a conversation between Father and Herr Schneider to demonstrate this.

Father informs Herr Schneider that he has joined the Nazi Party. "I have become a member of the NSDAP because I believe it's of advantage to my family and myself" (p. 70). From what he hears at party meetings, he believes the situation for Jews in Germany is going to get worse and urges Schneider to leave with his family immediately.

Schneider explains that, like so many other German Jews at this time, he has decided to stay because he and all his extended family are German, they are unlikely to be accepted better elsewhere, and the violence "will quiet down eventually." He speculates that Jews might be able to "put an end to our wanderings by not taking flight any more" (pp. 72–73).

Flora and Annette asked their peers to examine the choices the two fathers made and then to compare and contrast these with a difficult choice each of the students had made in their own lives. They said they hoped that this analysis would show that neither father is a "bad" person, because the context justifies their points of view. They did not make it clear how they came to this conclusion.

Were they implying that Father is morally justified to have joined the Nazi Party? Is he "good" when he warns Schneider? Might Father be consciously or unconsciously encouraging the Schneiders to emigrate so that he would not have to take moral or political responsibility to either give refuge to his neighbors or report them to the authorities?

Is Herr Schneider not morally justified to stay after his Nazi neighbor cautions him? Did the students understand that Herr Schneider cannot predict what is going to happen to Germany's Jews and that trying to leave could be just as risky as staying, even if they could find a place to go and had the means to get there?

Those who study *Friedrich* face such ethical considerations throughout the book. Many students found this work to be difficult, because Richter's mixed messages about moral culpability confused them and blinded them to the ethical problem presented by moral relativism.

Making Ethical Decisions

The question of moral culpability comes into clearer focus when the narrator, on his way home from school, participates in the pogrom (pp. 88–94). He is now thirteen years old and recently has attended Friedrich's bar mitzvah.[2] Getting caught up in the violent destruction, he is exhilarated, until he comes to his senses and becomes disgusted with himself. Shortly thereafter he returns home, only to find that the mob is now pillaging the Schneiders' apartment. "Mother began to weep loudly. I wept with her" (p. 95).

In their lesson about the narrator's moral confusion, Henry, Manny, and Jason (Section 3) set up a role-play to investigate why he took part in the pogrom. After dividing the class into groups, they asked one student in each group to step into the role of narrator and explain to different people in his life—Grandfather, Mother, teacher, Jungvolk leader, and Friedrich—why he joined the antisemitic rampage.

One student in role explained to Grandfather, an unabashed antisemite, that he liked feeling the power he had. To his best friend, Friedrich, he admitted realizing that he should have stopped but got swept up in the fervor of the crowd. To Mother he said that he just wanted to be accepted. To his teacher he said he could not understand why he participated. And to his Jungvolk leader he exclaimed how he enjoyed smashing Jewish property. This student quite skillfully approximated, through these rhetorical shifts, how the narrator and other non-Jewish Germans who were not firm believers in Nazi ideology became morally corrupted and culpable.

Before this juncture in the story, the narrator has reacted, or not, to what is going on around him without assuming responsibility. Three years after the pogrom, he is faced with an important ethical decision, because he is privy to knowledge that has life-or-death consequences for his neighbors and could endanger his own family's status. This time, he knows what is at stake and that he will be responsible for his actions.

The narrator's moral quandary in "The Rabbi" (pp. 114–17) arises when he inadvertently learns about the rabbi who is being hunted by the Nazis. He has to decide whether or not to report the rabbi to the authorities. "I didn't know what to do. The rabbi was a stranger to me. And what about my mother and father? Didn't they stand closer to me than this Jew? Might I endanger myself and them for the sake of a stranger? . . . Would I be able to bear the secret or would I suffer under it like Herr Schneider?" (p. 117).

Jane and Kerri (Section 5), in their lesson on "The Rabbi," asked students to think about a parallel dilemma in their own lives and then to freewrite an answer to one of these questions: "Has someone ever hid something from you that you think you should have known? or Has someone ever told you something that you wished they hadn't? Explain the event and discuss how your knowledge or lack thereof affected your perception." Those students who were willing to do so shared what they wrote and related their experiences to the text, and a general discussion ensued.

Jane and Kerri did not provide enough scaffolding for students to engage readily, and the students' experiences didn't parallel the narrator's. Nonetheless, the discussion did address an important ethical question: How do we value people "beyond the boundary of family, tribe, ethnicity, and nation" (Sacks, 2015, p. 126)? Rabbi Jonathan Sacks cites caring for strangers as a biblical value by which we can compare the values of individuals and cultures. Appiah, analyzing cross-cultural universal values, calls this worldview "cosmopolitanism" (2006; see Chapter 4, "Universal Values or Moral Relativism").

Still disturbed by his moral dilemma, the narrator returns to the Schneiders' apartment and asks the rabbi why they are being persecuted this way. The rabbi replies, "Because we are different, just because we are different we are persecuted and killed" (Richter, 1987, p. 120). Then the rabbi tells a parable that gives the narrator much to think about in relation to the moral dilemma he faces.

In his parable, a king's warriors have been idle too long, are poorly paid, and have been unable to gather the spoils of war. Afraid of their discontent, the king gives them permission to kill all the Jews in a town and keep a third of their booty. During the subsequent massacre, a boy named Solomon (which is also Friedrich's Hebrew name) survives because his parents hide him and die to save his life.

Unlike in the parable, Friedrich's parents could not save their son, but the rabbi seems to imply that Friedrich's friend and family can. Richter does not reveal how this conversation affects the narrator's decision. The story foreshadows the Schneiders' and the rabbi's fate, though. Soon, the Nazis come to the Schneiders' apartment and arrest Herr Schneider and the rabbi. (Friedrich is not at home, and his mother had died shortly after the pogrom.) The arrested men acknowledge the narrator and Father as they are led downstairs, but Richter gives no concrete evidence that the narrator or Father has informed on them (pp. 124–25).

In another lesson examining ethical behavior, Benny, Anna, and Morris (Section 4) asked students to consider the teacher Herr Neudorf's ethical dilemma by applying James P. Gee's theory of primary and secondary discourse (see Chapter 2) to analyze Neudorf's rhetoric. In "The Teacher" (pp. 59–63), Richter narrates how an adult authority figure, who can make no claim of innocence, expresses core moral values and performs as a Nazi.

Gee's and Heath's studies indicate that if there is a gap between the discourse of home, which shapes a person's primary identity, and school-based discourse, students can have difficulty succeeding in school. Although by applying this theory to the teacher's situation they stepped far outside Gee's context and purpose, Benny, Anna, and Morris's unconventional application of the theory helped them to analyze how Neudorf could hold and express antisemitic beliefs as a Nazi functionary while also supporting Friedrich in other ways.

Benny, Anna, and Morris asked students to define what they thought were Neudorf's primary and secondary discourses. The students concluded that Neudorf identifies as a teacher who cares for and about his students, and this derives from his primary discourse. He shows his dedication to the students' education by teaching them about the history of antisemitic persecution prior to expelling Friedrich because he is a Jew. Neudorf warmly bids Friedrich farewell and urges Friedrich's classmates to remain his friends.

However, as the students also discerned, this discourse is complicated by Neudorf's deep and possibly unconscious antisemitic beliefs. In his brief lesson about Jewish history, he maintains that the Jews crucified Jesus because they did not believe he was the Messiah. He demeans Jews by saying that they are "crafty and sly" and "avaricious and deceitful," but only because they have to be so in order to survive. At the same time, he also calls them "a very capable people" and reminds his students that they "are human beings, human beings like us!"

As Friedrich leaves after everyone says *"Auf Wiedersehen,"* Neudorf "jerked up his right arm, the hand straight out at eye level, and blurted: '*Heil Hitler!*'" (p. 64). The students analyzed his secondary discourse as that imposed on him by Nazi policies. If he fails at "Nazispeak," his career is over. If he succeeds, he compromises his core ethics and his ability to teach moral values.

Neudorf's remarks and behavior present readers with particularly thorny challenges, as they are infused with fiction as much as fact and carry antisemitic messages intertwined with humanitarian ones. How can readers distinguish between the realistic historical narrative in Neudorf's lecture and the antisemitic stereotyping and mythology that riddles it?

Is Neudorf walking a tightrope, balancing his liberal values with his fear of Nazi retribution? Or is he two-faced, appearing to be sympathetic to Jews while insidiously promoting Nazi ideology? To what extent is he culpable if he both resists and promulgates Nazism? The students grappled with these questions, coming to no consensus.

Contemporary Connections

For their practice lessons, the students appropriately focused much of their attention on the text, but the reader response process also led them quite naturally to consider the text's relevance to their lives today. As a result, in many lessons the teachers and their peer students linked life in Nazi Germany to contemporary life in the United States.

After demonstrating how the Nazis overplayed differences between Jewish and Gentile Germans, Cora and Jesse asked students to discuss how reactionary forces in our own society scapegoat outsider groups. They hoped the students would realize that "when we forget that all groups have differences, and emphasize the differences of a specific group above all others . . . it creates a social climate that allows for events such as the Holocaust to occur" (Cora and Jesse's lesson plan).

In the second half of their "Reasons" lesson, Flora and Annette presented two contemporary scenarios that compared the kinds of moral decisions people like the narrator and Father made in fascist Germany to those people might face today in societies defined as democracies. The first scenario was based on Flora's personal experiences as a Mexican American. A story that Doris Bergen (2016) tells in *War and Genocide* inspired this scenario.

Bergen recounts an incident in 1933 when a group of local Nazi functionaries eating in a restaurant harass an elderly Jewish lawyer who is also a customer, while the other non-Jewish Germans stayed silent. She writes, "All over Germany the silence of others like them sent a message back up to Hitler: it was safe to keep pushing" (2016, pp. 87–88).

Flora and Annette posed the following problem as a writing prompt and followed up with a role-play: "While a Mexican-American family is out to eat at a local restaurant, a police officer approaches [them] and asks to see some identification for them and their children. You are sitting at a nearby booth and begin to notice that the police officer is starting to get aggressive and continuously asking them for their 'papers.' What would you do?"

Students enthusiastically jumped into roles, trying to stand up to the police officer. The facilitators asked them questions about how they chose to respond; what interfered with them doing what they thought was right, such as peer pressure and the officer's response to their protests; and whether some civil rights are more important than others. (Notably, neither the student teachers nor their peers assigned any agency to the Latinx diners.)

Working through the scenarios, students gained a deeper understanding of how a book such as *Friedrich* could help students consider what it takes to fight oppression today and what the consequences are when people challenge or do not challenge threats to or violations of civil rights. However, they did not discuss how the contemporary scenario was similar to and different from the situation described by Bergen, or from the situations in *Friedrich* in which Jews were harassed or assaulted while bystanders passively looked on.

Without adequate analysis, drawing parallels between the Holocaust and our world today is risky. Flora and Annette's scenario was a good parallel, as the scene was in a restaurant, a public official was doing the bullying, and there were civilian bystanders. But when trying to resist oppression in a contemporary scenario like this, depending on the outcome of the role-play, the students could get a false sense of empowerment or conversely could feel that there is no point in fighting back. It is important to follow up such a role-play with further investigation and discussion.

How is it similar and different to resist oppression in a fascist state and in an ostensibly democratic one? Bergen suggests that the onlookers in her scenario would not have been at risk. In Flora and Annette's example, the same might be true. At the time of this role-play, the United States was enforcing draconian measures against migrants, but these laws and policies were being challenged in the courts, and a mass movement supporting the migrants was developing.

However, does the risk change depending on who resists? Would there be a difference between what would happen if a white middle-aged man tried to intervene and if a young black man, transgender person, or Latinx person tried to intervene?

People's acquiescence to Nazi violence emboldened the regime, and Nazis scaled back violence when people resisted, up to a point. What are the consequences of silence in the United States today when citizens do not counteract racist violence? Does this embolden white supremacists to perpetrate violent acts against people of color and other minorities? Does it create room for fascists to gain influence through manipulation of social and media networks and political processes?

What happens when people do resist—individually or through collective action? Does this prevent bigots from gaining traction? Flora and Annette were unable to take the discussion very far in this direction, but the potential was there to do so.

The second scenario was about a gay student who is bullied, based on the following writing prompt from Flora and Annette's lesson plan: "Jake is a junior in high school, he has been bullied his entire life, always being considered one of the 'losers.' Jake no longer feels safe walking through the halls of the high school and cannot stand the idea of facing his bully one more time. Jake brings a gun to school. What would you do?"

The class did less with this scenario. The simplest explanation for this is that the class spent most of the time playing out and discussing the first scenario. Another reason could be that the student teachers placed the action beyond the point where school officials, parents, and other students could have intervened to stop the bullying.

In any case, Flora and Annette's intent was well meaning because homophobic violence and gun violence are serious and life-threatening problems. To make a contemporary scenario meaningful, distinctions would need to be made between this kind of individualized violence against LGBTQ people, based on reactionary gender and sexuality socialization, and the kind of state-sanctioned violence to support a regime's antisemitic and ultranationalistic worldview that *Friedrich* depicts. (Note, however, that in some countries LGBTQ people still face state-sanctioned violence, and even in the United States, they do not yet have full legal protection.)

Janice, John, Roger, and Dave (Section 2) created another hypothetical contemporary dramatic scenario. Their stated goal was to better understand authoritarianism in Nazi Germany's educational system, based on "The Encounter" (pp. 85–88). In this chapter, the narrator's physical education instructor drills his class of boys through a grueling physical workout that doubles as indoctrination into Nazi hypermasculinity and antisemitic aggression, during which they march through the town singing strident anti-Jewish songs as they pass Friedrich and his Jewish classmates.

In the students' scenario, a teacher bullied his students into hyperpatriotic performances of the Pledge of Allegiance. Their role-play was intense and harsh. John, in role as the teacher, yelled at students, threatened to fail them all, and called them unpatriotic, causing them a great deal of emotional discomfort even though everyone knew this was a fictitious situation.

Neither the content nor pedagogy was appropriate. Replicating oppression by forcing an emotional response detracts from the students' abilities to analyze the oppression rationally. Given the power differential between teachers and students, if a high school teacher, even in role, bullied his or her students this way, the incident could result in the students at least temporarily losing trust in and respect for their teacher.

Despite the problems, however, this drama created an important learning moment. The discussion that followed was useful because the students were able to analyze the pedagogical problems in the lesson and to discuss the differences between this kind of bullying and the state-sanctioned intimidation Friedrich endures and indoctrination that the narrator receives.

Also during the discussion, some students in the class shared their own experiences with discrimination and how difficult it was to handle them. These students included one whose father was "a cop in Chicago who has racist and homophobic ideas" and a student whose second cousin was engaged to a black man to whom the family responded with racist hostility.

In their written reflections, the peer students criticized the harshness of the role-play but stated that it made them think and feel more about the book than they had before. Everyone commented that the discussion that followed was rich and productive. However, they noted that the drama seemed to reinforce the belief that most of us are too weak to resist, because no one challenged the ultranationalist teacher in the role-play. Neither the teaching group nor their peers speculated why that was.

Other drama techniques, however, can help people practice resistance. For example, in a variant of Boal's Forum Theatre based on "In the Shelter" (pp. 133–36), students might explore ways people in the air raid shelter could stand up to the Nazi landlord Herr Resch when he forbade allowing Friedrich to enter during an air raid.

In traditional Forum Theatre, actors take on the roles of the oppressed to experiment with resisting and countering oppression based on class divisions. In this situation, because they are compliant bystanders, everyone in the shelter is Friedrich's de facto oppressor. The problem would be to try to transform their positions from compliant bystanders to rescuers, building on evidence of potential resistance that appears in the text.

The teacher would need to guide them so they didn't create unrealistic heroes or facile solutions. They might not even succeed in saving Friedrich. However, experimenting with plausible alternatives could help students understand the dynamics of the situation and could then prompt them to consider contemporary connections.

Employing drama exercises recommended by Edmiston (2013) or Wilhelm (2002), teachers also might ask students to create a dialogue between or among characters through which the students speculate on future repercussions for those who did not resist Herr Resch. Would they have regrets? Would they later stand up to oppression? Would they continue to be complicit? How would they respond to the economic and immigration issues that divide Germans today?

To further explore the characters' internal reactions to these situations, students also might try a "voices in the head" stratagem, in which actors speak what characters are thinking as well what they are saying so spectator/researchers can observe and analyze the differences (Neelands, 1990, p. 58).

How to resist oppression and how to connect *Friedrich* with the students' contemporary experiences also factored into Jane and Kerri's lesson on Friedrich's dilemma in "The Rabbi" (see this chapter, pp. 91–92). They asked their peers to consider, "When does the innocence of childhood change to the knowledge of adulthood?" (Jane and Kerri's lesson plan). Specifically, Jane and Kerri wanted them to think about how innocence and knowledge affect one's understandings of and behavior in response to moral challenges.

This relates to the concern that many of the education students taking the course had regarding how and when to talk about the Holocaust with children and young adults. Richter insisted that he did not write *Friedrich* specifically for children; nevertheless, the book provides us with a way to think about age appropriateness in Holocaust education. He provides examples of what children of different ages might experience and might be capable of understanding and doing in response to discrimination and violence.

Is there some way that the eight-year-old narrator and his friend could have been better prepared to react when the Jungvolk leader tormented Friedrich? In our society today, do schools, parents, and other institutions that instill moral values have a responsibility to teach children of this age about discrimination and appropriate ways they can respond?

By the age of thirteen, should people have developed the moral fortitude not to participate in the kinds of hate speech and acts that the narrator perpetrated in "The Encounter" and "The Pogrom"? How might adults today prepare young teens to resist participating in and to counteract such violence?

At sixteen and seventeen, faced with the situation of a friend being unprotected and endangered as was Friedrich, should a person have the wherewithal and ethical determination to aid their friend? Should they be aware of resources that might help such a person today? And what about helping a stranger even in the face of potential danger to one's own family?

Such questions can guide teachers when they consider which Holocaust texts are appropriate for children at various stages of moral development. They also can help students make meaningful connections between and among the text, the reader, and the world.

REFLECTIONS

At first read, *Friedrich* might seem to be a straightforward, easy-to-comprehend story with a simple message. A teacher might decide that it is the perfect novel to adopt for a quick dip into Holocaust literature. Dive beneath the surface, however, and we see that the book is so much more complicated and demanding than that. Still, its brevity, simple vocabulary, and conventional narrative structure free teachers and students to concentrate on revealing and deconstructing *Friedrich*'s wealth of meaning and insights.

The book thus provides an effective entry into studying and teaching Holocaust literature. Together, the students and I uncovered some of the core pedagogical and content-based issues confronting those who teach Holocaust studies. The students predominantly attended to ethical considerations, and appropriately so. Reflecting on the data I collected, we have some additional concerns, which we discuss next.

Antisemitism

The students needed ongoing support as they developed their background knowledge and applied unfamiliar theories to their practices. Cambourne's (2003) conditions for learning, and Blau's (2003), Grossman's (2001), and McCann and his colleagues' ideas about what education students and pre-service teachers need in order to gain competence and confidence all indicate that students need multiple opportunities to demonstrate and approximate what they are learning and to receive helpful and supportive feedback. Likewise, identifying and responding to antisemitism takes practice and analysis.

By beginning the course with the unit on antisemitism, I had hoped students would be able to identify and analyze Jewish stereotypes and anti-semitism when they came across them in the literature and would rely on accurate and relevant sources for their research. Yet students still found it difficult to recognize antisemitism in *Friedrich*. They struggled with this again when they studied Art Spiegelman's *Maus* (see Chapter 7), but Spiegelman consciously and explicitly articulates the antisemitic stereotypes that he fears his depictions of his father evoke, which helps them.

Barbara's journal, excerpted above in this chapter's "Ethics and Morality" section, provides another example of how antisemitism eluded the students when she writes that "some Germans did sympathize with Jews." Not referring to German Jews as such is a mistake that several students made in this first unit. By so doing, these students unconsciously replicated the Nazis' antisemitic strategy to denationalize the Jews.

Drama Pedagogy

Some of the pedagogical problems that arose were due to the students' inexperience. This was especially apparent in role-plays like Janice, John, Roger, and Dave's about the bully teacher. Had I reviewed all the lesson plans before they taught them, I would have caught these problems in advance. Had I deliberately incorporated educational drama practices into the curriculum, such pedagogical missteps might have been avoided.

Be that as it may, these problematic role-plays provided visceral learning opportunities. Through them, the students experienced the potential hazards of superficial and insensitive role-plays but also learned experientially how powerful educational drama can be when it blends cognitive and affective learning to gain more insight into literary texts.

Reader Response

Using reader response theory proved to be problematic as well. Many of my students, lulled by how easy *Friedrich* is to read for surface comprehension, missed its subtlety and sophistication as well as Richter's complex positionality, especially when they initially responded. Some completely missed Richter's points, overlooked important themes, and reproduced prejudices that Richter both affirms and rejects.

In their lesson plans, some students tried to apply reader response techniques, with varied results. Their backgrounds—being literature students fascinated with literary tropes and high theory—sometimes interfered, and when teaching they sometimes regressed, using only leading questions and imposing unnecessary constraints on discussions, thus denying their students opportunities to plumb the text for all its rich meaning and ambiguities.

However, by following through the complete reader response cycle when researching their lessons, even rudimentarily, most of them developed a more nuanced understanding. They created new knowledge, empowering themselves as readers and future teachers, which they would less likely achieve through highly structured reading and teaching assignments that might have prohibited them from exploring their own ideas.

Pedagogical Content Knowledge

At this early stage in the course, the concept of pedagogical content knowledge was barely on their radar or mine. Most students thought about how to teach and what to teach and attended to the lesson plan criteria. Some did research to expand their background knowledge. But it was a stretch to expect students to integrate sufficient content knowledge with what they were learning about pedagogy when teaching their first practice lessons.

For example, Martha and Jill's (Section 9) goal for their lesson about Hitler's antisemitism was for students to investigate "why the Germans made the decision they did during the Holocaust" and the differences between German and Jewish perspectives. (Note that the students again distinguished between Jews and Germans, replicating the antisemitic misconception that Jews were not Germans.)

Starting with their history lecture, they set up a teacher-centered lesson by linking specific passages in *Friedrich* to their flawed lecture. By linking these excerpts and asking students to read and interpret them, in conjunction with their lecture, Martha and Jill denied their students the opportunity to ask their own questions and interpret what they were reading for themselves. A (possibly unintended) result was that they led their peer students toward justifying why Gentile Germans went along with anti-Jewish Nazi policies and actions, as if these Germans had no choices.

Others managed to come fairly close to demonstrating pedagogical content knowledge. Benny, Anna, and Morris applied Gee's discourse theory unconventionally. At the time, I was concerned that they were misinterpreting the theory, but when reflecting on the lesson afterward, we realized that using the theory this way helped them correlate pedagogy with content. They applied the discourse theory within the framework of Cambourne's approximation stage of learning. In this way, they helped their peers notice Neudorf's inconsistencies and moral dilemma.

Standards

In their lessons, students demonstrated various approaches to using standards in their lesson planning, some more useful than others.

The main language arts standard that Martha and Jill cite in their lesson plan, Common Core W.8, relates to using and evaluating various sources in order to answer a research question. Martha and Jill applied this standard to their own work rather than to the students' work. They, not their students, did the research that they presented in their PowerPoint, much of which was inaccurate. Because they did not cite their sources, it was impossible to evaluate the sources' strengths and limitations. By misinterpreting the standards and doing faulty research, Martha and Jill's lesson was counterproductive.

On the other hand, Henry, Manny, and Jason, in their lesson plan for the role-play exploring why the narrator might have participated in the pogrom, cited NCTE Standard Four, which supported their goals and strategies. This standard requires students to examine how people communicate with different audiences for different purposes. Consequently, they could see more clearly that there was no morally acceptable justification for the narrator's actions and that Richter was trying to help his readers and perhaps himself come to terms with the fact that ordinary non-Jewish Germans engaged in morally reprehensible behavior.

Teaching Risky Texts

The antisemitism that Richter replicates in *Friedrich* calls to mind the controversy about teaching *Adventures of Huckleberry Finn*. Should teachers avoid that book or teach it in a way that unpacks the stereotypes Mark Twain simultaneously embraces and challenges? Should *Friedrich* be struck from reading lists, or should teachers and students talk about how pervasive, even today, Jewish stereotypes are and that Richter harbored antisemitic prejudices while simultaneously critiquing antisemitism?

Too often, preservice and beginning teachers avoid complicated or controversial texts that cause students and teachers discomfort and require them to acquire historical background knowledge and cross-cultural understanding to interpret successfully. Playing it safe is part of an unwritten script meant to deprofessionalize teachers and disempower those who promulgate social justice.

It is therefore up to teacher educators to prepare and empower preservice teachers to teach complex texts like *Friedrich* in morally responsible ways. Teaching such texts is difficult and risky business but necessary if teachers are to help their future students understand the past and negotiate the moral and ethical challenges our world presents to them today. Standing up for justice can make a difference and is one of the fundamental reasons why teaching about the Holocaust is important today.

Flora and Annette were headed in the right direction with their restaurant scenario, but the students were not prepared to challenge the police officer effectively. Had I encouraged the students to analyze their own hesitations about standing up to oppression, they might have become more self-aware and thought more about what they could do in such situations.

To augment the few instances of resistance in *Friedrich*, teachers might add texts or other media that depict people who resisted Nazism and rescued Jews. This might help students envision what resistance looks like. The documentary film *Children of Chabannes* (Gossels & Wetherell, 2014) is a good example.

CONCLUSION

We can understand that the prospect of teaching *Friedrich* could easily overwhelm any teacher who is unfamiliar with Holocaust studies and literature. Working with this text in secondary English classes and in teacher education courses certainly is a formidable undertaking.

Most students came into the course with very little if any cultural and historical literacy concerning this era in European history, before and during the Third Reich. The previous units on antisemitism and the history of the Holocaust provided some background, and the research some did for their lesson plans taught them more. Viewing or reading survivor testimonies by Jewish people who grew up during this time would help clarify Jewish perspectives, particularly in relation to Richter's work, which mostly excludes such perspectives.

A number of students were hindered by their lack of knowledge. Some did not seem ready or willing to integrate new knowledge, leading to significant errors, misjudgments, omissions, and avoidances. Others, however, did benefit from their study in the previous units and from their research, resulting in effective lesson plans and teaching presentations.

Despite the challenges, under the guidance of a well-prepared teacher, and supplemented with the texts and topics just mentioned, studying *Friedrich* can help students come to a rich and nuanced understanding of the years leading up to the Holocaust, what Jewish people experienced as Nazi racial laws were implemented, and what were the ethical challenges that Nazism raised for non-Jewish Germans. Teaching *Friedrich* also affords ample opportunities to make the Holocaust relevant to today's students as they grapple with how to respond to moral and ethical challenges in their societies today.

NOTES

1. The USHMM's exhibit catalog *State of Deception: The Power of Nazi Propaganda* (Bachrach & Luckert, 2009) provides a comprehensive and profusely illustrated examination of the subject.

2. The bar (Hebrew for "son")/bat (Hebrew for "daughter") mitzvah (commandment) is a Jewish coming-of-age ritual in which a thirteen-year-old boy or twelve-year-old girl leads prayers in the synagogue and reads from the Torah, thus taking on the responsibilities and privileges of an adult member of the Jewish community.

Chapter 6

"Esther's First Born" and "The Shawl"

Women and Children in the Concentrationary Universe

The ultimate blasphemy of the scene, it seems to me, is not that the woman denied her child but that Nazi racists built an environment so deprived of ethical meaning that a woman would be given the occasion to deny her child to save her own life. What the woman did shocks us morally, but that the woman was placed in this situation should appall us much more.

(Literary critic James F. Farnham [1983, p. 66] commenting on Tadeusz Borowski's *This Way for the Gas, Ladies and Gentlemen* [1976])

After studying the novel *Friedrich*, the class turned to short stories, a genre that is convenient to read and explore in a high school classroom because of the texts' brevity and their concise attention to delimited topics. Totten (2001, pp. 128–29) suggests a variety of short stories that are appropriate for the classroom and that humanize major Holocaust themes. "Holocaust Fiction," a USHMM website, also contains a very useful annotated bibliography that includes short stories, literary anthologies, novels, and literary criticism.

In this course, the students read two stories found in *Truth and Lamentations* (Teichman & Leder, 1994), an anthology of Holocaust-themed short fiction and poetry. These stylistically contrasting stories, Sara Nomberg-Przytyk's "Esther's First Born" (1994, pp. 86–89) and Cynthia Ozick's "The Shawl" (1994, pp. 107–11), exemplify the dilemmas women and children faced in Nazi concentration camps, where human dignity and family life were stripped away and the fascist sociopolitical system distorted morality and moral choice for the incarcerated. Taken together, they also exemplify how truth can be revealed differently through fiction and nonfiction.

"Esther's First Born," originally published in Nomberg-Przytyk's book *Auschwitz: True Tales from a Grotesque Land* (1966/1985), is a semifictionalized, realistically rendered memoir of her experiences there. Esther, a pregnant concentration camp prisoner, decides to keep her baby even though she is aware that in the camp newborns and their mothers are automatically condemned to death.

In the story, the infamous Nazi doctor Joseph Mengele offers a twisted rationale for this policy, claiming that since Jews no longer live in freedom, and conditions in a concentration camp do not allow for normal child development, it is unethical to let the child live. However, Mengele states, "It would not be humanitarian to send a child to the ovens without permitting the mother to be there to witness the child's death. That is why I send the mother and the child to the gas ovens together" (p. 87).

Most pregnant women in Auschwitz gave birth secretly, and other inmates who served as midwives killed the newborns immediately in order to save the mothers' lives. Despite knowing that she and her offspring face certain death, Esther proudly insists she give birth to her baby in the camp's infirmary and does not save herself by surrendering the infant to the midwives.

By contrast, Ozick's "The Shawl," originally published in 1989, is a more fantastical rendering of mothering in a Lager where Rosa hides her own starving fifteen-month-old baby, Magda, in a shawl that appears to have magical qualities: "it could nourish an infant for three days and three nights" (p. 108). She keeps Magda safe until fourteen-year-old Stella, her niece, who is hungry, freezing, love-deprived, and jealous, steals the shawl.

Now Rosa can no longer comfort Magda or save the crying child from the guard who viciously murders Magda by throwing her against an electrified fence. Rosa does not cry out or go to her child. Instead, at the story's end, she chokes back her response because "if she lets the wolf's screech ascending now through the ladder of her skeleton break out, they would shoot" and kill her (pp. 110–11).

Both stories present examples of how Jewish women resisted persecution. In "Esther," the midwives try to save the mothers but at the price of the children's lives. Esther defiantly keeps her baby and confronts Mengele with her newborn, but mother and child are marked for death. In "The Shawl," Rosa hides her child but then has to watch Magda die when the child runs into the yard. These decisions exemplify the double binds prisoners agonized over.

GENDER IN HOLOCAUST LITERATURE

This chapter specifically concentrates on women's experiences. Lawrence L. Langer finds gendered analyses of Holocaust texts to have limited value. He studies testimonies of Holocaust survivors and argues, "Even when we hear stories of mutual support among women in the camps, . . . these narratives show us how seldom such alliances made any difference in the long-range effects of the ordeal for those who outlived it" (1998, p. 351).

While women and men were threatened and humiliated differently because of their particular gender roles, he points out, "the ultimate sense of loss unites former victims in a violated world beyond gender." He cautions against using gendered experience to "dredge up from this landscape of universal destruction a mythology of comparative endurance" (p. 362).

However, feminist scholars such as philosopher Joan Ringelheim (1998) encourage us to be explicit about the experiences of women in the Holocaust, whose stories have been suppressed. She writes, "If in the gas chambers or before the firing squads all Jews seemed alike to the Nazis, the path to this end was not always the same for women and men. The end—namely annihilation or death—does not describe or explain the process" (p. 350).

Sara Horowitz (2009) observes that "the victims of rape, forced prostitution, or sexual barter are almost exclusively women. . . . Literature by women explores the effects of these harsh circumstances on women's lives and psyches." Male writers, Horowitz claims, tend to depict women's situations and behaviors "as viewed externally rather than experienced internally. . . . [T]he sexual violation of women is presented in the background or on the periphery," as in Jerzy Kosinski's *The Painted Bird* (1995/1965), or eroticized, as in William Styron's *Sophie's Choice* (1992/1979).

Apropos of the short stories read in this class, Horowitz warns that while the themes of childbirth and motherhood are important, when we study women in the Holocaust we should not concentrate on women exclusively as sexual and reproductive beings. Nevertheless, as she also emphasizes, the themes of childbirth and motherhood are important and should not be overlooked. "Esther" and "The Shawl" effectively expose the plight of women in the concentration camps; the other texts included in the curriculum do not address women's issues directly.

Hans Richter and Art Spiegelman primarily depict the female characters in relationship to male protagonists, not as agents in their own right,[1] conforming with Horowitz's observation. For example, in *Friedrich*, both mothers defer to their husbands when there are moral or ideological decisions to make, and they participate mainly within the domestic sphere. The book presents examples of hypermasculinist indoctrination, but Richter either was unconscious about or not interested in drawing out the gendered structure of Nazi society.

This points to one of the limitations of the curriculum analyzed in this research. Participants did not read any text that sheds light on non-Jewish German women's participation in the persecution of Jews, especially in their roles in the Lagers (camps) or on the home front to procreate and rear the next generation of "Aryans." Teachers should be cognizant of how fascists exploited and shaped gender socialization, for both males and females, to seize and maintain power.[2]

ETHICS AND MORALITY IN THE CONCENTRATIONARY UNIVERSE

Two critically important ethical concepts—"the gray zone" and "choiceless choices"—are associated with the concentrationary universe, in which the normal functioning of society is replaced by a vicious totalitarian order and ethics and morality are profoundly distorted. The "gray zone" refers to situations in which prisoners in the concentration camps and residents of the ghettos compromised their ethics in order to survive. This concept is discussed in Chapter 7.

"Choiceless choices" are double binds in which Jews were forced to choose "between one form of 'abnormal' response and another, both imposed by a situation that was in no way of the victim's own choosing" and either of which led to degradation, disease, or death—one's own and/or others (Langer, 1988, p. 120). In the Lagers, even simple concepts and words related to choice and morality were rendered meaningless.

Langer analyzes an all-too-common story told by concentration camp survivors of a prisoner drowning a newborn infant to save the baby's mother. The situation allows "no heroic response, no acceptable gesture of protest, no mode of action to permit *any* of the participants, including the absent mother, to retain a core of human dignity. The *situation* itself forbids it, together with the Nazi 'law' stating that mothers who refuse to surrender their newborn infants to death must accompany them to the gas chamber" (p. 121).

Knowing "how utterly the Nazi mentality corrupted moral reality for the victims, may enable us to comprehend better how little discredit falls to these victims" (p. 120). There is a difference between the rationale prisoners give to kill babies in order to save their mothers and Mengele's rationale to murder mothers along with their children. The Nazis perverted morality and negated the ideas and values that shaped the Enlightenment, the philosophical movement of the eighteenth century, when rationalism began to replace religiosity.

The story Langer retells is similar to Nomberg-Przytyk's. It could be argued that Esther does behave heroically when she proudly shows her baby to Mengele, thereby retaining her dignity even though both she and her baby will be murdered.

The prisoners who serve as midwives in "Esther" also are caught in a double bind. They believe killing newborns immediately after birth to save the mothers is the lesser of two evils. Esther's baby will die one way or another, but if they had murdered the infant, Esther might have survived Auschwitz and conceived again, thus fulfilling her desire for motherhood. In the end, though, they respect Esther's right to make her own tragic choiceless choice.

In "The Shawl," Rosa chooses to hide Magda, trying to protect her as a mother under normal circumstances might. As long as the child is alive, Rosa has hope. She endangers her own life by giving up her ration to Magda, but even so the child clearly is starving. In this way, she prolongs the suffering of this innocent, voiceless, powerless toddler.

The only alternative would be to commit infanticide, which is anathema. In the horrific moment when she witnesses the Nazi guard throwing Magda against the fence, Rosa's choiceless choices are to be silent and save herself, run after the child and be shot, or scream and be shot. She instinctively saves herself—but the consequence is madness.

Understandably, Stella is jealous of Magda, who Rosa keeps warm in the shawl and feeds, while Stella is chilled to the bone and emaciated with hunger. She is faced with the choice of starving and freezing to death or depriving Magda of her protection and sustenance, which would be tantamount to murder. Barely more than a child herself, Stella's moral values are negated by the instinct to survive.

How different these situations are from the moral choices faced by the non-Jewish characters in *Friedrich*. In the shelter, Herr Resch says, "You follow my orders. . . . Otherwise I'll report you" (Richter, 1987, p. 136). There might have been consequences had he carried out that threat, but not deadly ones. There is no double bind here. Unlike Rosa's and Esther's dilemmas, the people in the shelter, especially the officer, could have stood up to the landlord. Their capitulation unequivocally was a moral failure.

In the Lagers, choices and actions cannot be judged as they would be under normal circumstances, because the normative system of morality was rendered inoperative. John K. Roth (2008) counsels:

Moral judgment should focus on the persons and decisions, the institutions and policies that created the Holocaust and every other form of genocide. Accompanying that judgment should be an intensification of responsibility to resist such people and to intervene against those circumstances, to honor those who do so, to embrace the survivors with compassion, to mourn and remember those who were murdered, and to restore—as far as possible—what was lost. (p. 17)

TRAUMA IN HOLOCAUST LITERATURE

"Trauma" is a word so commonly used today to describe an array of experiences and conditions that it is easy to assume we know what it means. It is unlikely that anyone reading these stories would deny that the events described were traumatic. However, teachers of Holocaust literature should not rely on unexamined, unarticulated, vague understandings of this term. Having a clear, even if rudimentary, understanding of trauma theory would help teachers to interpret and teach literature that represents concentrationary experiences.

The word "trauma" comes from the Greek word for "wound" and originally was used to describe a wound to the physical body caused by an external force. Psychoanalyst Sigmund Freud defines a traumatic experience as "any excitations from outside which are powerful enough to break through the protective shield [of the ego]" (quoted in Wilson, 1995, p. 14). Psychiatrist Judith Herman writes that traumatic events "overwhelm ordinary human adaptations to life" (1992, p. 33), and traumatic responses occur "when neither resistance nor escape is possible" (p. 34). Psychologist Kai Erikson recognizes that trauma can be generated from "a *constellation of life experiences* as well as from a discrete happening, from a *persisting condition* as well as from an acute event" (1995, p. 185).

Freud theorizes that "such an event . . . is bound to provoke a disturbance on a large scale in the functioning of the organism's energy and to set in motion every possible defense measure" (quoted in Wilson, 1995, p. 14). During the time of the initial events, the victim uses various unconscious strategies to endure the torment. Herman records terror, rage, pain, "freezing" or catatonia, or a numbness in which the victim maintains awareness but becomes dissociated from reality (1992, pp. 42–43).

Holocaust and genocide researchers have added new dimensions to the understanding of trauma. When applied to Holocaust survivors, comparative literature scholar Bella Brodzki (2004) describes it as "massive, cumulative psychic trauma . . . when vast numbers of people . . . were subjected for months and years to loss, terror, dehumanization, and death, in a social and moral framework seemingly designed to make normal ego functioning impossible" (p. 126).

Horowitz also describes a particular gendered aspect of trauma when she writes about Rosa that she represents the "protective capacity of motherhood, and the fragmentation of a survivor who could not, ultimately, do the work of mothering. When women cannot feed and shelter their children, and protect them from pain and from death, maternal love itself becomes an instrument of torture" (1998, p. 374).

In "The Shawl," we see the conditions of life in the camp that traumatized Rosa, Magda, and Stella: the starvation, the breakdown in morality, the humiliation, and the terror. We see Rosa hallucinating—hearing voices in the wire of the electrified fence and other such imaginings. In "Esther," we see how the protagonist protects herself from absorbing the brutal reality of her situation by inventing the fantasy that Mengele will save her baby when he sees how beautiful he is.

Reaction to the effects of trauma may be delayed. During a period of latency, the victim may not react to or feel the effects, but, over time, symptoms of what is now termed post-traumatic stress disorder (PTSD) may set in. Comparative literature scholar Cathy Caruth (1995) writes:

> Most experts agree that [PTSD] is a response . . . to an overwhelming event or events, which takes the form of repeated, intrusive hallucinations, dreams, thoughts, or behaviors stemming from the event, along with numbing that may have begun during or after the experience, and possibly also increased arousal to (and avoidance of) stimuli recalling the event. (p. 4)

Ozick writes about the aftereffects of trauma in a sequel to "The Shawl," the novella *Rosa* (1989), which tracks Rosa's life in Florida, where she maintains a fantasy relationship with Magda. This delayed response also is exemplified in *Maus*. People who are intimate with survivors may experience some of the symptoms of trauma too. Descendants of historical traumas such as genocides and mass enslavement take on the legacies of these traumas. *Maus* exemplifies how trauma is sometimes transmitted to the families of Holocaust victims and survivors.

The Pedagogy of Trauma

Other than by reading *Night*, secondary English students rarely study the concentrationary universe of the Holocaust. Understandably so: these Holocaust settings are among the most violent. Yet without paying close attention to life in the concentration camps and ghettos, teachers cannot say they have fully engaged with the history of the Holocaust. Those who study the Holocaust—seriously listen, observe, read, and view—cannot do so without having a psychic response. One question, then, is how should the Holocaust be taught without causing secondary trauma or extreme distress.

Marianne Hirsch and Irene Kacandes discuss how to process intensely emotional responses, attending to "the disturbing tension between affect and analysis." They cite historian Saul Friedländer, who "acknowledges this tension as constitutive" (Hirsch & Kacandes, 2004, p. 19). In his own work,

Friedländer intentionally links personal voice with historic analysis. He cautions that,

> the major difficulty of historians of the *Shoah* . . . is to keep some measure
> of balance between the emotion recurrently breaking through the "protective
> shield" and numbness that protects this very shield. . . . [T]he numbing or distan-
> cing effect of intellectual work on the *Shoah* is unavoidable and necessary; the
> recurrence of strong emotional impact is also often unforeseeable and necessary.
> (1992, p. 51, quoted in Hirsch & Kacandes, p. 20)

The antidote to this is twofold. First, keep bringing attention back to ethical and cognitive analysis, raising essential questions about what representations of the Holocaust teach us, as Mary M. Juzwik recommends (2013; see Chapter 2, "Integrating Cognitive and Affective Learning"). Second, provide opportunities for emotional expression. Hirsch and Kacandes recommend combining cognitive and affective responses by building "space for the expression of affect into the syllabus, precisely so that students, in the face of their strong emotional reactions, can still analyze issues such as represen-tation" (2004, p. 20).

After viewing videotapes of survivors' testimonies, comparative literature scholar Shoshana Felman's college-level literature students "felt alone, [the] class was entirely at a loss, disoriented and uprooted" (1992, p. 48). She helped them overcome the crisis they experienced by having them discuss their feelings and write their own testimonies (p. 52).

Hirsch and Kacandes, Felman, and compositionist Sondra Perl all recom-mend writing assignments that help students and teachers find the balance between affect and analysis. Perl writes about the transformative power of response journals (2004), and Hirsch and Kacandes provide two good college-level assignments—for a reading journal and for a media folder and course diary—that high school and middle school teachers easily could adapt (2004, p. 21).

Students who are psychologically vulnerable could experience a post-traumatic response despite teachers' best intentions and practices. Therefore, it behooves teachers to forewarn students of the potential for such reactions and be prepared to refer students to appropriate services when necessary. However, by virtue of Holocaust literature being representational rather than embodied, such texts do provide enough distance to shield most people from harm.

Many students in the course were noticeably upset by what they read and viewed. Some of these students had experienced significant trauma them-selves or had family connections to the Holocaust or other genocides. Writing in their journals and speaking in subsequent discussions about how the stories related to their own lives helped them process and put into perspective some of their emotional discomfort. Encouraging these students to further elucidate and analyze how their personal connections and emotional responses affected their interpretations of the texts would have benefited them.

JOURNALS AND DISCUSSIONS

Each student chose one of the stories to write about in their journals. Some students related these painful stories to their own lives, while others kept their distance and found it difficult to empathize with people who had such profoundly different life experiences from themselves. Their responses also included questions about ethical decision-making, how the stories relate to the world today, how and why the authors conveyed meaning through narrative and poetic language, and how fiction and creative nonfiction might get at truth in ways that other nonfiction Holocaust texts do not.

Reading and Responding to "Esther's First Born"

Making Personal Connections

Most students were deeply moved by Nomberg-Przytyk's story, and a number of students were extremely upset by the cruelty it depicted. Those who had experienced trauma themselves, had connections to the Holocaust through their families and heritage, or were mothers experienced the strongest emotions. (All the students quoted in these paragraphs about journals and discussions, except for Manny, were in Section 5.)

Jenny, a mother of two young children, writes, "I couldn't imagine killing them to save myself." Those who were not mothers found other ways to empathize with Esther. Carol looks forward to someday being a mother: overidentifying with Esther was very painful. Ann relates the story to hearing her mother say that if she had to make a choice, she would choose her children over her husband.

Others reacted strongly, too, but their points of connection were to other aspects of their lived experiences. In her journal, Edith describes two memories that surfaced as she read. Minor brain surgery she had endured was a painful, disruptive, and scary event, but, she emphasized, it was not torture. She submitted to it willingly, and it was medically necessary.

She also mentions being terrified to learn that one of her close friends was imprisoned but sees now that her friend's sentence—"for a limited time and with some deprivation but no brutality"—paled in comparison to the traumatic starvation and violence of the camps. Edith seems to have learned from previous discussions how to avoid inappropriate comparisons. Yet, while she rightly avoided overidentifying, she also downplayed the significance of her and her friend's experiences.

For others, relating was more difficult initially, but they were able to establish personal connections to the stories through interaction with their fellow students in small-group dialogue. Robert states in his journal that he cannot identify with the women in the stories because he is a man. However, after explaining his point of view to his small discussion group, he acknowledges that the stories do have some meaning for him because he has a mother and sister who are important to him.

Manny (Section 3) also changed his position on the value of reading such literature after discussing "Esther." In his journal, he acknowledges the limits of his understanding. "I never experienced anything this traumatic in my entire life. I can relate because I am Jewish and I have a compendium of historical facts about this period in my head. But I wasn't there. And I'm aware enough to KNOW I don't understand Esther's sorrow and suffering."

He expresses his strongest feelings about his relationship to the Holocaust in a story he shared about reading "Esther" to his fiancée:

> When I was done . . . she said, "I never thought of the babies. . . ." I thought this absurd—I have thought about the children, about the families, about the tragedy. . . . I had nightmares about this as a child. But after meeting with our groups they all said the same thing. . . . [They] "never thought of the children, or pregnancy, or childbirth in concentration camps." What to me was "just know" was shocking news to others.

Personally, he writes, he does not like reading stories about the Holocaust because he has heard the stories and contemplated the horrors enough. But when his group discussed the story, he reexamined this literature's significance, even for himself. "This story humanized a number—six million Jews died, that number is cold, detached, and hardly imaginable. Esther's story is present, visual, and shocking. Esther puts a face on a massive tragedy."

Literary Interpretations

Students struggled to understand what motivated Esther to bear her child under these genocidal circumstances. Did the story's title character understand the consequences of giving birth? Was she naïve? Shocked to see Esther's response to her gruesome situation, Edith wonders: "How can Esther be so happy to have a baby? How can there be hope in a place of death? Why is the narrator willing to take such risks to protect the mother?"

Responding to Edith during a whole-class discussion, Jenny speculated that Esther might have been delusional. Remembering our biblical incursion during our study of *Friedrich*, I suggested we might find some answers to Edith's questions in the "Megillah Esther" ("The Book of Esther" in the Hebrew Bible).

As a Jewish woman, the story's Esther would be familiar with the biblical Esther, who Jews traditionally view as a hero because she saves her people from Haman, a jealous and prejudiced adviser to the Persian king Xerxes, who convinces the king that all the Jews should be killed. After Xerxes's wife Vashti refuses to dance nude in front of his guests, Esther agrees to dance in her stead. She thus curries Xerxes's favor, and he takes her as another wife. Esther then strategically waits for the right moment to tell Xerxes that she is Jewish and then convinces him to reverse his order to kill her people.

Whether Nomberg-Przytyk's Esther is delusional, ignorant, or defiant, when she convinces herself that Mengele will save her and her beautiful child, perhaps she believes (consciously or unconsciously) that she embodies the compliant, beautiful, and smart Queen Esther. Perhaps, in her mind, Mengele represents Xerxes and her baby the Jewish people. However, in a perversion of the biblical story, Mengele instead reveals himself as more like the villain Haman, bent on destroying the Jews.

Nothing in "Esther's First Born" confirms or denies this biblical connection. However, making this connection can enrich our efforts to plumb the depth of Esther's thoughts in the story, and it raises an important question. Might this confused and oppressed woman who resists killing her baby be a courageous hero? Or, as Langer contends, is there no possibility for heroism and dignity in the Lager?

Reading and Responding to "The Shawl"

Making Personal Connections

Most students had difficulty finding their way into "The Shawl." They found its allusions and magic realism perplexing. Others, like Jesse, Deena, and Doris, made visceral, almost primal connections.

Jesse writes that he "never had to do anything as traumatizing as what happens in 'The Shawl.'" Nevertheless, he finds a way to empathize. "I have experienced blistering cold . . . on a Boy Scout retreat during the winter and we had to spend long periods of time outside. . . . My hands felt useless all the time and my whole body stung with cold. I can't imagine Stella's situation, but I can imagine how much the cold would have affected her after being without warmth for so long."

Deena writes that she did not have a nurturing mother: "I couldn't get the 'milk' from her," so relied on her sister "to give me life and give me the nourishment that I needed." Doris reacts to the same passage in Ozick's story: "Magda relinquished Rosa's teats . . . ; both were cracked, not a whiff of milk. . . . Magda took the corner of the shawl and milked it instead" (p. 107). Doris remembers that she "carried around a Barney doll and I would sleep with it and slobber all over it and it had a very comforting smell."

Kerri, who had a fifteen-month-old child, did not think she could withstand these horrors as a parent:

> Every thought, emotion, action of Rosa's seems to be my own. I can feel her uncertainty and fear. . . . I can feel her excitement and joy. . . . With every new development of my son I laugh or cry or shout out to anyone who will listen. . . . I can almost feel her devastation at watching her little girl die against the electric fence—can almost feel her positivity . . . die as her baby hits the ground. This story would not be the same for me if I did not understand motherhood; and yet . . . I still feel helpless in understanding this kind of tragedy.

Literary Interpretations

Many students were intimidated by Ozick's imaginative fiction. In his journal, Robert explains, "I'm not a fan of Ozick's usage of alliteration and repeating words or phrases to show depth nor a fan of her particular usage of metaphors."

> When I first finished reading "The Shawl" . . . I wasn't really sure how to react. For example, the very end when she writes ". . . so she took Magda's shawl and filled her own mouth with it, stuffed it in and stuffed it in, until she was swallowing up the wolf's screech and tasting the cinnamon and almond depth of Magda's saliva" (p. 111), kind of gross.

To gain insight into "The Shawl" and Ozick's motivation to write it, students viewed the video "A Conversation with Cynthia Ozick" (n.d.). Reflecting on her own life from 1942 to 1945, when she was a high school student living safely in the Bronx, she says, "I am bewildered by my happiness." She explains that she was inspired to write the story after reading William Shirer's *The Third Reich*, in which he describes a Nazi guard throwing a baby onto an electrified fence.

Prior to reading "The Shawl" and hearing Ozick speak about her work, some students were less open to Ozick's story and literary style because, they said, she was not a survivor, as was Nomberg-Przytyk. The video gave Robert some insight: "I think Ozick really wanted to capture how dark and how lonely these camps really were—and how frightening the experience was. . . . ['The Shawl'] is, in a way, a cry to all of those who survived, and all who passed away, saying 'I still remember and I am sorry.'"

Ozick uses magical and poetic literary devices, which may or may not be rooted in Jewish mysticism, to represent a horrific human reality that is almost impossible to imagine. The setting and time are ambiguous, leading to the characters' spatial and temporal disorientation. Ozick uses disturbing, stark, compressed, metaphoric language: "Stella, cold, cold, the coldness of hell. . . . Her knees were tumors on sticks, her elbows chicken bones" (p. 107). Yet the shawl temporarily, supernaturally, provides warmth and nourishment for Magda.

In an interview with Holocaust literature scholar Lillian Kremer, Ozick, who is immersed in and very knowledgeable about Jewish culture and thought, denies any metaphorical relationship between the shawl in the story and a *tallit* (the Jewish prayer shawl). Nevertheless, one can draw parallels, as does Holocaust and Judaic studies scholar Alan L. Berger (Kremer, 1999, pp. 153–54).

Traditionally in Orthodox Judaism, only men wear the tallit, which symbolizes comfort and protection during religious observances. The blue-threaded twined and knotted fringes at the corners are meant to remind the wearer of the *mitzvot*, or Jewish moral obligations (Numbers 15:37–41; Telushkin, 1991, p. 659). Magda sucks the corners of the shawl in lieu of her mother's nipples, replacing the patriarchal religious symbolism of the tallit and its knotted fringes with magical feminine nurturing qualities. Robbed of this protection, Magda is flung to her death.

To help them interpret Ozick's expressionistic story, students read Horowitz's "The Figure of Muteness," a study of "the trope of muteness in fictional responses to the Holocaust" in *Voicing the Void* (1997, pp. 33–45). Horowitz explains that many survivors found it so difficult to communicate in words the horror of their existence during the Shoah that they became determined never to speak about their life in the concentrationary universe. In Horowitz's research on literature by those who did try to represent their experiences in fiction, she found that mute characters frequently figure prominently.

"Muteness expresses not only the difficulty in saying anything meaningful about the Holocaust," Horowitz proposes; "it comes to represent something essential about the nature of the event itself. The radical negativity of the Holocaust ruptures the fabric of history and memory, emptying both narrative and life of meaning" (p. 38). Muteness resonates "in the discontinuous plot and chronology of some fictional narratives, in the deflated rhetoric and peculiar lacunae of others" (p. 39).

Logically, students applied what they learned from Horowitz by zeroing in on Magda's muteness. Doris points to the cognitive dissonance Rosa experiences between Magda's silence and her cry at the climax of the story:

She was terrified and overwhelmed with happiness all at once. She was happy because she didn't think her baby was able to cry anymore, she thought the child had gone deaf or dumb, as she put it. Hearing the baby cry made Rosa realize her baby was still physically able to be like other children. . . . I think this part shows a true struggle in the mother—between her wish for her baby to be healthy and normal and her wish for her baby to survive.

Kerri gleans a different insight:

The muteness is not just a lack of speech but a chosen silence. All of a sudden, we begin seeing how silence affects the whole situation. Is Magda just a child, or is she representative of those who remain silent? . . . [H]er shawl . . . separates her from the pain and tragedy that others endure. She does not speak until her protection is ripped away. . . . Rosa's fear reverberates through this story and forces us to reflect on what happens after someone speaks.

Kerri might be on to something that gets to the heart of what Ozick is trying to accomplish. The idea that Magda's muteness stands in for a greater silence, and that she is an infant—the most vulnerable—who carries this terrible burden to be silent, brings an archetypical quality to the muteness. When she finally speaks, her cry becomes the universal howl of every motherless child—of everyone engulfed in the Holocaust.

PRACTICE TEACHING

Making the transition between teaching *Friedrich* and the two short stories was tricky. Reading, writing about, and teaching lessons on *Friedrich* did not prepare the students adequately to comprehend the mass incarceration and genocide that happened in the Lagers. There an entire population was subjected to uninterrupted physical and psychic assault over months and years. Death could happen at any moment. Morality was beside the point. Comparing the students' contemporary experiences with the concentration camp experience was implausible.

When reflecting on the problems students had getting to the moral complexity of *Friedrich*, I hypothesized that if they had been able to develop their questioning strategies, they would be able to lead their students toward making deeper connections among the text, their lived reality, and the historical, sociological, philosophical, and political contexts for both. We had discussed how to craft questions (see Chapter 2, "Authentic Discussions"), but I was looking for yet another strategy that might help them fathom the significance of these stories.

Searching for an alternative, I found a video featuring Los Angeles master teacher Yvonne Hutchinson ("Using Anticipation Guides," n.d.), which I showed to the class. In the video, Hutchinson discusses with her students a text that raises social issues, in an environment characterized by rich discourse and critical thinking, through a prereading activity. Developed by H. L. Herber (1978), whose research focused on reading in the content areas, the anticipation guide encourages literacy development and engagement by taking students through a process to consider some underlying idea represented in a text before reading the text.

The process entails the teacher presenting a series of provocative statements to which each student answers "true" or "false," drawing on prior knowledge. Next, students discuss their answers, giving evidence to explain their positions, stimulating further interest in the topic. Then individually they read the text, and after reading, return to the group to discuss how evidence from the text affected their earlier positions. Several students in my class were eager to try this approach, although the lessons could only be hypothetical, because everyone had already read the stories. This chapter highlights two lessons in which students used anticipation guides.

Truth in Historical Fiction

Nancy and Charles (Section 9) created a lesson for "The Shawl" in which they were interested primarily in exploring how historical fiction conveys truth. Charles gave an introductory lecture on elements of Jewish mysticism that he related to the text. Then the two led an "anticipation guide style discussion," but posing questions, not statements. Nancy asked, "Is a child's life worth more than an adult's? Do you think any means to survive are acceptable? What is acceptable in the pursuit of *others'* survival? Would you sacrifice your own well-being for the sake of another's?"

Janet replied, "My child is more than equal to others. If I were in Rosa's place, I would favor my child over my niece." Cynthia responded, "I can't judge the value of someone else's life. Another's life is not necessarily worth more than mine." Barry speculated that the answer might vary with context. "If there's a riot going on, I'm going to keep the baby safe."

At this point, Charles asked, "Is nurturing innate or learned?" Lisa came down on the side of biological determinism: "Women have more estrogen than men." Rick countered with a social constructionist argument: "Then what about Stella? Most people are generally nurturing. It depends on the environment. Stella is probably an only child, and there's more working against her that would affect her ability to care about Magda."

Charles brought contemporary events and popular culture into the mix. "How far would you go to get food? Think of Hurricane Katrina, when the flooding spoiled food and the government didn't get food into the hands of the people. What do shows like *Survivor* [Burnett et al., 2000–present] and *Hunger Games* [Bissell et al. & Ross, 2012] say about how far people will go to get things they need?"

Kendall told a story about her eleven-year-old brothers who, at a party, got into a fight over a Klondike bar. One of them was pushed down a flight of stairs, the other slammed into a wall. Nancy wondered where the authority figure was who could call a time out. But then, in a disturbing twist that seemed like a rationale for the violence, she added, "I'll bet that was the best Klondike bar, to the one who got it. Anything taken in battle tastes twice as sweet."

Charles asked, "What's the most disgusting thing you would be willing to eat?" "I know people who ate paper and dirt because they were hungry," replied Nancy, priming the pump. "My grandfather's parents in Germany ate drywall," answered Jill. Barry quipped, "I'd eat maggots for money, but not for survival." Nancy pressed on: "If you and a friend are on a desert island, are you going to eat your best friend?" (She was trying to link the discussion to the passage in "The Shawl" in which Rosa feared that Stella "was waiting for Magda to die so she could put her teeth into the little thighs" [p. 108].)

The teaching team got so caught up in the discussion themselves, which at a certain point became gratuitous, that they allowed it to stray quite far from their objective to analyze whether and how Ozick conveyed the truth of the Lagers. As a result, the anticipation sequence became an end in itself rather than a means.

Charles did return to the original goal in the final portion of the lesson, a lecture on historical fiction, defining it as "set in the past and in a real place, with realistic characters, and including both fiction and truth." The truths here are the baby thrown against the fence and the concentration camp setting. The characters and story have mystical elements, which make it fiction, but are "like an insider's account," Charles said. The story contains "cultural truth."

This lesson engaged the students, and the discussion was a meaningful way for the students to explore parallels between the story and contemporary culture, until it jumped the track. Still, neither the discussion nor the lectures uncovered how Ozick uses literary tropes, including metaphor and hyperbole, to articulate the interior life of prisoners who endured the horror of the camps, an important component in attending to Nancy and Charles's original question about how truth is conveyed in historical fiction.

Distorted Ethics

Kylie and Sandy (Section 8), who taught "Esther's First Born," state in their rationale that they hope to invoke "passionate discussion of ethical belief in order to provide a starting point for thesis writing and idea development." They, too, developed an anticipation guide designed to generate discussion. They asked students to respond to statements that were relevant to and grounded in the text, including: "Hospitals exist to help people," "Killing babies is wrong/bad," and "I would be willing to sacrifice someone else's life to save my own."

This generated an enthusiastic discussion, similar in intensity to the one Nancy and Charles facilitated, but more related to their objectives. The teaching team then asked how the statements in the anticipation guide were explicitly related to the story, and they asked the students to consider whether the story impacted the students' views, which they did, albeit superficially.

The second half of their lesson was dedicated to writing: "Write about an issue you are passionate about, something you are willing to die for." Thinking that their anticipation guide was enough preparation to answer a question like this, they invited people to tell the class what they had written. A few volunteered. For example:

> I am very passionate about animals. . . . It kills me to see that dogs get killed because there is not enough room in a kennel for them. I can honestly not say if I would die for this cause.
>
> I am extremely passionate about Christianity. I would, I hope, be willing to die for it because to me it is more important than the things of the world or even my own life.

For their final activity, Kylie and Sandy asked students to create a thesis statement with a claim, a summary of supporting evidence, and a qualifying statement based on what they wrote. For homework, students were to write a first paragraph of an argumentative essay containing their thesis statement.

This writing lesson was problematic. Kylie and Sandy, like all their peers, had not yet taken the teaching of writing course. They did not understand that formulaic writing, and teaching writing formulaically, have serious limitations. (In the English Education program at Central State, literature methods and composition methods are taught sequentially, with the literature course first. This is a perfect example of problems that arise when the teaching of writing is separated from the teaching of literature.)

The way they used standards also is problematic. Rather than primarily attend to the story's moral significance and how the writer conveyed that meaning, they chose as their lesson's foundation CCW 9–10.1: "Write arguments to support claims in an analysis of substantive topics or texts, using valid reasoning and relevant and sufficient evidence." Discussing the ethical dimensions of "Esther" became merely a subtext.

Beginning with the statement "Hospitals exist to help people," Kylie and Sandy could have directed students to read closely for how Nomberg-Przytyk explains the twisted purpose of the "hospital" and how Mengele distorts the medical profession, getting to the idea that the Nazi worldview subverted universal moral values.

They could have cited CCRL 9–12.1, 4, 6, 7, and/or 9. These standards have to do with key ideas and details, craft and structure, and integration of knowledge and ideas. Had they even tried to work with the reading standards, instead of the writing standard, they might have come closer to the heart of the story more easily.

REFLECTIONS

The Problem of the Outsider Standpoint

One of the hardest tasks facing Holocaust educators is how to convey the almost total annihilation of ethics in the concentrationary universe. Nothing in most people's experiences compares to the unsolvable moral dilemmas facing the prisoners in the Lagers, nor to the perpetrators' amoral worldview and inhumane cruelty. How can they span the chasm between a moral society in which people acknowledge universal values and the concentrationary universe where, as Roth observes, ethics and moral sensibilities were "overridden, misused, and perverted" (2008, p. 8)?

Teachers always should help students find points of reference in their own lives in order to ensure students' engagement and protect their locus of control. Yet as long as people exclusively reference their own personal moral stances, they will not be able to judge a concentration camp survivor's actions in a social environment designed to negate universal moral values, nor speculate logically and rationally about how they would behave in such impossible circumstances.

When the student teachers used anticipation guides as a route toward comprehending the stories, they and their peers speculated about what choices they might make, but from the standpoint of a normative moral universe. The questions and statements in their anticipation guides set up hypotheticals that sidestepped a direct confrontation with the context of the concentration camps in the stories.

Literary critics like Horowitz and writers like Ozick, who did not live through the Holocaust, testify to how difficult, if not impossible, it is to understand the Holocaust from a standpoint outside of it. Holocaust survivor Primo Levi writes about this problem in *The Drowned and the Saved* (1989; see Chapter 7, "Ethics and Aesthetics of Representing the Holocaust"). And yet, it is precisely this understanding that those who study and represent the Holocaust urgently pursue.

Critical Questioning and Comparative Analysis

Many students who wrote journals and joined in reader response discourse also stayed within a more normative moral realm. However, a few students, like Manny and Edith, comprehended that "Esther's First Born" and "The Shawl" represented something for which they had no comparison.

None of the students, however, proceeded beyond the second stage of reader response, that of the shared response. To teach these two stories most effectively, a teacher would need to guide students through the discriminating response and research phases by posing critical questions. They would need to work with students to compare and contrast the two stories, provide historical context, and bring to bear theoretical perspectives.

Critical questioning can lead us from our limited, personal perspectives outward to the text and the world. After students read and respond to the text, the teacher could extrapolate from or extend questions that come up in discussion, crafting the kind of inquiry discussed in Chapter 2. Take Kylie and Sandy's anticipation statement, "Hospitals exist to help people": rephrased as a nonjudgmental question, a teacher might ask, "What are hospitals for?"

Using Christenbury and Kelly's questioning circles, that question would be located in the circle of the world. The personal connection—the reader—might be made by inviting students to talk about a hospital experience they have had. Then, bringing together the text, the reader, and the world, the teacher might ask, "How does our understanding and experience of hospitals apply or not to the concentration camp hospital in 'Esther'?" This question is what Christenbury and Kelly would call a "dense question" and might be the only question a teacher would need to ask.

Asking the students to read both of the stories instead of having them choose one or the other might have helped answer some of the questions that groups raised about the individual stories. A comparative analysis could incorporate the authors' uses of syntax, semantics, and metaphor; the contrasting choices each major character in each story makes; how each story says something about the lives of women and children in the concentration camps; the importance of setting in each story; and what each reveals about different dimensions of the concentrationary universe.

Such an analysis would have helped the students see how the authors attempted to represent the truth of the concentrationary universe through fiction and creative nonfiction. By closely reading the texts and comparing literary devices and then contrasting the characters' experiences to their own lives, students could have specified how the camps differ from the students' world, especially seeing how these constitute different moral universes.

For instance, "Esther" opens on the view from a passenger train window on a spring day. An orchestra plays, and women are planting flowers. These were the "lucky" prisoners, providing a cover to the "stinking, sordid life" just out of view (p. 86). Nomberg-Przytyk's ironic juxtaposition of images immediately jolts us out of our contemporary zones of consciousness, inducing cognitive dissonance and demonstrating the gulf between the normality of everyday life and the monstrosity of Auschwitz.

By contrast, Ozick creates that dissonance through extreme and disturbing metaphors and imagery. The story opens with Rosa, carrying Magda concealed in a shawl, and Stella stumbling along on a forced march. Rosa's complexion is "dark like cholera," the duct in Rosa's nipple "extinct, a dead volcano, blind eye, chill hole" (p. 107). When Magda dies, Rosa hallucinates "steel voices" in the electrified fence tormenting her, urging her to run toward her child (p. 110).

Historical Context

A few students escaped from the dissonance they experienced reading Ozick's story by consigning it to fantasy. The anticipation guides they created decontextualized and dehistoricized the story. Because the activities they engaged in were not anchored to the concentrationary universe, these students did not consider how this universe was constructed and why. To do this they would need to study more carefully the transition from the years of persecution to the years of extermination, when the Nazis adopted and implemented the so-called Final Solution.

There are a number of ways teachers could better prepare themselves and help meet their students' need to understand the historical context. They could:

- draw on a combination of historical texts, such as Bergen's (2009) *War and Genocide* or McKale's (2002) *Hitler's Shadow War*;
- show scenes from filmmaker Claude Lanzmann's *Shoah* (1985) and testimony retrieved from the Fortunoff, USHMM, or USC archives;
- provide more information about Nazi "medical research" and "treatment," and the process by which prisoners were selected to live or die, that Mengele and others engaged in and oversaw; and
- share information about the camps' social structures and hierarchies, using the USHMM website as a resource.

Theoretical Context

To comprehend the deep meaning of these stories, students eventually will need to try on some theoretical lenses, such as ethics, gender theory, and trauma theory. Langer's essay "The Dilemma of Choice in the Deathcamps" (1988) is short and effective and written in fairly plain language, so that eleventh- and twelfth-graders might be able to read it. Probably no short text better lays out the concept of choiceless choices.

Teachers would benefit from reading Roth's (2008) lecture "The Failure of Ethics," which may be too advanced for most high school students but offers deep insights. Brodzki (2004) provides a basic introduction to trauma theory and applies it to Holocaust education. Horowitz gives feminist perspectives on trauma (1998) and on Jewish women in Holocaust literature (2009).

CONCLUSION

Like *Friedrich*, these stories present daunting challenges to teachers and students. Unlike *Friedrich*, they are difficult even at the surface because of their brutal content and literary complexities, which will lead some students to resist them. However, these two very short texts provide significant insights that are central to Holocaust education.

Specifically, they powerfully represent the excruciating physical and psychic suffering that arises from having to make choiceless choices. They both illustrate the horrific conditions women and children endured in the concentration camps. The characters resist and succumb to the dehumanization their Nazi tormenters foment, showing both resilience and vulnerability. Nothing is sugarcoated here.

Perhaps most significantly, studying the stories can help students comprehend the vitally important concept that in the Lagers, the normative values that shaped European society were, for the most part, null and void. These values, by which most of us live our lives in contemporary society, do not apply when considering the actions of Holocaust victims and survivors. However, recognizing these disparities and what led to such a breakdown in morality is critical to living ethically in today's world.

What readers do not learn from either of these stories is what life was like for the characters before the camps. Nor do they learn what happens to the people who endured and survived the concentrationary universe (although Rosa does live on in Ozick's sequel, *Rosa*). The final text the students read in the course, *Maus* (Spiegelman, 1986 and 1991), synthesizes the life of a Jewish family before, during, and after the Holocaust, as narrated by the author's father. It is to that text that we turn next.

NOTES

1. This analysis descends directly from philosopher Simone de Beauvoir's gender theory proposed in the foundational second-wave feminist treatise *The Second Sex* (2011/1953).

2. For more on women and sexuality in Nazi Germany, see Elizabeth D. Heineman (2002), Dagmar Herzog (2002), and Claudia Koonz (1987).

Chapter 7

Maus

The Holocaust Years and the Aftermath

Why are children of Holocaust survivors still experiencing the effects of the Holocaust as if they themselves had actually been there? How do we explain that the so-called "second generation" seems to share the grief and terror of their traumatized parents? Was the trauma of the parents somehow transmitted to them?

(Kellerman, 2001, p. 256)

Maus: A Survivor's Tale, I: My Father Bleeds History, the first volume of Art Spiegelman's graphic auto/biographical memoir, stirred up the comics and broader literary communities in 1986 when it was published. Before *Maus*, Holocaust memoirs tended to conform to what could be called the tropes of Holocaust narratives, as journalist Christopher Lehmann-Haupt wrote in his 1986 book review: "the loss of property, the dawning sense of peril, the black markets, the 'selections,' the cellar hiding places, the briberies, the betrayals and finally the truck to the gate with the sign over it reading '*Arbeit macht frei*.'"[1]

However, Lehmann-Haupt goes on to say, Spiegelman has made four innovations: he examines the relationships between the survivors and their children, uses humor, presents the narrative in the form of a comic book, and portrays the characters as anthropomorphized animals.

While *Maus* was unconventional and controversial, nevertheless it received worldwide acclaim, the Pulitzer Prize, and praise from literary critics and Holocaust scholars. Published in two volumes (*My Father Bleeds History* in 1986; *And Here My Troubles Began* in 1992), *Maus* unfolds in 1972, when Art Spiegelman asks his father, Vladek, to tell his story of the Holocaust years. From 1972 to 1982, Art interviewed his father for more than forty hours. He retells and illustrates the story, interweaving it with family history and various present-day interactions among Vladek, other people in Vladek's life, and himself.

During the interviews, Vladek told his story, from the mid-1930s when Vladek met his girlfriend Lucia, and then his first wife (Art's mother), Anja, through Vladek and Anja's imprisonment in Auschwitz and their liberation when the war ended in 1945. Vladek tells of his marriage to Anja in 1937, the birth of their first son Richieu, and Germany's buildup to war with Poland. He is drafted into the Polish army in 1939. Shortly thereafter, the German army invades Poland and Vladek is captured, but he escapes and finds his way back home to Sosnowiec, Poland.

Once the Germans occupy Poland, the Nazis relocate the Jews in Sosnowiec to the Srodula ghetto. Vladek and Anja go into hiding just as the ghetto is "liquidated" and send their son to live with Anja's sister in the Zawiercie ghetto. In March 1944, Vladek and Anja are arrested while trying to escape to Hungary and are sent to Auschwitz. They find out later that Anja's sister poisoned Richieu, her own children, and herself right before the Nazis came to deport them to a deathcamp.

At Auschwitz, prisoners work under intolerable conditions and suffer psychological and physical degradation, all the time watching their fellow inmates being brutally murdered or dying of starvation and disease. Vladek relies on his considerable negotiating and bartering skills and experiences in the trades to gain privileges, avoid some hard labor, and get extra food for himself and, at times, Anja.

In January 1945, friends of Anja are hanged for smuggling explosives to the Sonderkommandos who have blown up a crematorium. That same month, Vladek is transported to Dachau, where he contracts typhus. He is freed in a prisoner exchange in April. The war ends in May, and Vladek and Anja are reunited in Sosnowiec. They immigrate to the United States in 1951.

GENDER IN *MAUS*

In *Maus*, women figure prominently but mainly in relation to either Vladek or Art. One important way we get to know Vladek is through his relationships with women, especially his two wives and his girlfriend. Vladek also mentions in his narrative the women who help Anja and him hide and escape, and the women who betray them.

Vladek's most complicated relationship with a woman is with Anja, whom he initially courts because her family is wealthy but with whom he soon falls in love. Vladek is an opportunistic young man whose faults precede the Holocaust, although they may be rooted in the Jewish people's centuries-old struggle for survival in Poland and other parts of Europe. He chastises Anja for taking political risks due to her leftist sympathies. During the Holocaust, he also takes risks but acts out of masculinist obligations to fend for his family and himself, not because he is a freedom fighter.

After the Holocaust, Vladek, a psychologically damaged man, tries to ignore and bury his feelings. Anja, however, keeps what Vladek calls a diary but may have been more of a memoir. When Art is an adult, she completes suicide. Naturally, Art wants to see her notebooks, and his father promises to look for them but eventually admits that he destroyed them after Anja died.

"These notebooks, and other really nice things of mother . . . one time I had a very bad day . . . and all of these things I destroyed. . . . These papers had too many memories. So I burned them." Vladek does not admit to having read them but says he had a "look in." He reveals that Anja told him, "I wish my son, when he grows up, he will be interested by this" (*Maus II*, p. 159).

Devastated by Anja's death, but helpless domestically, Vladek marries Mala, who is also a survivor. Their marriage is marred by Vladek's constant acrimony toward Mala, her jealousy of his continuing love for Anja, and her fears that he will cut her out of his will.

Once, when Art is alone with Mala, she complains to him about Vladek's miserly pecuniary habits. Art suggests that he's being pragmatic, but Mala contradicts him. "Pragmatic? Cheap!! It causes him physical pain to part with even a nickel!" (*Maus I*, p. 131). (Art worries that by portraying his father accurately it will seem as though he is perpetuating an antisemitic stereotype.) Eventually, Mala leaves him, claiming that what is wrong with Vladek is not due to Holocaust trauma but to character flaws. Despite their stormy relationship, however, Mala comes back when Vladek is hospitalized.

Art's feelings about his mother are fraught with conflict. Three months after Art is released from a psychiatric hospital, where he was recovering from a breakdown, we see him coming home from a weekend away and finding that his father has just discovered Anja's lifeless body. Left alone, Art thinks, "Menopausal depression." "Hitler did it! Mommy! Bitch." He accuses his dead mother: "You . . . shorted all my circuits . . . cut my nerve endings . . . crossed my wires!" (*Maus II*, p. 103).

No such angst characterizes Art's relationship with his French wife, Françoise. She provides emotional support while Art struggles to connect with his father and learn more about Vladek's Holocaust experiences. She is patient but observes, "It's amazing how hard it is to spend a whole day with him" (*Maus II*, p. 74). However, she sometimes questions Art's loyalty to his father and is disturbed by Vladek's behavior.

In one scene, while driving the car, she picks up an African American man who is hitchhiking, and Vladek carries on in Polish (with Art translating), "@!*!! I just can't believe it! There's a *shvartser* sitting in here!" ("Shvartser" is a Yiddish derogatory term for a black person.) After Françoise drops off the hitchhiker, Vladek says he thought the man was going to steal his groceries. Françoise fumes, "That's outrageous! How can you, of all people, be such a racist! You talk about Blacks the way the Nazis talked about the Jews" (*Maus II*, pp. 98–99).

The relationship between Art and his father is gendered, also. Art's and Vladek's masculinities are subtexts throughout. Vladek describes how he survived Auschwitz in part by relying on traditionally male-identified trades and maintained his virility by currying favor with his male superiors to win extra rations and other benefits. He toughed it out through the innumerable physical challenges that the Holocaust presents before, during, and after Auschwitz.

Repeatedly, his father critiques Art's masculinity, a critique that Art internalizes. The elder Spiegelman, now weakened by a heart condition and diabetes, wants his son to climb on the roof to fix a drainpipe: Art replies, "I'm no good at fixing that kind of stuff" (*Maus I*, p. 73). Vladek does gymnastics every day: Art quips, "My only exercise is walking out for cigarettes!" (*Maus II*, p. 18).

Pointing to a photo of his dead brother, Richieu, Art complains, "The photo never threw tantrums or got in any kind of trouble . . . it was an ideal kid and I was a pain in the ass. . . . They didn't talk about Richieu but that photo was a kind of reproach. *He'd* have become a doctor, and married a wealthy Jewish girl . . . the creep. . . . It's spooky having sibling rivalry with a snapshot" (*Maus II*, p. 15). "No matter what I accomplish," Art bemoans to Pavel, his psychoanalyst, "it doesn't seem like much compared to surviving Auschwitz" (*Maus II*, p. 44).

TRAUMA: THE AFTERMATH

The previous chapter introduces trauma theory, focusing on the first phase— the traumatizing event or events. However, as also explained therein, trauma often is not fully experienced as it occurs. Its effects often are delayed. The aftermath has its own trajectory (Caruth, 1995, pp. 7–8).

By the time concentration camp survivors were liberated, many could not overcome the terror and shame that had been woven into the fabric of their being, nor could they shed the mistrust that they had needed in order to survive but that sometimes warped their perspectives after they were freed. So, they remained silent about their experiences.

Even when it was clear that the danger was past, and people married and had children and got on with their lives, many refused to talk about the trauma. Psychic wounds festered, and the trauma led to post-traumatic stress disorder (PTSD). Many experienced nightmares, depression, anger, and illness. Many, like Spiegelman's mother, Anja, completed suicide.

Spiegelman invites the reader to take a psychological perspective on *Maus*. In his narrative and visual representation of Vladek's and his family's tale, Art provides deep insight into and concrete evidence of PTSD. He also analyzes how Vladek's trauma affected his relationships with Art and his second wife, Mala, singling out his excessive frugality, controlling behaviors, vindictiveness, mistrust, and racism. However, Art finds it difficult to understand which aspects of his father's personality were shaped by the Holocaust and which derived from other experiences.

Research psychologists have studied the cross-generational transmission of Holocaust trauma. Psychologist Natan P. F. Kellerman cites research indicating that second-generation survivors find it difficult to cope with stress and are more likely to develop PTSD than other people with emotional problems. They tend to have "[i]mpaired self-esteem with persistent identity problems, over-identification with parents' 'victim/survivor' status, [and] a need to be superachievers to compensate for parents' losses, carrying the burden of being 'replacements' for lost relatives" (2001, p. 259).

In his own life, Art also feels the psychological effects of the trauma his parents experienced. Hirsch, in her article "Family Pictures: *Maus*, Mourning, and Post-Memory" (1992), notes that *Maus* works on two levels, as the story of the father and the story of the son. The stories reflect memory—that of Vladek, the survivor—and postmemory, that of Art, the child of the survivor, whose life is dominated by his parents' memories of what preceded his birth, which they transmit to him.

Art had been estranged from his father but renews his relationship with him in order to understand his father's story, better understand himself, and to try to heal their relationship. The interviews can be viewed as a form of therapy for the author and his father who, like many survivors, has not spoken previously about his experiences.

Art serves as a witness, too, affording Vladek a chance to tell his own story even though Vladek is not eager to do so. But this is a very difficult position for Art to manage as his son. At times, he steps out of his role as interviewer to snap at his father. In so doing, he shows that he is unable to maintain consistently the kind of empathy that witnesses and therapists need.

It is also useful to examine this emotionally charged story through a drama therapy lens. Drama therapy is "the intentional use of drama and/or theater processes to achieve therapeutic goals" (North American Drama Therapy Association, n.d., para. 1). As a graphic story and work of art, *Maus* applies elements also common to theater and film: portraying characters in conflict with one another, who interact in different settings through time and space using different media; and portraying them metaphorically with pathos and humor, using distancing techniques such as masks to explore multiple levels of meaning.

Also, Spiegelman depicts characters assuming various roles to develop a coherent and rich narrative. For example, Art plays multiple roles—son, husband, interviewer, witness, analyst, artist, and auto/biographer. As a skilled comics artist, Spiegelman uses a wide variety of artistic strategies to document what he is learning about his father and his relationship with him and to tell his story in the most engaging and understandable way for an audience.

By so doing, he creates enough distance between himself and his troubled and troubling father to allow him, paradoxically, to get closer, maintaining the necessary balance of reality and imagination, emotion and intellect to listen to and to tell his father's disturbing story without destroying one or both of them. The artistic tools Spiegelman uses are consistent with what drama therapist Robert Landy says is necessary in order to establish an aesthetic distance that integrates physical reality, emotion, and thought. "Because one is not overflooded with feeling, one can think. Because one is not overly analytical and withdrawn, one can feel" (1983, p. 184).

Using these same techniques, Spiegelman depicts the impact of trauma on the lives of survivors and their descendants without overwhelming readers/viewers with the horror or interrupting his narrative with didactic explanations of PTSD. We are further cushioned from the actual experience because we are conscious that Vladek is narrating the story and Art is drawing it after the fact.

But Spiegelman does not let us remain so distant that we lose emotional engagement. He does not let us forget that the animals represent actual people. At different moments, he depicts all the characters as people wearing animal masks, as in a sequence of panels showing first Art at his drawing board, then predatory reporters and businessmen verbally assaulting him to exploit his success, and then in a session with his psychoanalyst where he continues to reflect on his problems identifying with Vladek and writing *Maus* (*Maus II*, pp. 41–47).

Spiegelman explains in *MetaMaus* (2011) that he used the masks to indicate a new present tense—after his father had died; a new topic—his psychological crisis as he faced writing about Auschwitz; and a new relationship to his father—in the form of transference to Pavel. As Art says, "I had to fully acknowledge myself as the author wrestling with making a book. It became useful to indicate that . . . there are human faces underneath these mouse heads, on the analyst's couch, grappling with my father's legacy" (p. 149). The masks bring us up short, reminding us that this is a story about real people, written and illustrated by a real person.

Eventually, Art is able to overcome his depression and move on with his narrative once he realizes, with the help of his therapist, that his father's apparent lack of empathy for Art reflects Vladek's guilty feelings for surviving the Holocaust and his wife's suicide. As a second-generation survivor, it is important for Art not to conflate his father's survivor's guilt with his own guilty feelings, particularly in relation to his success as the author of *Maus*.

READING COMICS/GRAPHIC TEXTS

For some of the preservice teachers who took the course, reading *Maus* was a literacy challenge. I had assumed that all the students would be competent readers of graphic literature, but in fact many found it difficult to read the combined text and graphics and fully appreciate the power of this medium to convey meaning differently than would text alone. Furthermore, none of the students knew the history of how Jewish artists contributed to and influenced comics. They all attended closely to my presentations and workshops on the early comics artists and the development of the comics genre, summarized below.

In the 1930s and 1940s, Jewish American artists found a niche in comics. During this antisemitic era in the United States, comics had low cultural status, and because of this, was one of the few industries that hired Jewish artists. (The film industry was another.) Many Jewish artists changed their names to protect themselves from discrimination and did not directly challenge antisemitism. Instead, they created anti-Nazi characters, including Superman (writer Jerry Siegel and artist Joe Shuster) and Captain America (writer Joe Simon and artist Jack Kirby, née Jacob Kurtzberg) (Kaplan, n.d.).

Cartoonist Scott McCloud's *Understanding Comics* (1994), which he presents in comics form, provides a useful and accessible introduction to the elements of cartooning. It begins with comics artist and critic Will Eisner's definition of comics as "sequential art." McCloud's working definition, embellishing Eisner's term, is "juxtaposed pictorial and other images in deliberate sequence, intended to convey information and/or produce an aesthetic response in the viewer" (p. 9).

"Words, pictures, and other icons are the vocabulary of the language called comics," writes McCloud (p. 47). He explains that the complicated interrelationships between visual images and text allow multiple levels of meaning and multiple ways to access meaning. Text is incorporated through thought- and word-balloons and text boxes and in a plethora of imaginative ways that artists invent.

Comics artists depict emotions, smells, movement, and other nontangible phenomena through use of expressive line, shadow, visual exaggeration, and other techniques. Graphic texts provide visual clues, including panels, "gutters" between panels, and "bleeds" that can fill the entire page. These clues prompt readers to use their imaginations to fill in missing details. Because of the rich stew that graphic artists and writers concoct, the reader's level of engagement tends to be high.

The term "graphic novel" is often applied to book-length comics, including *Maus*. While Eisner was not the first to use the term, it was his use of it that landed it a place in the comics lexicon. Author Michael Schumacher (2010) describes graphic novels as "book-length works of sequential art expanded in scope to include [fiction,] biography, memoir, history, and other types of non-fiction" (quoted in the University of Maryland Library's "Graphic Novels & Comics," n.d.).

However, using the term "novel" to include nonfiction seems problematic, given that the word traditionally has been used to connote a book-length work of fiction. Therefore, Eisner eventually settled on the terms "graphic literature" or "graphic story." These seem more appropriate as alternative descriptors for *Maus*, especially because Spiegelman (1991) famously excoriated the *New York Times* for categorizing his book as fiction.

Educators and marketers also distinguish comics from graphic literature to overcome the common association of comics with light entertainment, often humorous or in the realms of fantasy and science fiction, and not to be considered as serious literature. Spiegelman, in an interview with comics editor and publisher Gary Groth, says, "What happened in *Maus* was the absolute shock of an oxymoron: the Holocaust is absolutely the last place one would look for something to be made in the form of comics, which one associates with essentially trivial, simplified matter" (quoted in Geis, 2003, p. 5).

Langer, in his 1991 *New York Times* review of *Maus II*, defended Spiegelman's use of the graphic medium in *Maus*, characterizing it as "a serious form of pictorial literature." Now that literary scholars are engaging more readily with these complex texts, educators have embraced graphic literature, welcoming their addition to language arts curricula and as a way to enhance literacy development.

The building block of this literature is the icon, "any image used to represent a person, place, thing, or idea" (McCloud, 1994, p. 27). Comics artists imbue icons with significance in a process McCloud calls amplification through simplification: "When we abstract an image through cartooning, we're not so much eliminating details as we are focusing on specific details. By stripping down an image to its essential 'meaning,' an artist can amplify that meaning in a way that realistic art can't" (p. 30).

This simplification also stimulates the reader's identification with the characters and situations. As McCloud writes and illustrates, "Storytellers know that a sure indicator of audience involvement is the degree to which the audience identifies with the stories' characters" (p. 42). When viewers look at a photograph or realistic image of a person, they see it as someone else, but when they see an iconic cartoon image, they can project themselves into the image and identify with the character more easily.

In *Maus*, Spiegelman emphasizes and foregrounds every character's group affiliation by representing each ethnicity or nationality as a different animal. In their propaganda, the Nazis often depicted Jews scornfully as rats, thereby dehumanizing them and making it easier for non-Jewish people to accept violence against Jews, because everyone agrees that vermin need to be eliminated.

Spiegelman queers this trope by representing Jews as mice (less predatory than rats). He then assigns German Gentiles to be cats, as the cat-and-mouse theme works metaphorically. Other nationalities are represented by other animals—Poles as pigs, Americans as dogs, Swedes as reindeer, French as frogs, Roma and Sinti as gypsy moths, and British as fish—some carrying cultural or political significance, some arbitrary. (Nazi propagandists scornfully portrayed Jews as rats and Poles as swine, both of which Spiegelman ironically appropriated.)

In this way, he subverts Nazi propaganda and puts all ethnic and national groups on an equal footing while still emphasizing differences. He makes all the characters about the same size, thus eliminating any outward indication that the Nazis were inherently dominant.

When readers follow the narrative, they see that individuals, while sharing similar iconic visages, have a number of distinguishing visual characteristics, especially clothing. In *Maus*, Art always wears a dark vest and usually has a cigarette wedged between his fingers or dangling from his lips. Prior to the Holocaust, his father is seen characteristically wearing a trench coat or suit and tie and afterward also tends to wear suit or blazer and tie but with round eyeglasses perched on his nose.

In the Auschwitz scenes, however, in which he is in a striped uniform along with other prisoners, the mice are depersonalized completely, and the reader only recognizes Vladek through the context of the dialogue bubbles and text boxes. The generic uniforms help us understand the Holocaust as an event in which people were collectively categorized and treated based on ethnicity or other group affiliations rather than just being persecuted as individuals.

Using McCloud's (1994) book as a primary resource and presenting visual examples from *Understanding Comics* and *Maus* side by side, I demonstrated how Spiegelman incorporated the tools of comics art into *Maus*. Then, working individually and in small groups, students did a "treasure hunt," looking for their own examples of these different elements in *Maus* and recording them on a chart. In the next session, students applied what they were learning about comics to understand how Spiegelman puts to good use the graphic elements of comics, synthesizing text and image to make meaning.

For example, using both words and image, he indicates Vladek's emotional reaction when his Nazi boss in Auschwitz invites him to eat a substantial meal. Vladek narrates: "Here I saw rolls! I saw eggs! Meat! Coffee! . . . You know what it was to see such a thing?" Spiegelman depicts the table with the various foods on display. By drawing a spiky white arc over the array of food, as though the food itself is emanating rays of light, and through the use of exclamation points, Art represents the amazement Vladek felt (*Maus II*, p. 32).

The detail with which Art draws the food on the table exemplifies a feature of many graphic texts: characters are portrayed iconically, and background is drawn in detail. In this way, the reader/viewer can identify with, empathize with, and universalize the characters but understand that the characters are located in a specific time and place.

Spiegelman uses graphic devices to depict past and present simultaneously. In scenes set in the past, he presents Vladek's present-day narrative in word boxes placed over, under, or superimposed at the top or bottom of panels. In some cases, he both pictorially and verbally indicates past and present, as when he shows father and son walking along a sidewalk, Vladek telling his story and Art taking notes.

In a word balloon, Vladek says, "And the Poles of Srodula, we Jews had to pay to move them to *our* houses in Sosnoweic . . . and here in Srodula would be our ghetto to live in ever after." The two figures and the word balloon are superimposed on an image of a Nazi checkpoint at the entrance to the Jewish ghetto. At the bottom of the picture, more of Vladek's narrative appears in a word box (*Maus I*, p. 105).

Spiegelman also constantly indicates the broader historical context of the story. For instance, in a scene in which Vladek and Anja are traveling on a train, they look out the window at a Nazi flag, which features a swastika at its center. In subsequent panels, the other passengers then recount, and Spiegelman illustrates, how Nazis were gobbling up territory and terrorizing Jews. The image of the swastika comprises the background of each panel (*Maus I*, pp. 32–33). Searching for such examples, students began to understand the power of graphic texts to viscerally convey multiple layers of meaning while gripping the reader's attention.

ETHICS AND AESTHETICS OF
REPRESENTING THE HOLOCAUST

Like many who represent the Holocaust in literature and the arts, Spiegelman questions his own renditions, acknowledging ethical dilemmas. For example, on page 41 of *Maus II*, he sits at his drafting table, distraught about his success as a writer and artist whose work is grounded in the suffering of others. In five panels, starting with a close-up and panning out, ending with a large panel depicting him huddled at his drafting table, which is perched on the decomposing bodies of Holocaust victims, he addresses the reader:

> Between May 16, 1944, and May 24, 1944 over 100,000 Hungarian Jews were gassed in Auschwitz. . . . In September 1986, after 8 years of work, the first part of *Maus* was published. It was a critical and commercial success. At least fifteen foreign editions are coming out and I've gotten 4 serious offers to turn my book into a T.V. special or movie. (I don't wanna.) In May 1968 my mother killed herself. (She left no note.) Lately I've been feeling depressed.

For decades, philosophers and cultural critics, including Theodor Adorno (1983/1951), Berel Lang (2002), Lawrence L. Langer (2000), and writers such as Paul Celan (2002), Charlotte Delbo (1995), Primo Levi (1989), and Cynthia Ozick ("A Conversation," n.d.) have questioned the ethics and aesthetics of creating cultural representations of the Holocaust. Horowitz summarizes these arguments, writing, "the literary imagination after Auschwitz is said to domesticate, to trivialize, and to falsify what it seeks to represent" (1997, p. 17). Some critics hold literature to the test of history, demanding that writers represent only the facts.

Yet history may not edify us about the moral issues or the emotional devastation that people experienced. Spoken testimonies can do that, Horowitz says, but even these are constructed by survivors, as they seek "to articulate memories so horrible as to lie almost beyond the pale of recollection" (p. 21). Fiction, by contrast, can fill in "cognitive and psychological absences in history," maintaining historical veracity while providing opportunities for readers to morally and emotionally engage (p. 24).

Louis Begley, author of the novel *Wartime Lies* (1997), claims that truth and fiction in his work are irrevocably "scrambled." His comments, writes Horowitz, "suggest ways in which a fictional life can be constructed to reveal something truthful—about this fragmented self under siege, about memory, about trauma—that may otherwise elude expression" (p. 24). She finds an analogy in *midrash*—commentaries on the Torah that fill in the gaps in the original ancient text and offer ways for readers to access deeper meaning in the Torah (pp. 22–24).

So, what might constitute an ethics and aesthetics of Holocaust literature? Horowitz wants it to focus not just on the writer's stylistic competence—she and other critics emphasize that polished literary accounts can gloss over the Holocaust's chaos, ugliness, and horror—"but also the truth, authenticity, and morality of the writing, its connection with the philosophical, political, metaphysical implications of the Nazi genocide." Further, she cautions that the Holocaust should neither be trivialized nor exploited for gratuitous shock value or to satisfy popular culture's appetites (pp. 25–26).

Despite their own and cultural critics' warnings and concerns, artists and writers like those mentioned above and the authors of the texts students read in the course were and are compelled to search for ways to represent the Holocaust through literature and the arts that are authentic, even if they are not exclusively factual, historically accurate renderings.

THE GRAY ZONE IN THE CONCENTRATIONARY UNIVERSE

As we saw in the short stories, the problems in representing the concentration camps are particularly troubling. Both Ozick and Nomberg-Przytyk find creative ways to represent the moral quandaries facing prisoners who must make choiceless choices. In *Maus*, Spiegelman is faced with the challenge of depicting the ethical morass that Levi calls "the gray zone."

In *The Drowned and the Saved*, Levi's 1989 account of life in Auschwitz, he describes a phenomenon of immoral behavior he observed there, whereby some prisoners were able to gain a modicum of power and privilege by taking on functionary roles that further oppressed their fellow inmates. This gray zone could be found in the concentrationary universe outside the camps, as well, and was inhabited by both Gentiles and Jews.

We humans, Levi postulates, want to understand the ethical world simply as divided between them and us and good and evil. So, in the concentrationary world, we expect there to be victims—those who are incarcerated—and perpetrators, the Nazis. But this view, he continues, is too simplistic. The horrific situation facing the prisoners led many to seek relatively privileged roles in order to avoid starvation and postpone or avoid death.

These functionary roles included low-level occupations, such as household servants, cooks, and craftsmen who served Nazi officers; and professionals, such as doctors and accountants. All these prisoners were treated more humanely than other inmates. Women who were conscripted as sex workers, both official and unofficial, to serve privileged prisoners and camp personnel, received some privileges but submitted to constant sexual assault and abuse, which often led to death.

Other prisoners committed brutal atrocities in exchange for preferential treatment. These included the kapos, guards who enforced the rules of the Lagers. These workers were given better food, clothing, and shelter than the prisoners they controlled and often felt a false sense of empowerment and entitlement.

The Sonderkommandos marched people into the gas chambers, carted the bodies to the ovens in the crematoria, fed the corpses into the flames, and disposed of the ashes. In exchange for their labor in hellish conditions, these workers had all the food and liquor they wanted for a few months, after which they were killed. Some wagered that they would be liberated or could escape in that time, but most died in the camps.

Seeking advantages under circumstances in which Jews had to endure incomprehensibly horrific conditions in the ghettos, the boxcars, and the Lagers was understandable. As Levi writes, "nobody knows for how long and under what trials his soul can resist before yielding or breaking" (1989, p. 60). He argues that the opportunity to resist corruption under these circumstances requires a preexistent immutable moral fiber.

Still, many who gained "privileges" used their protected status to resist the Nazis and to save others. They passed contraband weapons, food, and other supplies to those organizing escapes and sabotage; facilitated communications among prisoners; and helped friends and loved ones by sharing food and in other ways.

Vladek lives by his wits and is able to obtain favors. From the beginning of the book when he deserts his girlfriend Lucia to be with Anja, whose family was wealthy, we see that he acts primarily out of self-interest. When confronted with the threats of living under Nazi rule, he makes decisions that help him survive and protect his family. He works the black market, cultivates relationships with anyone who has influence, and keeps one step ahead of the Nazis until another Jew, who discovers Anja and his hiding place, alerts the authorities.

In the camps, he convinces the Nazis that he has valuable skills and gains privileges as a shoemaker and tinsmith. Because he is multilingual, he teaches a Nazi officer English, which gives him more protection. He has enough freedom of movement to sneak food and messages to Anja. He is not completely self-serving, though. Occasionally altruistic, he takes risks to help others, as when he obtains shoes, a belt, and a spoon for his desperate fellow prisoner Mandelbaum (*Maus II*, pp. 33–34).

PRACTICE TEACHING

Before teaching *Maus*, the students had made a great deal of progress toward creating meaningful lessons, as they learned more about the Holocaust and became familiar with and more adept at applying teaching and learning theories and practices that would most benefit their students. They continued further along this path during this final unit. In their *Maus* lessons, the students synthesized what they had learned about the history of the Holocaust, Holocaust literature, and pedagogy since the beginning of the semester.

The themes they explored in *Maus* ran the gamut, reprising and deepening inquiry into topics raised in previous lessons. The students looked into how extreme conditions affect morality and ethical behavior, as in previous lessons, but saw that the effects on individuals differed depending on circumstances. They broadened their study of the Holocaust's impact on relationships, because they now could see how the Holocaust affected an extended family across generations.

They did workshops in which they investigated the characteristics of the comics genre. They analyzed how Spiegelman simultaneously promotes and challenges stereotyping, but unlike Richter, does so transparently. They continued to examine how their lives and choices parallel and differ from those who lived through the Holocaust, putting to use what they learned from *Maus* to what they were learning about their own lives.

At the same time, they asked their students to support ideas with textual evidence and discuss how themes emerge and develop and how characters interact and express conflicting viewpoints, aligning their lesson plans mostly with the skills-based Common Core Reading Literature Standards, CCRL1-3 and 6 for grades nine to twelve. As the semester progressed, the teaching teams more successfully defined lesson goals that aligned with appropriate standards while still engaging their students in meaningful learning. Most did not rely on the standards to determine which concepts they would teach but rather to support their pedagogical goals.

Ethics and Morality

Adrienne, Mona, and Ari (Section 1) guided students through an analysis of Vladek's and his family's moral decisions in "The Noose Tightens" (*Maus I*, pp. 71–93). Their goal was for students to consider how this analysis might help them think through their own moral decisions.

Vladek explains how the world was closing in on the Jews, their struggle to survive was getting harder, people were being guided by survival instincts, and public executions were becoming commonplace. In order to survive and provide for their families, Vladek and his associates bought and sold goods on the black market. The metaphor of the noose works well in this chapter, but it is not just a metaphor: Vladek narrates and Art illustrates Vladek witnessing his former black-market business partners hanging in the public square (*Maus I*, p. 83).

In this chapter, also, we see Vladek's father-in-law, Mr. Zylberberg, extracting favors from the local Jewish committee (*Gemeinde*) in exchange for his philanthropy. Later, the Gemeinde collaborates with the Nazis to gather all the Jews in the ghetto, some twenty-five thousand people, into a stadium to be sorted for deportation and death or to remain behind to work.

Vladek narrates a stark example of the gray zone as it affected his extended family (*Maus I*, p. 87). The Jewish police (the equivalent, in the ghettos, of kapos) come to his father-in-law's house to take away Anja's grandparents, who had been hiding in a secret bunker. (The Nazis were deporting all people over seventy years old to the deathcamps.) Vladek explains, "Some Jews thought . . . [i]f they gave to the Germans a few Jews, they could save the rest. And at least they could save themselves." The Jewish police hold Vladek's father-in-law hostage until the family gives up the grandparents, who are sent to Auschwitz and gassed immediately.

In their lesson, the three student teachers divided the class into groups, directing each to study one of these scenes. The students closely read the scenes, analyzing the moral issues with which the characters had to deal, what decisions they made, and whether those decisions could be considered ethical under any circumstances. They then discussed situations that required them to make moral or ethical decisions, how the stakes in such decisions differed from those in *Maus*, and whether the decisions the characters in *Maus* make are understandable given their extreme circumstances.

Intergenerational Relationships

For their lesson on the intergenerational effects of trauma, Jean, Ann, and Robert (Section 5) asked students to define trauma first and then use and revise their definitions by analyzing several emotionally intense scenes from the book. In *Maus I* (pp. 100–103), Art has a mental breakdown and Anja kills herself. Later, he learns that Vladek has burned his mother's journals and calls his father a murderer (pp. 158–59). At a vulnerable point, Art complains about having to compete with his dead brother, Richieu (*Maus II*, p. 15).

After participating in this exercise, many students who had felt considerable frustration with Art's anger at his father developed more empathy for him. Looking realistically at the way all these Holocaust-related incidents affected both Art and his father helped to create a more nuanced understanding about the aftereffects of the Holocaust and its impact on the next generation.

Cora, Debby, and Dave (Section 2) guided students to analyze the Holocaust's effect on Art and Vladek's relationship by exploring the concept of dehumanization during the Holocaust years. To begin the lesson, they asked students collectively to examine how Spiegelman depicts the ways Nazis dehumanized the Jews and then discuss the effects this had on Jewish survivors, particularly on Vladek. Following this, the teaching team asked students to examine whether Art's perception and judgment of his father changed when he learned more about what Vladek endured during the Holocaust.

Next, the group asked students to discuss how what they, as adults, now know about their parents may have changed the way they understand and judge them. Cory, Debby, and Dave designed the lesson to help their students build more empathy for Vladek and understand Art's anger and seeming lack of empathy for his father by reflecting on their intergenerational conflicts with their own parents.

Linking Text and Image

Several students chose to teach specifically about the comics genre. In their lessons, they investigated how the graphic novel communicates thoughts and feelings and how images and texts work together to create something complex and unique.

Cynthia and Kendall (Section 9) gave students several panels from *Maus* with text deleted and asked students to create their own texts to accompany those images. They envisioned this as a prereading activity. Each student's solutions were different, so they saw how particular images elicited varied responses. Then Cynthia and Kendall cut off that discussion and asked students to debate which genre was more effective: text only, or comics.

Setting up an either/or binary proved counterproductive. Students resisted engaging with this directive and lost interest. This disappointed the teachers at first, but the experience helped them gain insight about the danger of imposing simplistic binaries as well as unnecessary constraints on exploratory talk.

Mindy and Lisa (Section 9), who deeply appreciated the genre's richness and complexity, approached the interaction of text and image from the opposite direction. They rewrote a scene (*Maus I*, p. 46) in which Vladek narrates how his father prepared him to fail his physical to save him from being drafted into the Polish army without any description of setting and without dialogue:

Three months before the examination, he started with me. He would wake me up in the middle of the night and tell me I was sleeping too much. . . . And when I would eat, he would tell me I was eating too much. . . . And a few days before the exam, I was allowed no sleep and no food. . . . And when finally I went for my medical examination, an officer said I was a healthy one. But the doctor disagreed and told me to build myself up for a year and then he'd review my case.

Mindy and Lisa then gave students the images without the text. They asked the students to match the text with the images and to analyze how text and image worked together to enhance meaning. They also asked students to read closely, noticing the effects of the number and type of words used for each panel and how this affected the story.

In addition, the lesson included a list of general related questions, including:

- "How is the story as a whole affected by the use of pictures in place of some words? How does it affect setting or character description, for example?"
- "What are some examples of things that represent cultural meanings of the time period that would be hard to use words to describe?"
- "How are graphics used to make important statements about the time and the history regarding the Holocaust that would not be as effective as text alone?"

There were problems with the lesson that are common to new teachers. First, these questions do not suggest the possibility that there are times when text alone might be more effective. Second, asking questions that are not open-ended or have an implied bias stifle rich discussion and disempower students. Third, as they and other student teachers did with so many lessons during the semester, Mindy and Lisa asked more from the students than what they should expect in one fifty-minute lesson. The questions would be appropriate for homework and another day's discussion.

However, the questions did help the students pay attention to specific ways in which text and image interact. Studying the book from this perspective strengthens the reader's appreciation and interpretation, thus making the whole literary experience more meaningful.

Toward Pedagogical Content Knowledge

Comparing the lessons prepared by Nancy and Charles (Section 9) during the semester, their lesson for *Maus* was their most cogent. For *Friedrich*, in which they wanted to explore propaganda, they incorporated *Education for Death: The Making of the Nazi* (Disney & Geronimi, 1943), a racist, sexist, and borderline pornographic Walt Disney video that raised more problems than they were prepared to address. The goal for their lesson on "The Shawl" was to explore whether and how historical fiction can shed light on history (see Chapter 6, "Truth in Historical Fiction"), but too many digressions diverted them from their objective.

Although still focused on complex ideas, for *Maus*, Nancy and Charles asked students to carry out only one major task: investigate how Spiegelman represents Nazi ideology. They divvyed students into groups. Each studied different panels that the teaching team chose. Students then freewrote and shared what they had learned. These pedagogical strategies helped them attain their lesson goals and helped the students understand more dimensions of Spiegelman's work in its historical context.

This development toward understanding and applying pedagogical content knowledge also is evident in Flora and Annette's (Section 8) *Maus* lesson about how the Holocaust affected survivors and their children. Their teaching strategies helped students understand how complex Vladek and Art's relationship is. In their lesson rationale they write:

> We looked at . . . the laws that were being put into place with the story *Friedrich*. We then looked at relationships and what is considered to be right and wrong with the short stories we read. We . . . wanted our students to next focus on how this event changed people internally. . . . [Even though the mothers survived,] it is very likely that they still struggled for the rest of their lives. These struggles could have been passed on to their children or anyone else in their lives. . . . Just as any kind of life changing event in our students' lives can do the same.

In their lesson, they asked students to choose images from the text that illustrate trauma and explain how these images do that. They then asked students to reflect on a traumatic event they had experienced or someone they know had experienced and sketch how they would illustrate such an experience. Flora and Annette did not provide sufficient scaffolding for their students to create the artwork or talk about traumas in their lives very easily. Nevertheless, when the groups shared their ideas and showed their drawings, the discussion was energetic, thoughtful, and rich in questions about what trauma is and how it affects people's lives.

A GERMAN EDUCATOR'S VIEW OF *MAUS*

After teaching the methods course, I taught a graduate course about problems in teaching Holocaust literature, including *Maus*. Reading Spiegelman's book deeply influenced one student, Monika, a teacher and exchange student from Germany. Her personal connection to the Holocaust and professional status enabled her to apply her pedagogical content knowledge directly to her teaching. Her story also is significant because of her perspective as a non-Jewish German citizen.

While taking the course, Monika spoke to her family several times, asking them questions about the Holocaust and their experiences during World War II, but they were reluctant to answer her questions. She decided that she wanted to do something to make it easier for people to talk about the Holocaust in Germany by introducing *Maus* into her high school's curriculum. For my course, she wrote a rationale for this curriculum unit.

In her paper, "Teaching the Holocaust Using Art Spiegelman's *Maus* in German Classrooms in Germany," she explains her family's perspective. When the war began, her grandmother was six years old and her grandfather eleven, but her other grandfather was twenty when he lost his entire family in the war. He fought in Russia, was captured, and became a prisoner of war. Monika's grandparents talked a little about how World War II affected them but never openly discussed the Holocaust.

> I don't know if they really dealt with it privately, but even when my parents were young, that was not something that was talked about. . . . I just think it is a trauma that [my grandparents] wanted to forget as much as they could in order to live a normal life. It's sad to think that so many stories will be lost with this generation, although . . . I can respect their wish to start over after the war. But it was great to read *Maus* and see how some families do work through this and thus preserve this part of history . . . for future generations.

Maus became a means for Monika to explore more about what happened in Germany and to her own family and how what they experienced affected her. "I read the graphic novel . . . [as] a portrayal of the conflict between the legitimate interest of the general public in the personal stories of survivors, and in [the survivors'] own right to silence and a life after the war," she writes in her *Maus* journal. She compares her grandparents to Vladek, who could not see beyond his own individual traumatic story.

Like Art Spiegelman, Monika said she could see the bigger picture. She appreciated that in *Maus I*, he tried to learn as much as he could about the history and what his father experienced during the Holocaust. But she was especially moved by *Maus II*, because in it Spiegelman investigates the effects of the Holocaust on himself and, Monika writes, "people who weren't even alive [during the Holocaust]," which she describes as the major significance the books have for her.

Peter Fritzsche (2016) explains that World War II, unlike World War I, was to a great extent an assault on civilians. This, Fritzsche reasons, explains to some degree why so many went along with the Nazi persecutions of Jews and others and why today they are still reluctant to speak about the Holocaust.

Opportunism and greed motivated civilians, fear paralyzed them, and disregard for others blinded them. The war erased whole horizons of empathy as people crouched within their own little worlds of tenuous security. Neighbors failed one another. The terms for *Jew* and *Aryan* quickly became part of everyday speech, widening the gulf between the two groups, who experienced very different wars. (p. xiii)

This book had not been published when Monika took the course but could have helped her explain the difficulties she encountered speaking with her family, especially about why they would not look beyond their own adversity or come to terms with how the Nazis targeted the Jews during Hitler's regime.

Monika's reading of *Maus* helped her fill in some of the silences in her grandparents' narratives. She hoped that by teaching *Maus* she could help her students attain similar insights. (During the semester, I mentioned the film *The Nasty Girl* [*Das Schreckliche Mädchen*; Berger, Senftleben, & Verhoeven, 1990], about a German Gentile teenager who researches her town's involvement in the Third Reich's fascist agenda, which I hope she had a chance to view and share with her students.)

MAUS AS A CAPSTONE TEXT

Maus is an excellent text to complete a Holocaust unit; or it could be the main text of a shorter unit, supplemented where needed. It provides a broad historical sweep, from the mid-1930s through the 1980s. Spiegelman weaves evidence-based historical information into his father's personal narrative. The book also incorporates psychological perspectives, and the visual aspect of the text is guaranteed to secure most students' attention.

In *Maus*, Spiegelman raises many issues related to Holocaust studies: moral and ethical dilemmas; problems in representation; the stages of trauma and recovery; the victim, survivor, perpetrator, bystander, resister, rescuer, and witness roles; and the Holocaust's aftereffects. The book effectively exposes how stereotypes distort reality, and teachers can use it to demonstrate when and how writers use stereotypes to expose them, subvert them, or perpetuate them (consciously or not). It affords many opportunities to experiment with different teaching strategies and to work across genres and academic disciplines.

Student teachers have to grapple with the delicate balance between affective and cognitive learning, and between distancing and creating empathy. In schools where interdisciplinary teaching is encouraged and supported, the possibilities for team teaching are many. English teachers could cooperate easily with art, drama, and social sciences teachers to deliver a truly inspiring holistic educational experience.

Maus also provides opportunities to discuss linguistic and cultural diversity. Art painstakingly transcribes how Vladek incorporates some of the grammatic features of the multiple languages he spoke, invents words derived from English, and intersperses words from other languages into his English discourse. Nonnative English language learners often use such linguistic strategies. However, students unfamiliar with linguistic diversity may assume that he was illiterate, as did some students in this course. In fact, Vladek was fluent in several languages.

Applied linguistics and bilingual education researchers Suresh Canagarajah (2013) and Vivian J. Cook (1999), among others, counter the view that when nonnative English language learners integrate other languages into their English speech and writing, this interferes with their fluency. These scholars describe literacy for these nonnative speakers as a translingual practice (Canagarajah). They view second language users not as though they were failed native speakers but rather as "multicompetent language users" who strategically navigate between language codes (Cook).

In English-only classrooms, students who are English language learners, people whose home languages are nonstandard English, and those preparing to teach them can benefit socially and linguistically when the curriculum includes texts like *Maus* that feature nonstandard-English writers and speakers. In the context of English as a world language, incorporating such examples of language diversity into the curriculum demonstrates appreciation of and respect for the many forms of English that people speak.

Maus raises many issues that have parallels in today's world. For example, when looking at mass migration from areas affected by environmental and political disasters, how do displaced persons cope with the trauma? What resources are available to help them? How do host countries treat these survivors? What role does propaganda have in shaping peoples' ideas about otherness? What happens when host countries turn refugees and asylum seekers away? How is trauma transmitted across generations and promoted through the actions of the broader society?

As my students and I did when studying *Maus*, teachers and their students can open up such questions by analyzing the rhetorics of photojournalism, documentary and animated films, and graphic texts. Such representations, both fictional and nonfictional, help articulate ideas and feelings that words or pictures alone cannot convey.

NOTE

1. The hideously ironic sign at the entrance of the Auschwitz-Birkenau slave labor and death camps, translated as "Work sets you free."

Chapter 8

Some Final Considerations

What happens . . . to a member of the third generation who learns the truth about his heritage only as an adolescent? What happens today to a student unrelated to Jews whose innocence is ended by a history class, a piece of literature, or a film? Once one knows, what is the next step, and how does that step differ from person to person? How does such new knowledge inspire and affect university students who plan to become teachers?

(Karen Shawn, [2017, Spring], *PRISM*, p. 1)

We can only claim to provide, in this book, a narrow glimpse into the vast terrain of Holocaust studies. Our conclusions about teaching Holocaust literature are by necessity tentative. However, the research does offer a realistic picture of what meaningful teaching of Holocaust literature entails, freighted as it is with obstacles and pitfalls, and enlightening when taught appropriately. Our hope is, first, that reading this book sparks dialogue among its readers and with others about linking literature, history, ethics, and contemporary life with relevant teaching practices.

Further, while no single book could provide all that is needed to teach Holocaust literature with accuracy and sensitivity, this book should provide sufficient guidance to teachers as they continue to research Holocaust and genocide studies and venture to teach Holocaust literature responsibly. Nevertheless, we hope that the book inspires readers to teach their students this subject matter with eyes and hearts wide open to, but not unduly intimidated by, how challenging and complex a practice this is.

As we bring this endeavor to its conclusion, we offer educators and policy makers some final thoughts, recommendations, and encouragement.

EXPANDING THE CURRICULUM

After teaching the pilot course, I continued to integrate Holocaust literature into both undergraduate and graduate English studies courses. Those courses afforded me opportunities to teach a few texts and topics that were not as germane to an introductory Holocaust literature course within a teacher education setting but are significant nonetheless.

In an undergraduate course on contemporary LGBTQ literature, the texts included the film *Paragraph 175* (Epstein, Friedman, Cole, & Ehrenzweig, 2000), about the persecution of gay men during the Holocaust. In some iterations of that course, students also read the biography *Aimée and Jaguar: A Love Story, Berlin 1943* (Fischer, 1994), and/or viewed the film *Aimée and Jaguar* (Rohrbach, Huth, & Färberböck, 1999). The book contextualizes historically a lesbian relationship between a Jewish woman and a Gentile woman in Nazi Germany; the film romanticizes it.

In one graduate course, students investigated gender and sexuality through feminist, queer, and anticolonial theoretical lenses. Among the texts we read was *Bent*, by Martin Sherman (2000), a play about gay men in a concentration camp, available as a script and movie. The play raises a number of controversial questions about internalized homophobia and the differences between the persecution of Jews and gay men during the Holocaust.

Sherman wrote *Bent* in 1976, but during the Holocaust itself, Jews created and performed theatrical productions, even in the ghettos and concentration camps (especially Theresienstadt). Theater historian Alvin Goldfarb (1999) directs attention to how theater and all the arts spiritually nourished prisoners in those desperate times. "Theater was another attempt by the victims to sustain one another and to try to preserve a semblance of normality in an obscenely abnormal universe" (p. 124).

The performing arts also provided many ways to covertly resist, using thinly veiled allusions that the Nazis overlooked or ignored. The children's opera *Brundibár* (Krása & Hoffmeister, 1938/1943) and the opera *The Emperor of Atlantis* (Ullman & Kien, ca. 1943) are examples. Playwright Tony Kushner and children's literature author Maurice Sendak's adaptation of *Brundibár* (2003) is readily available; various performances of the operas can be viewed on the internet. The National Jewish Theater Foundation maintains an online annotated bibliography of theater works related to the Holocaust from 1933 to the present.

In addition to the play, that graduate course also included Israeli author Nava Semel's novel *And the Rat Laughed* (2008). The protagonist is a young Jewish girl who is mentally and physically abused by the family that is hiding her from the Nazis and who their son repeatedly rapes.

Professor of German Sonja M. Hedgepeth and women's historian Rochelle G. Saidel (2010) document the widespread sexual abuse Jewish women endured during the Holocaust. This occurred despite the "purity of race" prohibition barring sexual relations between non-Jewish Germans and German Jews. Perpetrators included Jewish and non-Jewish men of various nationalities the women encountered while in transit, in camps, in ghettos, or in hiding, and after liberation.

Israeli and many other women and children survivors were, and still are, reluctant to tell what happened to them because of the stigma attached to survivors who have been sexually abused. In many cases, their families and the public hold the victims responsible for what happened to them, instead of the abusers. Semel confronts this problem directly in *And the Rat Laughed*, powerfully challenging the stigma and breaking the silence wide open.

This curriculum also included literary texts that provoke thorny questions about the contemporary meaning of the Holocaust and its relationship to the current conflict between Arabs and Jews in Israel-Palestine today. The students read Semel's novel *Paper Bride* (2012), wherein she takes on contemporary politics in Israeli society and asks the rhetorical question, "What kind of world was it if two peoples couldn't share the same homeland?" (p. 246).

Many Holocaust scholars, including Israeli historian and Holocaust survivor Saul Friedländer (2016), also raise such questions, as may middle and secondary school students. To address their students' questions responsibly, teachers and teacher educators could gain background knowledge about the Israel-Palestine conflict (e.g., Gelvin, 2014; Laqueur & Schueftan, 2016) and pay close attention to current Middle East developments.

Similarly, students may wonder about the parallels between white supremacist and ultranationalist movements in the United States and Europe today, and fascism in Germany during the Holocaust years. As teachers seek to draw contemporary parallels between the Holocaust and the present, keeping abreast of such issues through reliable news sources would be helpful. Consulting the USHMM website about such issues also would assist teachers as they work with their students to unpack the roots of contemporary Islamophobic, antisemitic, and xenophobic rhetoric, policies, and violence.

IMPROVING TEACHER PREPARATION

From the beginning of the course, I emphasized that the objective to develop students' pedagogical skills was built into the curriculum and explicitly linked to the literature the students read. Despite this, many students could not accept that by learning through Holocaust literature how to use reader response strategies and to teach within historical and cultural contexts, they would be better prepared to teach any literature.

Some students also continued to believe that pedagogy should first and foremost focus on standards and skill building rather than understanding that when students have meaningful and engaging encounters with literature, they will necessarily improve their literacy skills and be more motivated to develop them further.

Many students also were uncomfortable with the disturbing content of the texts in this course, for a variety of reasons. The topics were emotionally difficult, and a few students were particularly sensitive because of personal experiences with trauma. Some hesitated to talk about religion, afraid to offend. Others objected on principle to focusing on social justice issues when teaching English literature classes.

Those students in the course who objected to the Holocaust curriculum also complained they were not learning how to teach any of the specific texts they assumed they would be teaching. That students wished to practice teaching texts before dealing with them in their own classrooms was understandable, given their lack of confidence that they could teach a text they had not been taught (see Chapter 2, "Teachers as Learners").

Considering all the pressures and anxieties they were experiencing, the students' objections are credible. These problems with texts, contexts, and pedagogy raise a number of questions. Was the instruction inadequate to help students transfer their learning to different contexts and to move past their initial discomfort? Or would they discover the benefits as they developed their teaching practices? How could these novice teachers prepare to teach Holocaust literature given that they had few or no other opportunities to study the Holocaust in their teacher preparation program or as an elective?

While we cannot answer these questions definitively, we encourage teacher educators, their students, and inservice teachers to consider them as they think about their own teaching and learning. Two assessments students wrote might shed some light on this line of inquiry.

A student writing anonymously on the back of a standardized departmental course evaluation form comments, "It was like learning to teach while actually learning something." Unlike the students who objected to the course's emphasis on meaningful encounters with unfamiliar literature, this student understood the importance of pedagogical content knowledge. Others demonstrated their ability to apply this concept when they taught their practice lessons.

Two of my students (Andrea and Ruth, Section 4), who emailed me after the semester ended, reported on how even some dissatisfied students progressed:

> Some students made it clear that they "didn't learn much" from the methods course . . . but we . . . noticed a tremendous change in our classmates. By the end of the semester, they were throwing around terms like "constructivism," "discourse communities," etc. . . . And from the way [they] put theory into practice in this and other courses [we took together], we could tell there was something right about what we were being taught. Thank you for enduring and being patient.

Those three students put positive spins on the course. They recognized that they had learned about pedagogy *and* about Holocaust literature. But the outcomes of the course suggest that unless teachers are deeply immersed in Holocaust studies for the equivalent of at least a semester, they are unlikely to be well prepared to teach Holocaust literature, even on a beginning level. Given the constraints of the teacher education curriculum, the likelihood that English education students would have a chance to study Holocaust literature in any depth is practically nil.

In their 2004 book, *Issues in Holocaust Education*, teacher educator Geoffrey Short and Holocaust educator Carole Ann Reed issued a rallying cry to incorporate Holocaust studies into all teacher education programs. Now, as then, the dearth of Holocaust studies in teacher education and in many universities makes it unlikely that prospective teachers will enter the profession prepared to teach this complex topic. For practicing teachers, much of professional development is voluntary, which makes it unlikely that inservice teachers will become better prepared during their careers.

The effort to change this situation requires the participation of teachers and school administrators; local, state, and national educational policy makers; colleges of education and academic departments; and professional education organizations. All these people and institutions need to lobby for and create the policies and programs necessary to teach Holocaust, genocide, and mass atrocities studies accurately and in ways that are culturally relevant. This is an even greater challenge during times of regressive school reform in which meaning-making takes a back seat to test-driven, high-stakes, standards-based curricula and accreditation hurdles and barriers.

In the short term, it is unrealistic to expect that school systems and universities will substantially change curriculum offerings, teacher preparation, and professional development regarding Holocaust education. Nor can we anticipate that states and school districts will support financially such professional development. Over the long term, we encourage readers to support and participate in the efforts of individuals and organizations that are pressuring state and local boards of education and universities to move in this direction.

Meanwhile, people who want to or are required to teach Holocaust literature may need to fashion their own self-education curriculum. Educators and education students can research the Holocaust and Holocaust pedagogy by visiting the websites this book references and other reputable resources that they might discover during their internet and library browsing. Reading any of the supplemental texts mentioned in each chapter also would be helpful.

Teachers can develop and strengthen their expertise by visiting Holocaust museums, enrolling in their educational programs, and studying their online resources. For example, the USHMM's Belfer National Conference for Educators is an intensive three-day experience for high school and community college faculty members from around the country. Israel's Yad Vashem, the World Holocaust Remembrance Center, provides online access to research and educational materials not available elsewhere.

Various other organizations and institutions offer conferences, workshops, and seminars for secondary school teachers, such as Syracuse University's Holocaust and Genocide Education Program and Florida Atlantic University's Center for Holocaust and Human Rights Education. They provide educational opportunities for their students and for people teaching in those areas of the country.

To find out about similar programs in their regions, teachers can contact the nearest Holocaust museum or academic program in Holocaust and genocide studies. The World Without Genocide website provides a list of academic programs in Holocaust and genocide studies.

Holocaust studies is often the only educational path by which students learn anything about Judaism or Jewish culture or in which Jews can see themselves reflected in the curriculum. This can be problematic. Teaching about the Jewish people only in the context of the Holocaust can be harmful and perpetuate stereotypes. Studying the Holocaust can and should be much more than a reminder of Jewish persecution and victimization.

Exploring the richness of Jewish life and culture prior to, during, and after the Holocaust helps us to humanize the people who the Nazis and other persecutors throughout history so dehumanized. Reading and viewing Jewish literature, theater, and film; visiting museums that feature Jewish art; attending relevant events sponsored by educational, religious, and community organizations and institutions: these are some of the ways educators can gain the cultural competence they need to teach Holocaust studies responsibly.

Words of Encouragement

Preservice teachers and teacher educators, and novice teachers and their mentors, should not expect to achieve mastery the first two or three times they teach any Holocaust texts. Proficiency happens over time, through a recurring process of reading, responding, research, and reflective teaching practice. All that educators realistically can expect of themselves and each other at any given point in this journey toward proficiency is that they teach responsibly, based on what they have learned so far about the texts and contexts, and apply their growing understanding of pedagogical content knowledge.

Learning about the problems that might appear when teaching about the Holocaust, as well as the exciting ways that the education students in this course met the challenges, should give more teachers the necessary insights and sound pedagogical strategies to take courageous but reasonable risks to teach this difficult subject matter. Key components of these endeavors include collaborating with others as much as possible, taking advantage of every opportunity for further learning, reflecting on what works and doesn't work, and revising lesson and unit plans, given the knowledge teachers gain each time they teach.

The lessons of the Holocaust remain as relevant today as always. Helping students understand the parallels between the social and political conditions that characterized the Holocaust years and the moral dilemmas people faced then, and the conditions and moral dilemmas people face today, should be a significant part of a Holocaust studies teacher's mission. Roth exhorts us to pay special attention to the Holocaust's gray zone, which "suggests that no question is more important than how—or even whether—ethics can be restored and revitalized after Auschwitz" (2008, p. 30).

We hope that this book encourages readers to take up the formidable challenge that teaching Holocaust literature, in all its complexity, presents. What we—education students, teacher educators, preservice teachers, and teachers—learn from the Holocaust should inspire us to help build, by teaching the next generations, a future in which genocides are less likely to occur. Even all today's educators' combined efforts could not prepare all their students to resist and prevent mass state-sponsored violence. Nevertheless, we see it as our responsibility to make that effort to the best of our abilities.

Pirkei Avot (*Ethics of the Fathers*) is a compilation of ethical teachings by various rabbis that is found in one of the key ancient Jewish texts, the *Mishna* (ca. 200 CE). In it, Rabbi Tarfon is quoted as saying, "It is not your responsibility to finish the work [of perfecting the world (*sic*)], but you are not free to desist from it either" (quoted in Telushkin, 1991, p. 479). It is in this spirit that I taught the course, that we wrote this book, and that we offer it to you.

References

Adorno, Theodor W. (1983). Cultural criticism and society. In Theodor W. Adorno, *Prisms* (pp. 17–34). (Samuel & Shierry Weber, Trans.). Cambridge, MA: MIT Press. (Original work published 1951)

Anti-Defamation League. (n.d.). Holocaust education: Why simulation activities should not be used. Retrieved from https://www.adl.org/education/resources/tools-and-strategies/why-simulation-activities-should-not-be-used

Appiah, Anthony Kwame. (2006). *Cosmopolitanism: Ethics in a world of strangers*. New York, NY: Norton.

Aupperle, Rebecca G. (2001). Face to face: The study of *Friedrich*, a novel about the Holocaust. In Samuel Totten (Ed.), *Teaching Holocaust literature* (pp. 73–102). Boston, MA: Allyn & Bacon.

Bachrach, Susan, & Luckert, Steven. (2009). *State of deception: The power of Nazi propaganda*. Washington, DC: United States Holocaust Memorial Museum.

Bakhtin, Mikhail. (1986). *Speech genres and other late essays by M. M. Bakhtin* (Vern W. McGee, Trans.). Caryl Emerson & Michael Holquist (Eds.). Austin, TX: University of Texas Press.

Barnes, Douglas. (1992). *From communication to curriculum* (2nd ed.). Portsmouth, NH: Boynton/Cook.

Bar-On, Dan. (1996). Attempting to overcome the intergenerational transmission of trauma: Dialogue between descendants of victims and of perpetrators. In Roberta Apfel & Bennett Simon (Eds.), *Minefields of their hearts: The mental health of children in war and communal violence* (pp. 165–88). New Haven, CT: Yale University Press.

Beauvoir, Simone de. (2011). *The second sex*. (Constance Borde & Sheila Malvony-Chevalier, Trans.). New York, NY: Vintage. (Original work published 1953)

Begley, Louis. (1997). *Wartime lies*. New York, NY: Ballantine Books.

Berenbaum, Michael. (2003). *A promise to remember: The Holocaust in the words and voices of its survivors*. Boston, MA: Bulfinch Press.

Bergen, Doris. (2009). *War and genocide: A concise history of the Holocaust* (2nd ed.). Lanham, MD: Rowman & Littlefield.

Bergen, Doris. (2016). *War and genocide: A concise history of the Holocaust* (3rd ed.). Lanham, MD: Rowman & Littlefield.

Berger, Senta, Senftleben, Michael (Producers), & Verhoeven, Michael (Director). (1990). *The nasty girl* (*Das schreckliche mädchen*) [Motion picture]. Germany: Miramax (U.S. distributor).

Bissell, Robin et al. (Producers), & Ross, Gary (Director). (2012). *Hunger games* [Motion picture]. United States: Lionsgate.

Blau, Sheridan. (2003). *The literature workshop: Teaching texts and their readers.* Portsmouth, NH: Heinemann.

Boak, Helen. (2013). *Women in the Weimar Republic.* Manchester, UK: Manchester University Press.

Boal, Augusto. (1985). *Theatre of the oppressed.* (Charles A. & Maria-Odilia Leal McBride, Trans.). New York, NY: Theatre Communications Group. (Original work published 1974)

Boden, Eliot H. (2011). The enemy within: Homosexuality in the Third Reich, 1933–1945. *Constructing the Past, 12*(1), article 4. Retrieved from http://digitalcommons.iwu.edu/constructing/vol12/iss1/4

Borowski, Tadeusz. (1976). *This way for the gas, ladies and gentlemen.* (Barbara Vedder, Trans.). New York, NY: Penguin Books. (Original work published 1959)

Bosmajian, Hamida. (2002). *Sparing the child: Grief and the unspeakable in youth literature about Nazism and the Holocaust.* New York, NY: Routledge.

Botzakis, Stergios, Burns, David Leslie, & Hall, Leigh A. (2014, March). Literacy reform and Common Core State Standards: Recycling the autonomous model. *Language Arts, 91*(4), 223–35.

Bourdieu, Pierre, & Passeron, Jean-Claude. (1990). *Reproduction in education, society and culture* (2nd ed.). (Richard Nice, Trans.). Beverly Hills, CA: Sage. (Original work published 1977)

Boyne, John. (2007). *The boy in the striped pajamas.* Oxford, UK: David Fickling Books.

Britton, James. (1982). Shaping at the point of utterance. In Gordon M. Pradl (Ed.), *Prospect and retrospect: Selected essays of James Britton* (pp. 139–45). Montclair, NJ: Boynton-Cook.

Britton, James. (1983, April). A quiet form of research. *English Journal, 72*(4), 89–92.

Brodzki, Bella. (2004). Teaching trauma and transmission. In Marianne Hirsch & Irene Kacandes (Eds.), *Teaching the representation of the Holocaust* (pp. 123–48). New York, NY: The Modern Language Association of America.

Brooks, Jacqueline Grennon, & Brooks, Martin. (1993). *In search of understanding: The case for constructivist classrooms.* Alexandria, VA: Association for Supervision and Curriculum Development.

Browning, Christopher R. (1992). *Ordinary men: Reserve Police Battalion 101 and the Final Solution in Poland.* New York, NY: Harper Perennial.

Burke, Jim. (2010). *What's the big idea? Question-driven units to motivate reading, writing, and thinking.* Portsmouth, NH: Heinemann.

Burnett, Mark, et al. (Producers.) (2000–present). *Survivor* [Television series]. New York, NY: CBS.

Cambourne, Brian. (1988). *The whole story: Natural learning and the acquisition of literacy in the classroom*. Auckland, NZ: Ashton Scholastic.

Canagarajah, Suresh. (2013). *Literacy as translingual practice: Between communities and classrooms*. New York, NY: Routledge.

Cargas, Harry James. (1991). *Reflections of a post-Auschwitz Christian*. Detroit, MI: Wayne State University Press.

Carillo, Ellen C. (2006, January). Reimagining the role of the reader in the Common Core State Standards. *English Journal, 105*(3), 29–35. Urbana, IL: National Council of Teachers of English.

Carroll, James. (2002). *Constantine's sword: The church and the Jews, a history*. New York, NY: Mariner Books.

Caruth, Cathy. (1995). *Trauma: Explorations in memory*. Baltimore, MD: Johns Hopkins University Press.

Celan, Paul. (2002). *Poems of Paul Celan: A bilingual German/English edition* (rev. ed.). (Michael Hamburger, Trans.). New York, NY: Persea Books.

Christenbury, Leila. (2000). *Making the journey: Being and becoming a teacher of English language arts* (2nd ed.). Portsmouth, NH: Heinemann.

Christenbury, Leila, & Lindblom, Ken. (2016). *Making the journey: Being and becoming a teacher of English language arts* (4th ed.). Portsmouth, NH: Heinemann.

Christmas, Danielle. (2015, March 15). The plantation-Auschwitz tradition: Forced labor and free markets in the novels of William Styron. *Twentieth-Century Literature, 61*(1), 1–31.

Cohen-Cruz, Jan, & Schutzman, Mady (Eds.). (1994). *Playing Boal: Theatre, therapy, activism*. New York, NY: Routledge.

Common Core State Standards Initiative. (2018). English language arts standards. Retrieved from http://www.corestandards.org/ELA-Literacy/

Cook, Vivian J. (1999). Going beyond the native speaker in language teaching. *TESOL Quarterly, 33*(2), 185–209.

Davey, Bruce, Gibson, Mel, McEveety, Stephen (Producers), & Gibson, Mel (Director). (2004). *The Passion of the Christ* [Motion picture]. United States: Icon Productions.

Dawidowicz, Lucy S. (1986). *The war against the Jews: 1933–1945*. New York, NY: Bantam.

Delbo, Charlotte. (1995). *Auschwitz and after*. New Haven, CT: Yale University Press.

Delpit, Lisa. (1998). The silenced dialogue: Power and pedagogy in educating other people's children. *Harvard Educational Review, 58*(3), 280–98.

Dewey, John. (2004). *Democracy and education*. Mineola, NY: Dover Publications. (Original work published 1916.)

Disney, Walt (Producer), & Geronimi, Clyde (Director). (1943). *Education for death: The making of the Nazi* [Motion picture]. United States: RKO Pictures. Retrieved from https://www.youtube.com/watch?v=6vLrTNKk89Q

Dixon, John. (1975). *Growth through English*. Urbana, IL: NCTE.

Donadio, Rachel. (2009, January 24). Pope reinstates four excommunicated bishops. *The New York Times*. Retrieved from http://www.nytimes.com/2009/01/25/world/europe/25pope.html

Douglass, Frederick. (1847). Love of God, love of man, love of country. Retrieved from http://www.teachingamericanhistory.org/library/index.asp?document=535

Deutsche Welle. (2003, September 29). Rosenstrasse film criticized for "distorting" history. Retrieved from https://www.dw.com/en/rosenstrasse-film-criticized-for-distorting-history/a-979395

Echoes and Reflections. (n.d.). Retrieved from https://echoesandreflections.org

Edmiston, Brian. (2013). *Transforming teaching and learning with active and dramatic approaches: Engaging students across the curriculum*. New York, NY: Routledge.

Edmiston, Brian, & Wilhelm, Jeffrey D. (1988). *Imagining to learn: Inquiry, ethics, and integration through drama*. Portsmouth, NH: Heinemann.

Ely, Margot, with Anzul, Margaret, Friedman, Teri, Garner, Diane, & Steinmetz, Ann McCormack. (1991). *Doing qualitative research: Circles within circles*. London, UK: The Falmer Press.

Epstein, Rob, Friedman, Jeffrey, Cole, Janet, Ehrenzweig, Michael (Producers), & Epstein, Rob, Friedman, Jeffrey (Directors). (2000). *Paragraph 175* [Motion picture]. United States: New Yorker Films.

Erikson, Kai. (1995). Notes on trauma and community. In Cathy Caruth (Ed.), *Trauma: Explorations in memory* (pp. 183–99). Baltimore, MD: Johns Hopkins University Press.

Errington, Edward. (1992). *Towards a socially critical drama education*. Gelong, Victoria, AU: Deakin University Press.

Facing History and Ourselves. (n.d.). https://www.facinghistory.org

Farnham, James F. (1983, April). Ethical ambiguity and the teaching of the Holocaust. *English Journal*, *72*(4), 63–68.

Felman, Shoshana. (1992). Education and crisis, or the vicissitudes of teaching. In Shoshana Felman & Dori Laub (Eds.), *Testimony: Crises of witnessing in literature, psychoanalysis, and history* (pp. 3–56). New York, NY: Routledge.

Finders, Margaret J., & Hynds, Susan. (2006). *Language arts and literacy in the middle grades* (2nd ed.). Boston, MA: Pearson.

Fischer, Erica. (1994). *Aimée & Jaguar: A love story, Berlin 1943*. New York, NY: HarperCollins.

Fisher, Berenice. (1993). The heart has its reasons: Feeling, thinking and community-building in feminist education. *Women's Studies Quarterly*, *21*(3), 75–87.

Fleet, Josh. (2012, March 28). History and meaning of the word "Holocaust": Are we still comfortable with this term? *Huffington Post*. Retrieved from http://www.huffingtonpost.com/2012/01/27/the-word-holocaust-history-and-meaning_n_1229043.html

Florida Center for Instructional Technology. (n.d.). A teacher's guide to the Holocaust. Retrieved from http://fcit.usf.edu/holocaust/

Forbes, Harry, & Mulderig, John. (2008). Constantine's sword. [Review of the book *Constantine's sword: The church and the Jews, a history*, by James Carroll].

Catholic Online News Service. Retrieved from https://www.catholic.org/news/national/story.php?id=27692

Fortunoff Video Archive for Holocaust Testimonies. (n.d.). Retrieved from https://web.library.yale.edu/testimonies/youtube

Foster, Gary, Krasnoff, Russ (Producers), & Jackson, Mick (Director). (2016). *Denial* [Motion picture]. United Kingdom: BBC Films.

Frank, Anne. (1995). *The diary of a young girl: The definitive edition*. Otto H. Frank & Mirjam Pressler (Eds.). (Susan Massotty, Trans.). New York, NY: Doubleday.

Freedom Writers Foundation. (n.d.). Retrieved from http://www.freedomwritersfoundation.org/

Freire, Paulo. (1993). *Pedagogy of the oppressed*. (M. B. Ramo, Trans.). New York, NY: Continuum. (Original work published 1979)

Freire, Paolo, & Macedo, Donaldo. (1987). *Literacy: Reading the word and the world*. South Hadley, MA: Bergin & Garvey.

Friedländer, Saul. (1992). Trauma, transference and "working through" in writing the history of the Shoah. *History and Memory* (4), 39–59.

Friedländer, Saul. (1997). *Nazi Germany and the Jews: The years of persecution, 1933–1939*. New York, NY: Harper Perennial.

Friedländer, Saul. (2007). *The years of extermination: Nazi Germany and the Jews, 1939–1945*. New York, NY: HarperCollins.

Friedländer, Saul. (2016). *Where memory leads: My life*. New York, NY: Other Press.

Fritzsche, Peter. (2016). *An iron wind: Europe under Hitler*. New York, NY: Basic Books.

Gee, James Paul. (1989). Literacy, discourse, and linguistics: An introduction. *Journal of Education*, *17*(1), 5–17.

Gee, James Paul. (1996). First language acquisition as a guide for theories of learning and pedagogy. *Linguistics and Education*, *6*(4), 331–54.

Geis, Deborah H. (Ed.). (2003). *Considering* Maus: *Approaches to Art Spiegelman's "survivor's tale" of the Holocaust*. Tuscaloosa, AL: University of Alabama Press.

Gelvin, James L. (2014). *The Israel-Palestine conflict: One Hundred Years of War* (3rd ed.). Cambridge, UK: Cambridge University Press.

Gilyard, Keith. (1991). *Voices of the self: A study of language competence* (4th ed.). Detroit, MI: Wayne State University Press.

Gold, Jonathan. (2016, May). Shifting out of neutral: A history teacher leaves the struggle for objectivity behind. *Education Digest*, *81*(9), 31–35.

Goldfarb, Alvin. (1999). Theatrical activities in the Nazi concentration camps. In Rebecca Rovit & Alvin Goldfarb (Eds.), *Theatrical performance during the Holocaust: Texts, memoirs, and documents* (pp. 117–24). Baltimore, MD: Johns Hopkins University.

Goodrich, Frances, & Hackett, Albrecht. (1986). *The diary of Anne Frank*. New York, NY: Dramatists Play Service. (Original work published 1955)

Gossels, Lisa, & Wetherell, Dean (Co-producers and Co-Directors). (2014). *Children of Chabannes* [Motion picture]. United States: Good Egg Productions and Wetherell & Associates.

Gray, Esther Cappon, & Thetard, Susan A. (2010). Inventing a drama world as a place to learn: Student discoveries while speaking and writing in role as fictional workers. In Peggy Albers & Jennifer Sanders (Eds.), *Literacy, the arts, and multimodality* (pp. 90–109). Urbana, IL: NCTE.

Grossman, Pamela L. (2001). Research on the teaching of literature: Finding a place. *Handbook of research on teaching* (pp. 416–32). Washington, DC: American Educational Research Association.

Gutierrez y Muhs, Gabriella, Flores Niemann, Yolanda, Gonzalez, Carmen G., & Harris, Angela P. (Eds.). (2012). *Presumed incompetent: The intersections of race and class for women in academia.* Boulder, CO: Utah State University Press.

Heath, Shirley Brice. (1990). *Ways with words: Language, life, and work in communities and classrooms.* Cambridge, UK: Cambridge University Press.

Heathcote, Dorothy, & Bolton, Gavin. (1995). *Drama for learning: Dorothy Heathcote's mantle of the expert approach to education.* Portsmouth, NH: Heinemann.

Hedgepeth, Sonja M., & Saidel, Rochelle G. (2010). *Sexual violence against Jewish women during the Holocaust.* Waltham, MA: Brandeis University Press.

Heineman, Elizabeth D. (2002). Sexuality and Nazism: The doubly unspeakable? In Dagmar Herzog (Ed.), *Sexuality and German fascism* (pp. 22–66). New York, NY: Berghahn Books.

Herber, H. L. (1978). *Teaching reading in the content areas.* Englewood Cliffs, NJ: Prentice-Hall.

Herman, Judith. (1992). *Trauma and recovery: The aftermath of violence—from domestic abuse to political terror.* New York, NY: Basic Books.

Herzog, Dagmar. (2002). *Sexuality and German fascism.* New York, NY: Berghahn Books.

Herzog, Dagmar. (2005). *Sex after fascism: Memory and morality in twentieth-century Germany.* Princeton, NJ: Princeton University Press.

Hilberg, Raul. (1985). *The destruction of European Jews.* New York, NY: Holmes & Meier. (Original work published 1961)

Hilberg, Raul. (1993). *Perpetrators victims bystanders: The Jewish catastrophe, 1933–1945.* New York, NY: Harper Perennial.

Hirsch, Marianne. (1992). Family pictures: *Maus,* mourning, and post-memory. *Discourse, 15*(2), 3–29.

Hirsch, Marianne, & Kacandes, Irene (Eds.). (2004). *Teaching the representation of the Holocaust.* New York, NY: The Modern Language Association of America.

Hirsch, Marianne, & Spitzer, Leo. (2010). *Ghosts of home: The afterlife of Czernowitz in Jewish memory.* Berkeley, CA: University of California Press.

Holocaust Educational Foundation of Northwestern University. (n.d.). "Holocaust studies centers, institutes, and programs." Retrieved from https://www.hef.northwestern.edu/links/holocaust-centers/

Horowitz, Sara R. (1997). *Voicing the void: Muteness and memory in Holocaust fiction.* Albany, NY: State University of New York Press.

Horowitz, Sara R. (1998). Women in holocaust literature: Engendering trauma memory. In Dalia Ofer & Lenore J. Weitzman (Eds.), *Women in the Holocaust* (pp. 364–77). New Haven, CT: Yale University Press.

Horowitz, Sara R. (2009, March 1). Holocaust literature. In *Jewish women: A comprehensive historical encyclopedia*. Jewish Women's Archive. Retrieved from http://jwa.org/encyclopedia/article/holocaust-literature

Horowitz, Sara R. (2012). Literary afterlives of Anne Frank. In Barbara Kirshenblatt-Gimblett & Jeffrey Shandler (Eds.), *Anne Frank unbound: Media, imagination, memory* (pp. 215–54). Bloomington, IN: Indiana University Press.

Hutchinson, Yvonne Divans. (n.d.). Using anticipation guides. Retrieved from http://insideteaching.org/quest/collections/sites/divans-hutchinson_yvonne/

Jacoby, Oren, Carroll, James, Solomon, Michael, West, Betsy (Producers), & Jacoby, Oren (Director). (2008). *James Carroll's Constantine's sword* [Motion Picture]. United States: Storyville Films.

Juzwik, Mary M. (2013). The ethics of teaching disturbing pasts: Reader response, historical contextualization, and rhetorical contextualization of Holocaust texts in English. *English Education, 45*(3), 284–308.

Kaplan, Arie. (n.d.). Jews in comic books: How American Jews created the comic book industry. In *My Jewish learning*. Retrieved from http://www.myjewishlearning.com/article/jews-in-comic-books/

Kellermann, Natan P. F. (n.d.). Transmission of Holocaust trauma—an integrative view. *Psychiatry, 64*(3), 256–67.

Kesselman, Wendy. (2000). *The diary of Anne Frank* (Acting edition). New York, NY: Dramatists Play Service.

King, Martin Luther, Jr. (2004, January 15). Beyond Vietnam: A time to break silence. (Speech originally delivered April 4, 1967.) Retrieved from http://www.commondreams.org/views04/0115-13.htm

Kolatch, Alfred J. (1987). *The concise family Seder*. New York, NY: Jonathan David Publishers.

Koonz, Claudia. (1987). *Mothers in the fatherland: Women, the family, and Nazi politics*. New York, NY: St. Martin's Press.

Kosinski, Jerzy. (1995). *The painted bird* (2nd ed.). New York, NY: Grove Press. (Original work published 1965)

Krása, Hans, & Hoffmeister, Adolf. (1938). *Brundibár*. (Josa Karas, Trans.). London, UK: Boosey & Hawkes.

Kremer, Lillian. (1999). *Women's Holocaust writing: Memory and imagination*. Lincoln, NE: University of Nebraska Press.

Kunzman, Robert. (2012). How to talk about religion. *College, Careers, Citizenship, 69*(7), 44–48. Retrieved from http://www.ascd.org/publications/educational-leadership/apr12/vol69/num07/How-to-Talk-About-Religion.aspx

Kushner, Tony, & Sendak, Maurice. (2003). *Brundibár*. New York, NY: Michael di Capua Books/Hyperion Books for Children.

Ladson-Billings, Gloria. (1992). Culturally relevant teaching: The key to making multicultural education work. In Carl A. Grant (Ed.), *Research and multicultural education* (pp. 106–21). London, UK: Falmer Press.

Ladson-Billings, Gloria. (1995). Toward a theory of culturally relevant pedagogy. *American Educational Research Journal, 32*(3), 465–91.

Landy, Robert J. (1983). The use of distancing in drama therapy. *The Arts in Psychotherapy, 10*(3), 175–85.

Lang, Berel. (2002, March 12). Uncovering certain mischievous questions about the Holocaust. Retrieved from https://www.ushmm.org/m/pdfs/20050726-lang.pdf.

Langer, Lawrence L. (1988). The dilemma of choice in the deathcamps. In A. Rosenberg & G. E. Myers (Eds.), *Echoes from the Holocaust: Philosophical reflections on a dark time* (pp. 118–27). Philadelphia, PA: Temple University Press.

Langer, Lawrence L. (1991, November 3). A fable of the Holocaust [Review of the book *Maus II: And here my troubles began*, by Art Spiegelman]. *New York Times.* movies2.nytimes.com/books/98/12/06/specials/spiegelman-maus2.html

Langer, Lawrence L. (1998). Gendered suffering? Women in Holocaust testimonies. In Dalia Ofer & Lenore J. Weitzman (Eds.), *Women in the Holocaust* (pp. 351–63). New Haven, CT: Yale University Press.

Langer, Lawrence L. (2000). *Preempting the Holocaust.* New Haven, CT: Yale University Press.

Lanzmann, Claude (Producer & Director). (1985). *Shoah* [Motion picture]. United Kingdom: British Broadcasting Company.

Laqueur, Walter, & Schueftan, Dan. (Eds.). (2016). *The Israel-Arab reader: A document history of the Middle East* (8th revised and updated ed.). New York, NY: Penguin Books.

Lee, Carol. (2007). *Culture, literacy, and learning: Taking bloom in the midst of the whirlwind.* New York, NY: Teachers College Press.

Lehmann-Haupt, Christopher. (1986, November 10). Books of the Times [Review of the book *Maus: A Survivor's Tale*, by Art Spiegelman]. *New York Times*, p. C21.

Lentin, Ronit. (2000). *Israel and the daughters of the Shoah: Reoccupying the territories of silence.* New York, NY: Berghahn.

Levi, Primo. (1989). *The drowned and the saved.* New York, NY: Vintage.

Levitt, Joy, & Strassfeld, Michael. (1999). *A night of questions: A Passover Haggadah.* Elkins Park, PA: The Reconstructionist Press.

Lewis, C. S. (2001). *The chronicles of Narnia.* New York, NY: HarperCollins.

Lindquist, David. (2012). Defining the Shoah: An opening lesson for a Holocaust unit. *The Social Studies, 104*(1), 32–37. Retrieved from https://doi.org/10.1080/00 377996.2012.660212

Lipstadt, Deborah. (1994). *Denying the Holocaust: The growing assault on truth and memory.* New York, NY: Plume.

Lipstadt, Deborah. (2006). *History on trial: My day in court with a Holocaust denier.* New York, NY: Ecco.

Lipstadt, Deborah. (2016). *Denial: Holocaust history on trial.* New York, NY: Ecco.

Littell, Franklin H. (1975). *The crucifixion of the Jews: The failure of Christians to understand the Jewish experience.* New York, NY: Harper & Row.

Loban, Walter. (1976). *Language development: Kindergarten through grade twelve.* Urbana, IL: National Council of Teachers of English.

London Jewish Cultural Center. (n.d.). The Holocaust explained. Retrieved from https://www.theholocaustexplained.org/

Martin, Nancy. (1996). Researchers and learners: Some changes in the direction of research in English. In Margaret Meek & Jane Miller (Eds.), *Changing English: Essays for Harold Rosen* (pp. 48–56). London, UK: Heinemann Educational Books.

Mayberry, Katherine J. (Ed.). (1996). *Teaching what you're not: Identity politics in higher education.* New York, NY: New York University Press.

Mayher, John. (1990). *Uncommon sense: Theoretical practice in language education.* Portsmouth, NH: Boynton/Cook.

Mayher, John, Lester, Nancy, & Pradl, Gordon. (1983). *Learning to write/Writing to learn.* Portsmouth, NH: Heinemann.

McCann, Thomas M., Johannessen, Larry R., Kahn, Elizabeth, & Flanagan, Joseph. (2006). *Talking in class: Using discussion to enhance teaching and learning.* Urbana, IL: National Council of Teachers of English.

McCann, Thomas M., Ressler, Paula, Chambers, Dianne, & Minor, Judy. (2010, October). Teaching English together: Leadership through collaboration. *English Leadership Quarterly, 33*(2), 10–13. National Council of Teachers of English.

McCloud, Scott. (1994). *Understanding comics: The invisible art.* New York, NY: Harper Perennial.

McKale, Donald M. (2002). *Hitler's shadow war: The Holocaust and World War II.* New York, NY: Cooper Square Press.

Meeks, Lynn Langer, & Austin, Carol Jewkes. (2003). *Literacy in the secondary English classroom: Strategies for teaching the way kids learn.* Boston, MA: Pearson.

Milner, Joseph O., Milner, Lucy M., & Mitchell, Joan F. (2012). *Bridging English* (5th ed.). Boston, MA: Pearson.

Mommsen, Hans. (1991). *From Weimar to Auschwitz: Essays in German history.* Princeton, NJ: Princeton University.

Morris, Charles R. (2001, January). The worst thing about my church: A compelling new history and Catholic anti-Semitism. *The Atlantic Monthly.* Retrieved from http://www.theatlantic.com/past/docs/issues/2001/01/morris.htm

Mouton, Michelle. (2007). *From nurturing the nation to purifying the Volk: Weimar and Nazi family policy, 1918–1945.* Cambridge, UK: Cambridge University Press.

National Council of Teachers of English. (2009). NCTE/IRA Standards for the English Language Arts. Analysis. Retrieved from http://www.ncte.org/standards/ncte-ira

National Jewish Theater Foundation. (n.d.). Holocaust theater catalog. Retrieved from htc.miami.edu

Neelands, Jonothan. (1990). *Structuring drama work.* Cambridge, UK. Cambridge University Press.

Nomberg-Przytyk, Sara. (1985). Esther's first born. In Sara Nomberg-Przytyk, *Auschwitz: True tales from a grotesque land* (pp. 67–71). (Roslyn Hirsch, Trans.). Eli Pfefferkorn & David H. Hirsch (Eds.). Chapel Hill, NC: University of North Carolina Press. (Original work published 1966)

Nomberg-Przytyk, Sara. (1994). Esther's first born. In Milton Teichman & Sharon Leder (Eds.), *Truth and lamentation: Stories and poems on the Holocaust* (pp. 86–89). (Roslyn Hirsch, Trans.). Urbana, IL: University of Illinois Press. (Original work published 1966)

North American Drama Therapy Association. (n.d.). What is drama therapy? Retrieved from http://www.nadta.org/what-is-drama-therapy.html

Novick, Rona Milch. (2010, Spring). German bystander inaction during the Holocaust: Lessons learned from social psychology and teachable moments for today's students. *Prism, 1*(2), 83–86.

Nystrand, Martin. (2006, May). Classroom discourse and reading comprehension. *Research in the Teaching of English, 40*(4), 392–412.

O'Neill, Cecily. (1995). *Drama worlds: A framework for process drama.* Portsmouth, NH: Heinemann.

Oppenheimer, Mark. (2017, April 22). Reclaiming "Jew." *New York Times.* Retrieved from https://www.nytimes.com/2017/04/22/opinion/reclaiming-jew.html

Oyez. (n.d.). National Socialist Party of America v. Village of Skokie. Retrieved from https://www.oyez.org/cases/1976/76-1786

Ozick, Cynthia. (n.d.). A conversation with Cynthia Ozick about her book "The Shawl" (short version). Retrieved from https://www.youtube.com/watch?v=cFIgXhScfzY

Ozick, Cynthia. (1989). *Rosa.* In Cynthia Ozick, *The shawl* (pp. 13–70). New York, NY: Knopf.

Ozick, Cynthia. (1994). The shawl. In Milton Teichman & Sharon Leder (Eds.), *Truth and lamentation: Stories and poems on the Holocaust* (pp. 107–11). Urbana, IL: University of Illinois Press.

Perl, Sondra. (2004). Writing the Holocaust: The transformative power of response journals. In Marianne Hirsch & Irene M. Kacandes (Eds.), *Teaching the representation of the Holocaust* (pp. 123–48). New York, NY: The Modern Language Association of America.

PEW Forum on Religion and Public Life. (2007, May). Religion in the public schools. Retrieved from http://www.pewforum.org/uploadedfiles/Topics/Issues/Church-State_Law/religion-public-schools.pdf

Piercy, Marge. (1999). Growing up haunted. In *The art of blessing the day: Poems with a Jewish theme.* New York, NY: Knopf.

Pine, Lisa. (2011). *Education in Nazi Germany.* London, UK: Bloomsbury.

Plaut, Joshua Eli. (2012). We eat Chinese food on Christmas. *A kosher Christmas: 'Tis the season to be Jewish* (pp. 65–86). New Brunswick, NJ: Rutgers University Press.

Pogany, Eugene L. (2012). Catholics and Jews: A review of *Constantine's Sword* [Review of *Constantine's sword: The church and the Jews, a history*, by James Carroll]. *Interfaith Family.* Retrieved from http://www.interfaithfamily.com/arts_and_entertainment/popular_culture/Catholics_and_Jews_A_Review_of_Constantines_Sword.shtml

Probst, Robert. (2004). *Response & analysis: Teaching literature in secondary school* (2nd ed.). Portsmouth, NH: Boynton/Cook.

Ressler, Paula. (2002). *Dramatic changes: Talking about sexual orientation and gender identity with high school students through drama.* Portsmouth, NH: Heinemann.

Ressler, Paula. (2010, December). Episodes on High F. *Journal of the Motherhood Initiative: Mothering, Bereavement, Loss and Grief, 1*(2), 33–45.

Richter, Hans Peter. (1987). *Friedrich*. (Edite Kroll, Trans.). New York, NY: Puffin Books.

Ringelheim, Joan. (1998). The split between gender and the Holocaust. In Lenore J. Weitzman (Ed.), *Women in the Holocaust* (pp. 340–50). New Haven, CT: Yale University Press.

Rohrbach, Günter, Huth, Hanno (Producers), & Färberböck, Max (Director). (1999). *Aimée & Jaguar* [Motion picture]. New York, NY: Zeitgeist Films.

Rosenblatt, Louise. (1969, March). Towards a transactional theory of reading. *Journal of Literacy Research*, *1*(1), 31–49.

Rosenblatt, Louise. (1993, April). The transactional theory: Against dualisms. *College English*, *55*(4), 377–86.

Rosenblatt, Louise. (1995). *Literature as exploration* (5th ed.). New York, NY: Modern Language Association. (Original work published 1938)

Roth, John K. (2008). The failure of ethics: The Holocaust and its reverberations. Retrieved from https://www.uvm.edu/sites/default/files/UVM-Center for Holocaust-Studies/RothHilbergLecture_000.pdf

Rothberg, Michael. (2009). *Multidirectional memory: Remembering the Holocaust in the age of decolonization*. Palo Alto, CA: Stanford University Press.

Sacks, Jonathan. (2015). *Not in God's name: Confronting religious violence*. New York, NY: Schocken.

Schneider, Jenifer, Crumpler, Thomas P., & Rogers, Theresa. (2006). *Process drama and multiple literacies: Addressing social, cultural, and ethical issues*. Portsmouth, NH: Heinemann.

Schön, Donald A. (1984). *The reflective practitioner: How professionals think in action*. New York, NY: Basic Books.

Schumacher, Michael. (2010). *Will Eisner: A dreamer's life in comics*. New York, NY: Bloomsbury USA.

Schweber, Simone. (2004). *Making sense of the Holocaust: Lessons from classroom practice*. New York, NY: Teachers College Press.

Seltzer, Robert M. (1980). *Jewish people, Jewish thought*. New York, NY: Macmillan.

Semel, Nava. (2008). *And the rat laughed*. Melbourne, AU: Hybrid Publishers.

Semel, Nava. (2012). *Paper bride*. Melbourne, AU: Hybrid Publishers.

Shawn, Karen. (2017, Spring). Introduction. *PRISM: An Interdisciplinary Journal for Holocaust Educators*, *9*, 1–2.

Sherman, Martin. (2000). *Bent: The play*. New York, NY: Applause Theatre & Cinema Books. (Original work published 1979)

Short, Geoffrey, & Reed, Carole Ann. (2004). *Issues in Holocaust education*. Burlington, VT: Ashgate Publishing.

Shulman, Lee S. (1986, February). Those who understand: Knowledge growth in teaching. *Educational Researcher*, *15*(2), 4–14.

Smagorinsky, Peter. (2002). *Teaching English through principled practice*. Boston, MA: Pearson.

Smagorinsky, Peter. (2007). *Teaching English by design: How to create and carry out instructional units*. Portsmouth, NH: Heinemann.

Solinger, Michael, Linder, Dixie, Sherman, Martin (Producers), & Mathias, Sean (Director). (1997). *Bent* [Motion Picture]. United States: MGM/UA Entertainment Company.

Spiegelman, Art. (1986). *Maus: A survivor's tale, I: My father bleeds history.* New York, NY: Pantheon.

Spiegelman, Art. (1991, December 29). A problem of taxonomy. *New York Times.* Retrieved from https://www.nytimes.com/1991/12/29/books/l-a-problem-of-taxonomy-37092.html

Spiegelman, Art. (1992). *Maus: A survivor's tale, II: And here my troubles began.* New York, NY: Pantheon.

Spiegelman, Art. (2011). *MetaMaus: A look inside a modern classic,* Maus. New York, NY: Pantheon.

Spurlin, William. (2008). *Lost intimacies: Rethinking homosexuality under National Socialism.* Oxford, UK: Peter Lang.

Stanley, Liz, & Wise, Sue. (1983). *Breaking out: Feminist consciousness and feminist research.* London, UK: Routledge & Kegan Paul.

Street, Brian V. (1995). *Literacy in theory and practice.* Cambridge, UK: Cambridge University Press.

Styron, William. (1992). *Sophie's choice.* New York, NY: Vintage. (Original work published 1979)

Sue, Derald Wing, Capodilupo, Christina M., & Holder, Aisha M. B. (2008). Racial microaggressions in the life experience of Black Americans. *Professional Psychology: Research and Practice, 39*(3), 329–36.

Sullivan, Andrew. (2001, January 14). Christianity's original sin. *New York Times.* Retrieved from https://www.nytimes.com/books/01/01/14/reviews/010114.14sullivt.html

Tanner, Daniel, & Tanner, Laurel. (1995). *Curriculum development: Theory into practice* (5th ed.). Englewood Cliffs, NJ: Prentice-Hall.

Teichman, Milton, & Leder, Sharon. (1994). *Truth and lamentation: Stories and poems on the Holocaust.* Urbana, IL: University of Illinois Press.

Telushkin, Joseph. (1991). *Jewish literacy: The most important things to know about the Jewish religion, its people, and its history.* New York, NY: William Morrow and Company.

Todd, Mary, & Millen, Rochelle L. (2014, Spring). Convictions in conflict: A dialogue about religious identity in the Holocaust classroom. *Prism: An Interdisciplinary Journal for Holocaust Educators, 5,* 113–18.

Totten, Samuel (Ed.). (2001). *Teaching Holocaust literature.* Boston, MA: Allyn & Bacon.

Totten, Samuel, & Feinberg, Stephen. (2009). *Teaching and studying the Holocaust.* Charlotte, NC: Information Age.

Ullman, Viktor, & Kien, Peter. (ca. 1943). *The emperor of Atlantis or Death's refusal.* Mainz, Germany: Schott.

United Nations. (n.d.). Genocide. Retrieved from http://www.un.org/en/genocideprevention/genocide.html

United States Holocaust Memorial Museum (USHMM). (n.d.). Guidelines for teaching about the Holocaust. Retrieved from http://www.ushmm.org/educators/teaching-about-the-holocaust/general-teaching-guidelines#methodology

USHMM. (n.d.). Holocaust fiction. Retrieved from https://www.ushmm.org/research/research-in-collections/search-the-collections/bibliography/holocaust-fiction#h136

USHMM. (n.d.). Indoctrinating youth. Retrieved from http://www.ushmm.org/wlc/en/article.php?ModuleId=10007820

USHMM. (n.d.). Introduction to the Holocaust. Retrieved from https://www.ushmm.org/wlc/en/article.php?ModuleId=10005143

USHMM. (n.d.). Origins of neo-Nazi and white supremacist terms and symbols: A glossary. Retrieved from https://www.ushmm.org/confront-antisemitism/origins-of-neo-nazi-and-white-supremacist-terms-and-symbols

USHMM. (n.d.). Protocols of the elders of Zion. Retrieved from https://www.ushmm.org/wlc/en/article.php?ModuleId=10007058

USHMM. (n.d.). Resources for educators. Retrieved from https://www.ushmm.org/educators

USHMM. (n.d.). Steven Spielberg film and video archive. Retrieved from https://www.ushmm.org/online/film/search/simple.php

USHMM. (n.d.). Teacher Training Programs. Retrieved from https://www.ushmm.org/educators/professional-events-and-resources

USHMM. (n.d.). Topics to teach. Retrieved from https://www.ushmm.org/wlc/en/article.php?ModuleId=10007262

USHMM. (n.d.). Victims of the Nazi era. Retrieved from https://www.ushmm.org/wlc/en/article.php?ModuleId=10007457

USHMM. (n.d.). Who were the Gypsies? Retrieved from https://www.ushmm.org/learn/students/learning-materials-and-resources/sinti-and-roma-victims-of-the-nazi-era/who-were-the-gypsies

University of Maryland Library Guides. (n.d.). Graphic novels & comics. Retrieved from http://lib.guides.umd.edu/comics

University of Southern California Shoah Foundation. (n.d.). Visual history archive. Retrieved from https://sfi.usc.edu/vha

Valkenberg, Pim, & Corelli, Anthony. (Eds.) (2016). *Nostra Aetate: Celebrating 50 years of the Catholic Church's dialogue with Jews and Muslims*. Washington, DC: The Catholic University of America Press.

Wagner, Betty J. (1995). *Dorothy Heathcote: Drama as a learning medium*. Portsmouth, NH: Heinemann.

Wagner, Betty Jane (Ed.). (1998). *Educational drama and language arts: What research shows*. Portsmouth, NH: Heinemann.

Waller, James. (2002). *Becoming evil: How ordinary people commit genocide and mass killing*. Oxford, UK: Oxford University.

Weinberg, Gerhard L. (1995). *Hitler and World War II: Essays in modern German and world history*. Cambridge, UK: University of Cambridge Press.

Weinberg, Gerhard L. (1998). The Holocaust and World War II: A dilemma in teaching. In Donald G. Schilling (Ed.), *Lessons and legacies II: Teaching the Holocaust in a changing world* (pp. 26–40). Evanston, IL: Northwestern University Press.

Weinstein, Gerald, & Mellen, Donna. (1997). Antisemitism curriculum design. In Maurianne Adams, Lee Ann Bell, & Pat Griffin (Eds.), *Teaching for diversity and social justice* (pp. 170–97). London, UK: Routledge.

Whitesides, John. (2011, January 12). Palin's "blood libel" charge ignites firestorm. *Reuters*. Retrieved from https://www.reuters.com/article/us-usa-shooting-palin-idUSTRE70B3W320110112

Wiesel, Elie. (2006). *Night*. (Marion Wiesel, Trans.). New York, NY: Hill and Wang. (Original work published 1960)

Wiesenthal, Simon. (1998). *The sunflower: On the possibilities and limits of forgiveness*. New York, NY: Schocken Books. (Original work published 1976)

Wiggins, Grant, & McTigue, Jay. (2005). *Understanding by design* (2nd ed.). Alexandria, VA: Assoc. for Supervision and Curriculum Development.

Wilhelm, Jeffrey. (2002). *Action strategies for deepening comprehension*. New York, NY: Scholastic.

Wilson, John P. (1995). The historical evolution of PTSD diagnostic criteria: From Freud to DSM-IV. In G. S. Everly, Jr. & J. M. Lating (Eds.), *Psychotraumatology: Key papers and core concepts in post-traumatic stress* (pp. 9–26). New York, NY: Plenum Press.

Wistrich, Robert S. (1992). *Antisemitism: The longest hatred*. New York, NY: Pantheon.

World without Genocide. (n.d.). Academic programs in Holocaust and genocide studies. Retrieved from http://worldwithoutgenocide.org/about-us/other-opportunities/academic-programs-in-holocaust-and-genocide-studies

Yamato, Gloria. (2004.) Something about the subject makes it hard to name. In Margaret L. Anderson and Patricia Hill Collins (Eds.), *Race, class, and gender* (5th ed.) (pp. 99–103). New York, NY: Thomson/Wadsworth.

Zinn, Howard. (2002). *You can't be neutral on a moving train: A personal history of our times*. Boston, MA: Beacon Press.

Zusak, Markus. (2007). *The book thief*. New York, NY: Alfred A. Knopf.

Index

About the Authors

Paula Ressler is associate professor emerita of English at Illinois State University. She is a former director of the English Education Program and faculty member in English, English Education, and Women's and Gender Studies.

Becca Chase is a former assistant director of the Women's and Gender Studies Program and faculty member in Women's and Gender Studies, English, and English Education at Illinois State University.